Shelagh Stephenson
Plays:
The Memory of Water, Five Kinds of Silence, An Experiment With An Air Pump, Ancient Lights

The Memory of Water: 'wickedly funny and moving . . . riotously well-observed . . . the play is also a shrewd meditation on the subjective, competitive and self-preserving nature of memory that so often distorts and tailors recollections . . . Stephenson has a sure instinct for the quirky side of life' *Independent*

Five Kinds of Silence: 'a humane and unsensational attempt to get inside the heads of an abusive Burnley man and the wife and two adult daughters who, driven to the limits of endurance, end his tyranny with a rifle' *Independent*

An Experiment With An Air Pump: 'one of the most imaginative tilts at millennium anxiety that you're likely to see . . . It is the way Stephenson anchors her exhilarating ideas in these domestic squabbles that makes her play a first-rate drama' *The Times*

Ancient Lights: 'a play of rare intelligence, humour and wisdom' *Daily Telegraph*

Shelagh Stephenson was born in Northumberland and read drama at Manchester University. Her first stage play, *The Memory of Water*, premiered at Hampstead Theatre in 1996 and subsequently transferred to the West End, where it won an Olivier Award for Best Comedy in 2000. Her second play, *An Experiment With An Air Pump*, opened at the Royal Exchange Theatre in Manchester. It was joint recipient of the Peggy Ramsay Award and later transferred to the Hampstead Theatre. Both plays subsequently ran at New York's Manhattan Theatre Club. Her third play, *Ancient Lights*, was produced at Hampstead Theatre in December 2000. She has written several radio plays, including the award-winning *Five Kinds of Silence*, which she adapted for the stage and which was presented at the Lyric, Hammersmith in 2000. Her screen adaptation of *The Memory of Water* was released in spring 2002 with the title *Before You Go*.

by the same author and available from Methuen Drama

Ancient Lights

Enlightenment

An Experiment With An Air Pump

The Memory of Water & Five Kinds of Silence

SHELAGH STEPHENSON

Plays: 1

The Memory of Water

Five Kinds of Silence

An Experiment With An Air Pump

Ancient Lights

introduced by the author

Methuen Drama

METHUEN DRAMA CONTEMPORARY DRAMATISTS

3 5 7 9 10 8 6 4

This collection first published in Great Britain in 2003 by
Methuen Publishing Limited,
Reprinted in 2006 by Methuen Drama

Methuen Drama
A & C Black Publishers Limited
36 Soho Square
London W1D 3QY

The Memory of Water first published in 1997 by Methuen Drama
Copyright © Shelagh Stephenson 1997, 2002
Five Kinds of Silence first published by Methuen Drama in 1997
Copyright © Shelagh Stephenson 1997, 2002
An Experiment With An Air Pump first published by Methuen Publishing Limited
in 1998
Copyright © Shelagh Stephenson 1998, 2002
Ancient Lights first published by Methuen Publishing Limited in 2000
Copyright © Shelagh Stephenson 2000, 2002

Introduction copyright © 2003 by Shelagh Stephenson

Typeset in Baskerville by MATS, Southend-on-Sea, Essex
Printed and bound in Great Britain by
CPI Cox & Wyman, Reading, Berkshire

Caution

All rights whatsoever in this play are strictly reserved and application for
performance etc. should be made to: Julia Tyrrell Management,
57 Greenham Road, London N10 1LN.
No performance may be given unless a licence has been obtained.

Contents

Shelagh Stephenson:
A Chronology

1996 (July) *The Memory of Water* premiered at Hampstead Theatre

Five Kinds of Silence broadcast on BBC Radio 4. Subsequently won the Writers Guild Award for Best Original Radio Play (1996); the Mental Health Media Award for Best Radio Play (1996) and the Society of Authors Sony Radio Awards for 1997 for Best Radio Play.

1999 (January) *The Memory of Water* transferred to the West End

1998 (February) *An Experiment With An Air Pump* opened at the Royal Exchange Theatre, Manchester

An Experiment With An Air Pump joint recipient of the Peggy Ramsay Award

An Experiment With An Air Pump transferred to the Hampstead Theatre

The Memory of Water opened at New York's Manhattan Theatre Club

1999 *An Experiment With An Air Pump* opened at New York's Manhattan Theatre Club

2000 (February) *The Memory of Water* won Olivier Award for Best Comedy

(May) *Five Kinds of Silence* adaptation presented at the Lyric, Hammersmith

(November) *Ancient Lights* produced at Hampstead Theatre

Introduction

When you're writing a play, you have a tenuous notion of
what it might be about, the world you feel you're exploring.
When you've finished it, you read it through and feel
uncertain as to whether you've achieved a tenth of what you
set out to do. The issue is clouded by the fact that at this stage,
you can't remember in any truthful way what galvanised you
in the first place. All you can do is ask yourself; does it have
three-dimensionality, rhythm, dramatic drive and structure?
Does it deal with truth? With luck you may be able to say 'yes'
to most of these questions. By the time you get into rehearsals,
you've handed the remaining intractable problems over to the
actors and director. Collaboratively, you try to bring the play
to its full potential. Sometimes it works better than others: it
can be a dispiriting business. But it can also be a joyous one.
All the plays in this collection were teased and out and refined
in the rehearsal room. Two of them, *The Memory Of Water* and
An Experiment With An Air Pump, were refined and restructured
further for their New York productions and this is the first
time the correct version of the latter play has appeared in a
British edition.

Looking back over the plays it's clear to me that whatever I
thought I was writing about at the time, they are in fact all
about death, dying, being dead, being afraid of death, being
obsessed with it. I'm not sure that I set out to do this, but even
on a cursory reading it's hard to avoid the conclusion. As to
why this may be, well, what else is there in the end?

I'm also fascinated by scientific exploration and intellectual
obsession. Mary, in *The Memory of Water* is a neurologist,
almost everyone in *Experiment With An Air Pump* is connected
with scientific exploration, Tad in *Ancient Lights*, is fascinated
by pathology. *Five Kinds of Silince* stands slightly apart. This
particular play emerged via a very different process. Originally

commissioned and produced as a radio play, it was later
adapted for the stage. The original idea, based on a true story,
was suggested to me by Jeremy Mortimer. I was reluctant at
first to take on such a bleak subject, but fortunately his powers
of persuasion were greater than my misgivings. The play has
been discussed a great deal since then – as play about abuse.
In the process of writing it, the word never once crossed my or
anyone else's mind. In rehearsals it was never mentioned. It's
a play about madness and control, violence and despair,
which happens to involve incestuous sex.

The other three plays in this collection are much more
similar in terms of their genesis in the sense that they were
commissioned specifically for the theatre. In performance
terms, they require a great deal of rhythmic energy and
precision: theatricality, in fact. The dialogue is heightened,
syncopated, not naturalistic in the televisual sense. When they
work, the plays should, with a bit of luck, produce extremes of
laughter and pathos, intellectual debate and emotional
resonance, hard on each other's heels.

Shelagh Stephenson
June 2003

For Eoin O'Callaghan

The Memory of Water

The Memory of Water was first performed at the Hampstead Theatre, London, on 11 July 1996, with the following cast:

Mary	Haydn Gwynne
Vi	Mary Jo Randle
Teresa	Jane Booker
Catherine	Matilda Ziegler
Mike	Alexander Hanson
Frank	Dermot Crowley

Directed by Terry Johnson
Designed by Sue Plummer
Lighting by Robert Bryan
Sound by John A. Leonard

Act One

Blackness. A pool of bluish-green light reveals **Vi**, *aged around forty. She is sitting at a dressing-table. The drawer is open. She wears a green taffeta cocktail frock circa 1962. She is sexy, immaculately made up, her hair perfectly coiffed. She wears earrings and a matching necklace, and carries a clutch bag, from which she takes a cigarette and lighter. She lights up. The pool of light opens up to reveal the rest of the room in a dim, golden, unreal glow: a bedroom, dominated by a double bed in which* **Mary** *lies, wearing a pair of sunglasses. She watches* **Vi**. *The room is slightly old-fashioned, with dressing-table and matching wardrobe. Some clothes are draped over a chair. There is a long diagonal crack running across the wall behind the bed. An open suitcase lies on the floor, half unpacked, a half-full bottle of whisky and a pile of books on the bedside table.*

Mary   What do you want?

Vi   Someone's been going through these drawers.

Mary   Not me.

Vi   What did you think you'd find?

Mary   Nothing.

She closes the drawer and looks over to the bed.

Vi   That crack's getting worse. Have you noticed anything about the view?

Mary   No.

Vi   It's closer.

Mary   What is?

Vi   The sea. Fifty yards closer. It'll take the house eventually. All gone without a trace. Nothing left. And all the life that happened here, drowned, sunk. As if it had never been.

Mary   D'you remember a green tin box with chrysanthemums on it?

Vi   No.

Mary   It had papers in it. It's gone. Where is it?

Vi   I've no idea.

Mary   What have you done with it?

Vi *picks up some books from the bedside table and looks through the titles.*

Vi   *Head Injuries and Short-Term Changes in Neural Behaviour . . . The Phenomenology of Memory . . . Peripheral Signalling of the Brain.*

She puts them down.

Bloody hell, Mary. What's wrong with Georgette Heyer?

Go to black. Fade up bedside lamp. **Vi** *has gone.* **Mary** *is lying prostrate. She stirs and gets out of bed, goes to the dressing-table, opens drawers, rifles through them. The phone rings.*

Mary   Hello? . . . What time is it? . . . I wouldn't be talking to you if I was, would I? I'd be unconscious . . . Where are you? . . . Jesus . . . you're what? So will you want me to pick you up from the station?

The door opens and **Teresa** *comes in.*

Teresa   Oh . . .

Mary   Hold on . . . (*To* **Teresa**.) It's not for you.

Teresa   Who is it?

Mary (*to caller*)   What? She's gone where? . . . OK, OK. I'll see you later. Are you sure you don't want me to pick you up –

She's cut off.

Hello? . . . Shit.

Teresa   Who was that?

Mary   A nuisance caller. We struck up a rapport.

Teresa   He's not staying here, is he?

Mary   Who?

Teresa   I'm presuming it's your boyfriend.

Mary   How much sleep have I had?

She picks up a portable alarm clock and peers at it.

Teresa   How's his wife?

Mary   Jesus. Two and a half hours.

*She flops back on the pillows. Looks at **Teresa**.*

Why are you looking so awake?

Teresa   I've been up since quarter past five. Presumably he's leaving her at home, then.

Mary   You've got that slight edge in your voice. Like a blunt saw.

Teresa   I'm just asking –

Mary   Of course he's bloody leaving her at home. She's gone to stay with her mother.

Teresa   I thought she was ill.

Mary   Maybe she went in an iron lung. Maybe she made a miracle recovery. I don't know. I didn't ask.

Teresa   Where's he going to sleep?

Mary   What?

Teresa   You can't sleep with him in that bed.

Mary   He's staying in a hotel.

Teresa   I thought it might be something important.

Mary   What?

Teresa   The phone. Funeral directors or something.

Mary   We've done all that. Can I go back to sleep?

Teresa   And where's Catherine?

Mary   She said she might stay over with someone.

Teresa   Does she still have friends here?

Mary   Probably. I don't know.

She turns away, settles down, and shuts her eyes. **Teresa** *watches her for a while.*

Teresa   She could have phoned to say. Anything could have happened to her. It's still snowing.

Mary   She's thirty-three, Teresa.

Teresa   The roads are terrible.

Mary   She'll get a taxi.

Teresa   Probably just as well she didn't come home. She'd have probably drunk four bottles of cider and been brought home in a police car. And then she'd have been sick all over the television.

Mary   She was thirteen when she did that.

Teresa   She was lucky she didn't get electrocuted.

Mary   It wasn't switched on.

Teresa   Yes it was, I was watching it. It was *The High Chaparral.*

Mary   No it wasn't. I wish you'd stop remembering things that didn't actually happen.

Teresa   I was there. You weren't.

Mary *gives up trying to sleep. Sits up.*

Mary   I was there.

Teresa   That was the other time. The time when she ate the cannabis.

Mary   That was me. I ate hash cookies.

Teresa   It was Catherine.

Mary   It was me.

Teresa   I was there.

Mary So where was I?

Teresa Doing your homework probably. Dissecting frogs. Skinning live rabbits. Strangling cats. The usual.

Mary Teresa. I'd like to get another hour's sleep. I'm not in the mood, OK?

She tries to settle down in the bed, and pulls something out that's causing her discomfort: a glass contraption with a rubber bulb at one end. She puts it on the bedside table and settles down again. **Teresa** *picks it up.*

Teresa Oh, for God's sake . . . Is this what I think it is?

Mary I don't know. What d'you think it is?

Teresa A breast pump.

Mary I found it on top of the wardrobe. I think I'd like to have it.

Teresa Why?

Mary Because you've got the watch and the engagement ring.

Teresa For Lucy. Not for me. For Lucy.

Mary OK. So you want the breast pump. Have it.

Teresa I don't want it.

Mary Good. That's settled. Now let me go to sleep.

Teresa You can't just take things willy-nilly.

Mary You did.

Teresa Oh, I see. I see what this is about.

Mary *sits up.*

Mary It's not about anything, it's about me trying to get some sleep. For Christ's sake, Teresa, it's too early in the morning for this.

Mary *pulls the covers over her head. Silence.* **Teresa** *goes to the door, turns back.*

Teresa   Could you keep off the phone, I'm waiting for Frank to ring and my mobile's recharging –

Mary   If you take that phone to the funeral this time –

Teresa   Oh, go to sleep.

Mary *sits up.*

Mary   I'm surprised Dad didn't burst out of his coffin and punch you.

Teresa   I didn't know it was in my bag.

Mary   You could have turned it off. You didn't have to speak to them.

Teresa   I didn't speak to them.

Mary   You did. I heard you. You told them you were in a meeting.

Teresa   You're imagining this. This is a completely false memory.

Mary   All memories are false.

Teresa   Mine aren't.

Mary   Yours in particular.

Teresa   Oh, I see, mine are all false but yours aren't.

Mary   That's not what I said.

Teresa   And what's with the Ray-Bans?

Mary *takes them off.*

Mary   I couldn't sleep with the light on.

Teresa   You could have turned it off.

Mary   I was frightened of the dark.

Teresa   When did this start?

Mary   It's all right for you. You're not sleeping in her bed.

Teresa   Oh, for goodness' sake.

Mary   You grabbed the spare room pretty sharpish.

Teresa   I was here first.

Mary   Have the sheets been changed?

Teresa   Yes.

Mary   When?

Teresa   What difference does it make?

Mary   I don't like sleeping in her bed, that's all.

Teresa   She didn't die in it.

Mary   She was the last person in it. It's full of bits of skin and hair that belong to her –

Teresa   Stop it –

Mary   And it makes me feel uncomfortable –

Teresa   What bits of skin and hair?

Mary   You shed cells. They fall off when you're asleep. I found a toenail before.

Teresa   Please.

Mary   I thought I might keep it in a locket round my neck. Or maybe you'd like it –

Teresa   Stop it, for goodness' sake.

She picks up a book from the bedside table.

You can't leave work alone for five minutes, can you, even at a time like this?

Mary   I've a very sick patient.

Teresa   You had a very sick mother.

Mary   Don't start, Teresa.

Teresa   Oh, she never complained. Because your job's important. I mean, doctors are second to God, whereas Frank and I only have a business to run, so obviously we could drop everything at a moment's notice.

Mary   It's not my fault.

Silence.

Teresa   Why do we always do this?

Mary   What?

Teresa   Why do we always argue?

Mary   We don't argue, we bicker.

Teresa   OK, why do we bicker?

Mary   Because we don't get on.

Teresa   Yes we do.

Mary   Oh, have it your own way.

She unscrews the whisky and takes a swig. **Teresa** *looks at her, aghast.*

Teresa   You haven't even got out of bed yet.

Mary   It's the only way we're going to get through this.

She offers it to **Teresa**, *who shakes her head.*

Teresa   D'you often have a drink in the morning?

Mary   Of course I bloody don't, what d'you think I am?

Teresa   Lots of doctors are alcoholics. It's the stress.

Mary   Someone dies, you drink whisky. It's normal, it's a sedative, it's what normal people do at abnormal times.

She takes another swig. Silence.

OK. Let's be nice to each other.

Silence.

What do people usually talk about when their mother's just died?

Teresa   I don't know. Funeral arrangements. What colour coffin. I've got a list somewhere.

Mary   There should be a set form. Like those books on

wedding etiquette. Sudden Death Etiquette. Lesson One. Breaking the news. Phrases to avoid include: guess what?

Teresa   I was distraught, I wasn't thinking properly –

Mary   I thought you'd won the lottery or something –

Teresa   It's quite tricky for you, being nice, isn't it?

Mary   Sorry. I forgot. How are you feeling?

Teresa *looks at her watch.*

Teresa   I was expecting him to phone an hour ago.

Mary   I'm not talking about Frank.

Teresa   I don't know how I feel. Everything I eat tastes of salt.

Silence. She crosses the room and takes the whisky from **Mary**. *She takes a swig and grimaces.*

Salt. Everything tastes of it.

Hands it back. Sits on the bed.

The funeral director's got a plastic hand.

Mary   God.

Pause.

What's it like?

Teresa   Pink.

Mary   What happened to his real one?

Teresa   How should I know?

Mary   Didn't you ask him?

Teresa   It didn't seem appropriate.

Mary   No. I suppose not.

Teresa   He was showing us pictures of coffins.

Mary   As they do.

Catherine (*off*)   Hi!

Mary   Oh God.

Teresa   In here.

Catherine *bursts in, wrapped in layers of coats and scarves, laden with carrier bags. She divests herself as she speaks.*

Catherine   God, it's bloody freezing out there. It's like *Scott of the Antarctic*, the cab was sliding all over the place and I had one of those drivers who kept saying, have you been shopping, are you going somewhere nice? And I said, yes, actually, a funeral. My mother's. I thought, that'll shut him up, but it turns out he knew her. I forgot what it's like up here. Everyone knows the butcher's daughter's husband's mother's cat. And he got all upset, we had to pull over, so anyway I invited him to the funeral. He's called Dougie. I bet he doesn't come. God, I've got this really weird pain at the very bottom of my stomach, here, look, just above my pubic bone. It keeps going sort of stab, twist, so either I've got some sort of cyst, but actually, God, I know what it is, I bet. I bet I'm ovulating. Isn't that amazing? I can actually feel the egg being released. Although, hang on, I don't think I'm due to ovulate. You can't ovulate twice in the same month, can you? It's not my appendix because I haven't got one. Fuck. It must be PMT. In which case I think I've got an ovarian cyst.

Silence.

Mary   D'you want us to take you to hospital or shall I whip it out now on the kitchen table?

Catherine   I'll be fine.

Mary   Good, because I'm over the limit for either activity.

Catherine   Oh brilliant, whisky.

She picks up the bottle and takes a slug.

Teresa   Where've you been?

Catherine   Shopping.

Teresa Shopping?

Catherine Well, you'd call it a displacement activity, but I call it shopping.

Teresa All night?

Catherine I went for a drink. I stayed with some friends.

Teresa What friends?

Catherine You don't know them. Oh God, there it goes again. Have you ever had this? Right here. Right at the bottom of your stomach?

Teresa No.

Catherine What d'you think it is?

Mary I've no idea.

Teresa We've been worried sick.

Catherine Look, just here –

*She takes **Mary**'s hand and holds it against her groin.*

Mary Wind.

Catherine Do any of your patients actually survive?

Teresa You could have picked up a phone. I mean, where've you been?

Catherine Down the docks shagging sailors, what d'you think?

Mary I'd have come with you if I'd known.

Teresa It's just a bit insensitive –

Mary Yes it is. There's a time and a place for everything –

Teresa Disappearing, leaving us to deal with all this –

Catherine All what? D'you like my shoes? I can't stop buying shoes. I even like the smell of them. Honestly, it's just like an eating disorder except it's not it's just shoes although sometimes it's underwear. D'you ever get that, you have to buy twenty pairs of knickers all at once, usually when you're a bit depressed –

Teresa   You can't wear those for a funeral. You look like Gary Glitter.

Catherine   I didn't buy them for the funeral.

Mary   I remember them the first time round. They were horrible then.

Catherine   I got them in a sale.

Mary   Oh well. That's some consolation.

Catherine   What's wrong with them?

Teresa   I thought you didn't have any money.

Catherine   Credit cards. What's wrong with them?

Teresa   You said you were broke.

Catherine   Oh, for God's sake, broke doesn't mean you can't buy things. I'm trying to cheer myself up, or is that not allowed? The minute I walk in the door I feel it in waves, the two of you waiting to pounce, looking for something to criticise. Christ, it's no wonder I've got low self-esteem.

Mary   You have an ego the size of Asia Minor.

Catherine   I'm just asking you to clarify your position *vis-à-vis* my shoes. I mean, quite obviously you don't like them, but why d'you always have to do this sneery superior thing? Why can't you just be straight and say you hate them?

Mary   I hate them. Can I go back to sleep now?

Teresa   I'm just wondering how you can afford to go out and buy all this stuff if you haven't got any money.

Mary   She shoplifts.

Catherine   Will someone tell me what I'm supposed to have done?

Mary   It was a joke.

Catherine   So all right, I know, Mum's dead –

Teresa   There's no need to put it like that –

Catherine   But you want me to sit down and cry about it and I can't.

Mary   I don't. I want you to go away.

Catherine   You always do this to me.

Mary   I'm tired.

Catherine   Some of the things you say to me are just, you know, not on. It's like I don't count. All my bloody life. And I'm not having it any more. I won't take it any more, OK?

Teresa   Have you been taking drugs, Catherine?

Catherine   Oh, for God's sake. I was in a really good mood till I walked in here.

Teresa   Your mother's just died, how can you be in a good mood? Try and be a bit more sensitive –

Catherine   No one's being sensitive to me.

Mary   We fucking are!

Silence.

Catherine   Did Xavier call?

Mary   Who?

Catherine   Xavier.

Mary   I thought he was called Pepe?

Catherine   You see, this is what you do to me. This permanent, constant, endless belittling.

Teresa   He didn't call.

Catherine   I'm about to marry him and you can't even get his name right.

Mary   You're always about to marry people.

Catherine   What's that supposed to mean?

Mary   And you never do.

Teresa   Oh shut up, both of you.

Silence.

Catherine   If I don't get some painkillers I'm going to die.

Mary   There might be some paracetamol in my case.

Catherine   Haven't you got anything more exotic?

Catherine *goes to the suitcase.*

Mary   Not for you, no. They're in the pocket. Now, will you both go away and let me get some sleep?

Teresa   Would anyone like some barley cup?

Catherine *finds the paracetamol and takes a couple.*

Catherine   I'd rather drink my own urine.

Mary   You may laugh.

Teresa   I do not drink my own urine.

Mary   Yet.

Catherine   Haven't we got any ordinary tea?

Teresa   That stuff in the kitchen's made from floor sweepings. You might as well drink liquid cancer.

Mary   God, you do talk absolute shite sometimes.

Teresa   Some people think that drinking your own urine –

Mary   Yes I know. And they're all mad.

Teresa   You're always so certain when it comes to things you know nothing about.

Mary   You know bugger all about bugger all.

Teresa   You've a completely closed mind, it infuriates me. You're so supercilious, you don't even listen –

Mary   If God had meant you to ingest your own urine, he'd have rigged up a drinking-straw arrangement directly from your bladder. To save you the indignity of squatting over a teacup. Now, please, I just want an hour.

Teresa   There are things to do.

Mary   They can wait.

Catherine   I'm going to have a hot bath and a joint. I can't stand this.

She goes.

Teresa   So once again it's me. Everything falls to me.

Mary   Go and have a lie-down, Teresa.

Teresa   I can't bloody lie down, I can't sit still. I can't cope, I need some Rescue Remedy.

She goes out.

Mary   I've got some beta blockers, they're much better –

Teresa (*off*)   I get agitated. I get like this. I don't need drugs.

She comes back, carrying her bag, chanting.

Teresa   Brown one and a half pounds of shin of beef in a heavy casserole. Remove and set aside. Sauté two medium onions in the casserole with two crushed cloves of garlic –

Mary   What are you doing?

Teresa   Recipes. I recite recipes. It's very soothing. I've tried meditation but my mind wanders. I think of all the phone calls I should be making instead of sitting there going 'om'. Carbonnade of beef seems to work best.

Mary   You're a vegetarian.

Teresa   I've tried it with nut loaf but it's not the same. And now I've got that salt taste in my mouth and I feel sick.

Mary   Psychosomatic.

Teresa   I know it's psychosomatic. I know it is, all right. I'd just like it to stop, that's all.

Catherine *comes in with a bundle of mail.*

Catherine   More fan mail.

Mary   I thought you'd gone for a bath to soothe your cyst.

Catherine   There's not enough water. So it's still sort of niggling, I wish it would stop –

She goes to her carrier bags and takes out various pieces of clothing. She opens the wardrobe door, holds them up against herself in front of the mirror.

I think it's stress. I mean, it's an incredibly stressful time, isn't it, and I always get things like this when I'm strung out. Last year I had this weird thing in my legs, like they were kind of restless or jumpy or something. Every time I tried to go to sleep they used to sort of twitch and hop. The doctor in Spain said it was quite common and I just needed to relax more, but I can't, I've got an incredibly fast metabolism and then I get that spasm thing in my stomach which is definitely stress-related, I'm sure it's irritable bowel syndrome. I mean, that starts up the minute I'm even a tiny bit tense, I notice it straight away because I'm very in touch with my body, I can sort of hear it speaking to me.

Pause.

Teresa   I think I'm going mad.

Catherine   Last night I dreamed I could do yogic flying. I bet that means something –

She tugs at the jacket.

I'm not sure about this, are you? I don't suit black, that's the problem.

Teresa   As soon as the phone went I knew.

Catherine   Can you wear trousers at a funeral?

Teresa   I said to Frank, I can't answer it. We should never have left her at the hospital like that. We should have stayed.

Mary   You weren't to know.

Teresa I'm not good with hospitals, I had to get away.
Everyone in her ward looked like they'd already died,
everyone was pale grey with a catheter.

Mary *is opening the mail. Reads.*

Mary 'With deepest sympathy on your sad loss, Mimi.'
Who's Mimi?

Teresa When Frank spoke to them they said, 'She's worse,
you'd better get up to the hospital.' I took the phone and said,
'She's dead, isn't she, you don't phone at three in the morning
unless someone's dead.' And then, this is the awful bit, I put
the phone down, and the thing I wanted to do more than
anything else was have sex, which is sick, I know, that's what
Frank said afterwards. I know I should have phoned you two,
but I had this idea, this flicker she might not be dead, even
though I knew she was really, but they wouldn't tell me over
the phone, and I'd have woken you up, and what would the
point be anyway, you were miles away –

Mary It's OK. Stop worrying about it –

Teresa That's why I didn't phone straight away. Mimi
used to live three doors down.

Catherine Can I borrow a skirt from someone?

Teresa I keep going over and over it –

Catherine Is anyone listening to me?

Mary Oh, shut up and sit down. Your cyst might burst.

Teresa And the doctor was about twelve, and embarrassed.
Eventually we had to say it for him. He kept fiddling with his
pen and giving us a rundown of everything that had
happened, until eventually Frank said, 'Are you trying to tell
us she's not coming back? Are you trying to tell us she's dead?'
And he said, 'More or less, yes.' And I said, 'What d'you
mean, more or less? She's either dead or she isn't, you can't be
a bit dead, for God's sake.' And then I looked at my feet and I
was wearing odd shoes. A black one and a brown one. Not
even vaguely similar. So I started to laugh and I couldn't stop.

They had to give me a sedative. Frank was shocked. They're not like us, his family, they've got Italian blood. Someone dies, they cry. They don't get confused and laugh.

Catherine   All I want to know is, can I borrow a skirt?

Mary   Oh shut up, Catherine, for Christ's sake!

Catherine   If I could get an answer out of anyone, I would –

Mary   Yes, you can borrow a fucking skirt!

Silence. **Teresa** *goes to her bag and takes out a bottle of pills. She takes two.*

Catherine   What are they?

Teresa   Nerve tablets. Have one, for heaven's sake. Have six. Have the lot. They're completely organic, no chemicals.

Catherine   I like chemicals.

Teresa (*emptying her bag on to the bed*)   All right, don't then. I've got a list somewhere. Things to sort out.

Mary   Do it later, Teresa.

Teresa   I can't. I can't sit still. I have to do it now.

Mary   You're a useless advertisement for the health food industry.

Teresa   Supplements. We do health supplements. Remedies. How many times do I have to tell you? You do this deliberately, you wilfully misinterpret what we do because you think it's funny or something, and actually I'm getting bored with it.

Catherine   You're making me incredibly tense, both of you.

Teresa   We're making you tense? Good God, you haven't stopped since you came in. Jumping around all over the place like you're on speed, which, thinking about it, you probably are, blahing on about your ovaries and your restless legs and your PMT. I don't give a toss about your insides. Has anyone seen my electronic organiser?

They look vaguely round the room. Silence.

Mary   What does it look like?

Teresa   I had it a minute ago, I had it –

Teresa *throws her bag down. Silence.* **Catherine** *offers her the joint.*

Catherine   D'you want some of this?

Teresa   No, thank you.

Mary   Maybe you should.

Catherine   It's completely organic. We grew it in the garden.

Teresa *takes a reluctant puff. Then another. Silence.*

Catherine   You know when you went to the hospital. When she was dead.

Teresa   Mmmm . . . ?

Catherine   Did you see her?

Teresa   Who?

Catherine   Mum.

Teresa   Of course I did.

Catherine   How did she look?

Teresa   Asleep. She just looked asleep.

Catherine *takes the joint back.*

Catherine   Oh good.

Silence.

Teresa   It's got the list on it. My organiser's got the list on it.

Catherine *opens an envelope and reads a card.*

Catherine   'My thoughts are with you at this sad time.
Your mother was a wonder woman. Norman Pearson.'
Norman Pearson?

Teresa *takes the card from her and looks at it.*

Teresa   Patterson. Norman Patterson.

Mary   Who's he? And what does he mean 'wonder woman'?

Teresa   I don't know. He's got an allotment.

Catherine   I'm starving. Is anyone else hungry?

Mary   Maybe they were having an affair.

Catherine   Munch munch munch, I'd really like some Shreddies. Have we got any Shreddies, d'you think?

Teresa   She was getting more and more confused. Everything was packing up. I tried everything. I offered her all sorts of things. I wanted to take her to that herbalist in Whitby. She wouldn't have any of it.

Mary   I don't think the colonic irrigation was a very good idea. Not for Alzheimer's disease.

Teresa   You don't know the first thing about colonics –

Mary   I do know that your colon is specifically designed to function independently, without recourse to a foot pump.

Teresa   She never took care of herself, that's the problem.

Mary   She was seventy-five. She died. Let her be.

Teresa   She still smoked.

Mary   So what?

Teresa   She died because her heart gave out because she never ever looked after herself properly.

Mary   I don't think that's strictly true.

Teresa   You're a doctor, you know it's true.

Mary   OK. It's all her own fault. She ate sliced white bread so she deserved to die. Whereas you wouldn't have it in the house, so you'll probably manage to avoid death altogether. That's the general idea, isn't it? While the rest of us deserve all we get, because we've been recklessly cavalier in the diet department. Or we couldn't quite stomach six feet of plastic tubing being shoved up our bottoms –

Teresa   Thank God you're not my doctor –

Mary   Thank God you're not my patient –

Teresa   I'm just saying, if you eat properly –

Mary   And I'm just saying people die. You can't avoid it. Not even you.

Teresa   Well, you two managed to avoid it pretty comprehensively when it came to Mum. Most of the time you weren't even here.

Mary   Great. The guilt fest. I knew we'd get there eventually.

Catherine   It's no good trying to make me feel guilty because I don't.

Teresa   I didn't think for a moment you would.

Catherine   You'd like me to, though, and I won't. I refuse. I've nothing to feel guilty about at all. I didn't like her.

Mary   Who?

Catherine   Mum.

Teresa   Don't be ridiculous.

Catherine   She didn't like me.

Mary   Yes she did.

Catherine   How do you know?

Teresa   She was your mother.

Catherine   I had a horrible childhood.

Teresa   We all had the same childhood. It wasn't horrible.

Catherine   Mine was.

Mary   That's because you're an egomaniac.

Catherine   She thought I was the menopause.

Mary   Who told you that?

Catherine   She did. She had the cat put down without telling me. She shut me in a cupboard. She said it was an accident but it wasn't.

Mary   When did she do all this?

Catherine   I never had the right shoes. She wouldn't let me visit you in hospital when you had an exploding appendix. She did it deliberately. She excluded me from everything. She made me stay in the shop after closing time and count nails.

Mary   When I think of our childhood, we went on a lot of bike rides and it was always sunny.

Teresa   Well, it was for you. You couldn't put a foot wrong.

Catherine   When I think of it, it was always pissing down. And what bike? I never had one.

Teresa   I'm sure you came to the beach with us, I remember it —

Catherine   The only time I went to the beach, it was with you and you left me there. You forgot me. You didn't remember till you got home and Mum said, 'Where's Catherine?'

Teresa   That was Mary. She was too young, she was being a pain and showing off in Esperanto, so we ran away and left her. With no bus fare and the tide coming in.

Catherine   It was me!

Mary   No it wasn't. It was me.

Catherine   So how come I remember it?

Mary   Because I told you about it and you appropriated it because it fits. If it was horrible, it must have happened to you. And she didn't have the cat put down, it just died.

Teresa   It got run over by a combine harvester actually.

Catherine   I don't remember any of this.

Teresa   The amount of chemicals you've had through your system, I'm surprised you can remember anything at all.

Catherine   You did leave me at the beach. Someone left me at the beach. I remember it vividly. I've got a brilliant memory. I remember everything.

Teresa   You've forgotten Lucy's birthday every year since she was born –

Mary   You'd go mad if you remembered everything. What would be the point? Your head would burst. There's an illness actually, a sort of incontinent memory syndrome, where you recall everything, absolutely everything, in hideous detail, and it's not a blessing, it's an affliction. There's no light and shade, no difference between the trivial and the vital, no editing system whatsoever.

She looks at **Catherine.**

Actually, Catherine, maybe you should come in for a few tests.

Catherine   You're doing it again!

Teresa *has spied something under the bed. She picks it up: her electronic organiser.*

Teresa   I've found it. I've found my list.

She consults her gadget.

Insurance – undertakers 10.30, bridge rolls – I think there's just the flowers left –

Catherine   Do we have to do this now?

Teresa   It won't get done on its own. If it was up to you two, she'd have to cremate herself –

Mary   All right, all right –

Teresa   Because while you were doing Spanish dancing with Pepe in Fuengirola –

Catherine   His name's Xavier and I've never been to Fuengirola in my life –

Teresa   I was watching her fall apart. Twenty miles here, twenty miles back. Three times a week.

Catherine   I spoke to her a week ago. She wasn't that bad. She said she was off to the hairdressers.

Teresa   Oh, for goodness' sake, she was mad as a snake. And I'm the one who dealt with it all.

Mary   I'm sure when they publish a new edition of *Foxe's Book of Martyrs* they'll devote a chapter entirely to you.

Teresa   Every month something else went, another wire worked itself loose. Not big things, little things. She used to put her glasses in the oven. 'What day is it?' she'd say, and I'd say, 'Wednesday,' and she'd say 'Why?' 'Well, it just is. Because yesterday was Tuesday.' And she'd say, 'There was a woman here with a plastic bucket. Who is she?' 'Elaine. You know Elaine. Your home help.' And then she'd look at me and we'd start all over again. 'What day is it?' I mean, she wasn't even that old.

Silence. She takes some sheets of photographs from her bag.

Anyway. I got these photos from the florist. There's a number under each picture, so if you just give me the number of the wreath you want, I can phone in the order.

She hands the photos to **Mary**, *who gives them a cursory glance.*

Mary   I'll have the one in the shape of a football.

Teresa   I'm just trying to keep things in a neutral gear, that's all.

Mary   Choosing flowers for your mother's funeral is not what I'd call a neutral activity.

The phone rings. **Teresa** *and* **Mary** *both make a grab for it.* **Mary** *wins.*

Mary   Hello? . . . Hello?

Catherine   Is it Xavier?

Mary   Hello?

Teresa   Give it to me.

Mary   There's just a crackling sound. Hello, can you hear me?

Teresa *grabs the receiver.*

Teresa   Frank?

Catherine   It'll be Xavier.

Mary *grabs it back.*

Mary   Mike?

The line goes dead. She puts the receiver down. Silence.

It's like waiting for the relief of Mafeking.

Silence.

Catherine   Does anyone want a sandwich?

Mary *gets out of bed and rifles through her suitcase for clothes.*
Catherine *begins to go.*

Catherine   I went to this brilliant funeral in Madrid –

She goes out.

Mary   Brilliant. You went to a brilliant funeral.

Catherine *(off)*   He was a friend of Xavier's who fell off a roof and at the party afterwards they had little bowls of cocaine –

Mary   Oh, what a good idea. That'll go down well with the St Vincent de Paul Society.

Catherine *(off)*   And they dyed his poodle black. Just for the funeral. It was washable dye so it wasn't cruel, but anyway, it was raining and God, you should have seen the state of the carpets afterwards. So that was a bit of a disaster, but later on there was a firework display and he went up in a rocket.

Mary   Who?

Catherine (*off*)   The person who was dead. Not the poodle.

Mary   We're not doing that to Mum.

Catherine *reappears in the doorway carrying a bread knife.*

Catherine   I'm just saying that funerals don't have to be depressing. They can be quite happy.

Mary   Farcical even.

Catherine   Scrambled eggs. That's what I want. I bet we haven't got any eggs –

Exit **Catherine**.

Mary   I keep having dreams about her.

Teresa   Who?

Mary   Mum.

Teresa *opens a card.*

Teresa   Thank God. I thought you meant Catherine. It's bad enough having her in the same house without dreaming about her as well.

Mary   She's about fortyish and she's always wearing that green taffeta dress.

Teresa   'With deepest sympathy from Winnie and the boys. Sorry we won't be able to make the funeral due to a hip replacement op.'

Mary   I've never heard of any of these people, have you? And there's this smell in the dream.

Teresa   Can you dream smells?

Mary   I think so.

Teresa   I can't.

Mary   It was that perfume she used to wear. In a tiny bottle, she got it in Woolworths, and on Saturday night when she leaned over to say good night, she smelt of cigarettes and face powder and something alcoholic, and this perfume.

Teresa   Phul Nana.

Mary   Phul Nana . . . that was it . . . the whole room smelt of it.

Teresa   She always said, if you don't wear perfume you'll never find a man.

Mary   You'll never get a boyfriend.

Teresa   And then, frankly –

Mary   Unless you're a nun.

Teresa   You might as well cut your throat with the bread knife.

Mary   I don't know how she managed to give birth to three daughters and then send us out into the world so badly equipped. She'd have sent us up K2 in slingbacks. With matching handbags.

Teresa   She must have taught us something, otherwise we'd all be dead.

Pause.

Did she ever mention sex to you?

Mary *gives her a withering look.*

Teresa   No, I suppose not.

Mary   I found a box of sanitary towels in her wardrobe once. I was nine. I said, 'What are these?' I mean, I knew they were something bad, but I was desperate, I dared myself to ask. I was thinking all sorts of things. She snatched the box off me and said, 'Put that back. It's a home perm kit.'

There is a banging noise at the window.

Teresa   What was that?

Mary   There's something at the window . . .

Teresa   Hello . . . ?

The sound comes again.

Oh God, it's like *Wuthering Heights*.

Mary   Someone wants to come in.

Teresa   Well, open the window.

Mary   You do it.

Teresa   Oh, for goodness' sake –

She goes to the window and opens it, screams.

Mike   Sorry . . .

Mary   Mike . . . Oh Jesus . . . Teresa, this is Mike . . .

Teresa   Hello.

Mike   I've been ringing the doorbell.

Teresa   It's broken.

Mike   Yes.

Pause.

I'd like to come in, if that's not too much trouble. Otherwise, you know, I could just stand here and die, apparently it's a nice way to go, freezing, you don't feel a thing, you just drift off into oblivion –

Mary   Oh God, yes, sorry, I'll open the door –

Mike   For Christ's sake –

He climbs in through the window, covered in snow.

Mary   How long have you been there?

Mike   Hours.

Mary   Sorry. Here, give me your coat.

Teresa   We thought you were Heathcliff. At the window.

Mike   Drink. I need a drink.

Mary (*taking off his outer clothes*)   Heathcliff wasn't at the
window. He was inside. It was Cathy trying to get in.

Mike   Sorry?

Teresa   Are you sure?

Catherine *appears, eating a sandwich and smoking another joint. She
has a glass in her hand.*

Catherine   Who's this?

Mary   Mike, this is Catherine. Catherine, this is Mike.

He tries to smile.

Mike   Sorry, can't speak. Frozen.

Catherine   Mike the married boyfriend Mike?

Mary *fetches the whisky.*

Teresa   Would you like a cup of tea?

Catherine   You don't look a bit like you do on the
television. You're quite small really, aren't you?

Mike   People say this to me all the time, but I'm not
actually.

Catherine   Mind you, you'd never think Robert Redford
was only five foot five, would you?

Mary *snatches the glass from* **Catherine**.

Mary   Give me that.

Fills it and gives it to **Mike**.

Catherine   They always do this to me. So, how tall are
you?

Mike   I'm five eleven.

Catherine   Don't be ridiculous, I don't believe you.

Teresa *hisses at her.*

Teresa   Catherine . . .

Catherine   Sorry, would you like some drugs?

She holds the joint out to him. **Mike** *shakes his head.*

Are you not allowed?

Mary   He doesn't. Come here, sit down.

He sits on the bed and she rubs his hands, undoes his shoes and takes them off.

Mike   I think I've got frostbite.

Catherine   I won't tell anyone. Or I'll say you did but you didn't inhale.

Mike   I'm sorry?

Catherine   That's what celebrities usually say.

Mary   He's not a celebrity, he's a doctor.

Catherine   I saw your programme yesterday. That woman with the psoriasis. God. I thought you were really good.

Mike   Thank you –

Catherine   But you don't want to be caught with a joint in your hand, do you? On top of everything else. You can't be a drug addict and be having an affair. Can you imagine the papers? 'TV Doctor blew my mind says hospital consultant' –

Mary   Catherine, you're off your face –

Teresa   Why don't you come with me and make some tea for everyone?

Catherine   Our mother's just died.

Mike   I know. I'm very sorry.

Catherine *bursts into tears.*

Mary   I'm sorry about this, Mike. Catherine, stop it –

Catherine   God, is no one allowed to show their feelings around here? I'm depressed, I've suffered a bereavement, it's normal to cry, for God's sake –

Mary   Go away, stop doing this –

Mike   It's OK, it's OK, she's allowed to be unhappy –

Catherine   You see? It's only you two who are weird, you don't know what it's like –

Teresa (*storming out*)   That's it. I'm getting a gun.

Catherine *throws herself on the bed and howls.*

Catherine   We're orphans . . .

Mike *puts his arm around her. She holds on to him, puts her head in his lap.*

Catherine   And I'm the youngest, I had them for less time than everyone else did . . .

Mary   Catherine, get up off that bed and get out –

Mike   She's OK, she can't help it, what's the matter with you?

Mary   And you shut up, you know nothing. Catherine, if you don't get out of here, so help me God, I'll brain you.

Catherine *gets up weakly, weeping. She manages to look tiny and pathetic. She turns as she gets to the door.*

Catherine   I've got that pain again . . .

Mike   What pain? Where?

She totters over to **Mike** *and lifts her sweater up.*

Catherine   Just here . . .

Mary   There's nothing wrong with you.

Catherine   She keeps saying that to me –

The phone rings. She stops weeping immediately, and grabs it.

Hello? . . . Xavier? . . . Fuck . . . OK . . . OK . . . You're where? OK, I'll tell her.

She slams the phone down.

It's bloody Frank . . .

She storms out and slams the door.

(*Off*) Teresa!

Mary   I'm sorry. I'm sorry. You have to just ignore her. You don't understand.

Mike   Why are you being so horrible to her?

Mary   Where d'you want me to start?

Mike   OK, OK, OK, come here –

She puts her arms around him and they kiss. It grows passionate. Eventually she pulls away.

Mary   This is my mother's bed.

Mike   I know. Sorry. So.

Mary   So.

Mike   How are you?

Mary   Fine.

Mike   Good.

Mary   Is something wrong?

Mike   I've been stuck on a train in a snowdrift all night.

Mary   Sorry.

Pause.

Did you bring that paper I asked you for?

Mike *squirms apologetically.*

Mike   I couldn't remember the title.

Mary   'A Trophic Theory of Neural Connections'. Why didn't you write it down?

Mike   I didn't think, I mean, I didn't realise you needed it that badly. I thought you'd have enough on your plate. I mean, it's ridiculous, it's an obsession. What's the big deal

about this patient? You've seen post-traumatic amnesia
before, it's not that unusual –

Mary It's not an obsession. I've got close to him, that's all.

Mike How can you get close to someone who can't
remember his own name?

Mary Forget it. I'll look up the paper when I get back.

Pause.

Everything all right at home?

Mike The same, you know.

Pause.

Mary Mike.

Mike What?

Mary D'you love me?

Mike Yes.

Mary Say it then.

Mike I love you. Now you.

Mary Now I what?

Mike Now you say it. That's the form.

Mary Oh, this is ridiculous.

Mike You started it.

Silence.

Mary So. She's better then?

Mike Who?

Mary Chrissie.

Mike No. Why? What d'you mean?

Mary I saw a photo of the two of you. In the hospital
magazine. At a tombola, for Christ's sake. And there she was,

large as life. Fit as a fiddle. And I thought, where's the intravenous drip? What happened to her catheter? I suppose it spoilt the line of her dress, did it?

Mike   Mary –

Mary   I'm sorry, I can't help it, it brings out something horrible in me. I mean you always give the impression she's at death's door, practically in an iron lung –

Mike   Don't exaggerate –

Mary   I'm exaggerating? You said she could hardly walk. Well, forgive me, but either that picture's trick photography, or she's doing the shagging twist –

Mike   She was feeling a bit better.

Mary   God, what's the matter with me? It's Catherine, she makes me want to kill people, and right now I want to kill your wife, which is irrational and I'm sorry.

Mike   You're in shock.

Mary   I'm not in shock. But let me just say this: people don't get off their deathbeds for a tombola.

Mike   I'm sorry I went to a party with my wife. I'm sorry she's not as ill as you'd like her to be. Perhaps you'd prefer her to be dead too. For fuck's sake, Mary. What d'you want me to say?

Mary   I feel humiliated! I've rationalised, I've philosophised, I've come to terms with the fact that I'm living in some nether world with different rules where we don't do Christmas, we don't do bank holidays, and if you die I'll be the last to find out. I accept this because your wife's supposed to be incapable of crossing the street on her own, and now I discover her hopping round a dance floor like a bag of ferrets. I know I'm not supposed to feel things like humiliation or fury or jealousy because they're irrational but sometimes I do, sometimes I just do, OK?

Silence.

Mike   I'm sorry.

Pause.

I think I've got hypothermia. Can I get into bed? I'll keep my clothes on.

Mary   She'd probably quite like the idea of a man in her bed. Get in.

He gets into bed. She sits down on the chair.

Mike   Don't stay over there. Come and sit with me.

Mary   I'm fine here.

Mike   Come on. Please. I've come all this way. The heating broke down on the train, the lights went, and just when we thought we were out of the woods, there were frozen points, and the buffet car ran out of food. We sat in the middle of nowhere and I started to worry about who we'd eat first if things got really out of hand. The man opposite me looked like Margaret Rutherford. I tried to imagine filleting him with a pocket penknife.

Mary   I'll sit on the bed. I'm not getting into it.

She perches primly next to him. He kisses her. She brings her feet up, but pulls her mouth away from his. Lies next to him on top of the covers. He puts his arm round her.

I'm sorry. This is making me very tense. It just feels weird.

Mike   Sorry, sorry, sorry.

He puts his hands behind his head.

Mary   He can remember his own name actually.

Mike   Who?

Mary   That patient. It's coming back in bits. If you show him a bike, he can ride it. He can't remember what it's called, that's all.

Mike   I was talking to someone the other day who'd worked in this lab in France a few years back . . . or maybe he knew someone who worked there, I can't remember. Anyway, they were doing these experiments with water, because they were researching the efficacy of homeopathy, and what they came up with after months and months of apparently stringent tests was that you can remove every last trace of the curative element from a water solution and it will still retain its beneficial effect. And they decided that this meant water was like magnetic tape. That water had memory. You can dilute and dilute and dilute, but the pertinent thing remains. It's unseen, undetectable, untraceable, but it still exerts influence. I mean, they did a full range of tests. It wasn't just a shot in the dark.

Pause.

It's all complete bollocks, of course. Except . . .

Mary   Except what?

Mike   I've got an erection.

Pause.

Mary   We can't. We absolutely can't.

Mike   No.

Mary   It'll go away if we ignore it.

He leans over and kisses her. After a while she pulls away and gets up. She walks about the room, picking up objects from the dressing-table, putting them down.

Everything I look at makes me want to cry. I see these things and a life unravels in front of my eyes. I can't sleep for remembering.

Mike   What?

Pause. **Mary** *is nervous.*

Mary   Can you feel nostalgia for something that never really existed? I remember growing up here. I remember nightlights and a doll's house. I can see them in my mind's eye. And I'm not sure we had either. I find myself aching, longing for it. This half-imagined childhood.

Mike   You want to be a child again?

Pause.

Mary   I want to go through it again. The light on the landing, the bedtime stories. Even though I know some of the memories aren't real. It's like I've hooked up to some bigger, general picture, and it *feels* so real I can taste it.

Pause.

I think I'm pregnant.

Pause.

Mike   What?

Mary   You heard me.

Mike   You can't be.

Mary   I am.

Mike   You can't possibly be.

Mary   I know I'm geriatric, but I'm not completely desiccated –

Mike   Hang on a minute, this is ridiculous –

Mary   It's not ridiculous.

Mike   Have you done a test?

Mary   No, but I feel very strange.

Mike   What d'you mean, strange?

Mary   As in I'm-pregnant strange, what d'you think I mean?

Mike   I'm not going to believe this till you've done a test.

Mary   I'm the size of a house. Look at me.

Mike   You always look like that, don't you?

Mary   Observant. There's another thing you're not.

Pause.

I feel weird.

Mike   You can't. You can't feel weird.

Mary   Well, I do.

Mike   This is unreal. This is completely unreal. I don't believe this is happening –

Mary   Stop getting in a state, will you?

Mike   I'm not getting in a fucking state!

Silence.

What are you going to do?

Mary   What am *I* going to do? What happened to *we*?

Mike   OK, OK, we.

Mary   Well, I kind of hoped for the usual. You know, nine months' gestation followed by birth of something small and squalling. Preferably human. Or perhaps I'm asking for too much.

Mike   Let's not panic about it, OK?

Mary   I'm not panicking. You are.

Mike   I'm not. I'm not. I mean you're probably not. Pregnant.

Mary   I am.

She climbs on the bed next to him and kisses him. Puts her hand on his groin.

Brilliant. I'm pregnant. Instant detumescence.

Silence.

Mike   I think . . . I don't think . . . you know, I mean, the thing is, I'm trying to say –

Mary   It might make the papers, your wife will be humiliated, you can't cope and you're leaving me.

Mike   No, that's not what I'm trying to say.

Pause.

You're sure you're pregnant?

Mary Would you like it in writing?

Mike I have to tell you there's a problem here. The thing is. How can I put this? The thing is, it's not mine. I mean if you are, it's not mine –

Mary Just run that past me again, will you?

Mike I've had a vasectomy.

Silence.

Mary What?

Mike I've had a vasectomy.

Mary You've had a vasectomy.

Mike Yes.

Silence.

Mary When?

Mike Before I met you.

She stares at him.

I wanted to tell you. I was going to, and then . . . it didn't seem important, I suppose . . .

Mary It didn't seem important.

Mike No . . . I mean . . . I just . . . You never . . . I mean it never came up . . . I thought you didn't want children. You never said. I thought, you know, you had a career and everything.

Mary You've got a career. You've also got three children.

Mike I'm sorry. I'm sorry. Why didn't you say anything? Why didn't you tell me you wanted a child?

Mary I'm thirty-nine, Mike. I'm thirty-nine. Didn't you ever think?

Mike   I'm not a mind-reader. You never showed the slightest sign. You never even hinted.

Pause.

Mary   I thought you'd leave me.

Mike   You thought I'd leave you?

Mary   I thought you'd leave me if I said I wanted a child.

The door opens and **Teresa** *comes in carrying a lot of black bin liners.*

Teresa   You're going to hate me for this – oh, for goodness' sake.

Mary *and* **Mike** *spring apart.* **Mary** *gets up.*

Mary   We were just talking.

Mike *gets out of bed.*

Mike   Look, fully dressed –

Catherine *comes in with another joint.*

Catherine   Oh God, have you two been in bed? That's disgusting.

Mary   What? Look, Mike and I are trying to have a conversation –

Teresa   We have to sort out her clothes.

Catherine   Why do we have to do it now?

Teresa *is already taking clothes out of the wardrobe.*

Teresa   A friend of mine's sending a truck to Zimbabwe and I promised I'd have them ready this afternoon.

Mary   She's not even in her grave yet, and apart from that –

Teresa   If we wait until after the funeral, I'll get left with it all.

Mary   Teresa, listen –

Teresa   No. You listen. If it wasn't for me, nothing would ever get done. She'd be lying on the floor stoned out of her brains, you'd be having it off in our dead mother's bed and I'd be holding the fort –

Catherine   St Teresa of Avila –

Teresa   Somebody has to be practical! Somebody has to be in charge, you two can live in chaos but I can't –

Catherine   What chaos?

She is rifling through the clothing, holding frocks up in front of herself.

What's this made of, d'you think? Is it silk?

Mike   Maybe I should, you know –

Mary   Don't even think about it –

Mike   Fine.

Mary   I'm in shock, I still can't believe you –

Teresa   The sooner we get this over with the better. Right. I've worked it out. We divide it into two lots. Crap and good stuff.

Catherine   The crap we send to the poor bastards in Zimbabwe –

Teresa   The crap we take to the dump.

Catherine   I quite like this. Can I have it?

She holds up a dress in front of her and hands the joint to **Teresa**, *who puffs at it absent-mindedly as she sorts through the clothes.*

Mike   Um, what would you like me to do?

Mary   I don't know. Hang yourself.

She picks up the whisky and takes a slug.

Mike   D'you think you should be drinking? I mean –

Mary   Just lie down and die, will you?

Teresa   Mike, you take these bags. This one for rubbish, this one for good stuff. We'll hand it to you, you pack it.

Mike Right. OK. This one rubbish, this one good stuff . . .

Teresa *takes another armful from the wardrobe and throws it on the bed.* **Mary** *stands stricken, staring at it.* **Catherine** *is posing in mirrors, holding up frocks.*

Teresa Oh, for goodness' sake, Mary. I know it's not a very nice job, but it has to be done.

Mary OK, OK.

She picks up some clothes dispiritedly. **Catherine** *picks up a gaudy floral number.*

Catherine God, d'you remember this? What a mistake.

She dances round with the dress in front of her.

Teresa I think that can go in the crap pile.

Catherine They might like it in Zimbabwe.

Teresa She wore that terrible hat with it, d'you remember?

Catherine *scrabbles through the pile. She picks up a hat.*

Catherine Here it is, here it is –

Teresa *begins to giggle. She takes another puff of the joint.*

Mary Is this what you add up to? A wardrobe full of tat and three pelican children?

Teresa Oh dear, I do feel light-headed . . . have some of this, Mary, it's all so much easier . . . pure thingy . . .

Catherine Grass.

Teresa Exactly, no chemicals.

She takes one more draw and hands the joint to **Mary.** **Catherine** *has put the hat on, and is draping the dress around her.*

Teresa Cousin June's wedding. 1969.

Catherine It was horrible even then. D'you remember we didn't want to sit next to her in church.

Mary   Give it to me. (*Takes it, hands it to* **Mike**.) This is for the rubbish.

Mike   Are you sure? Maybe we should have another bag for kind of in-betweens.

Catherine *snatches the dress back.*

Catherine   No, no it's you, Mary, it's perfect –

She holds it against **Mary** *who throws it aside.* **Mike** *puts it in the rubbish.* **Teresa** *yells.*

Teresa   Aargh, look at this –

She pulls out a sixties cocktail frock from the pile on the bed.
Catherine *doubles up with laughter.*

Teresa   She can't have worn this, surely.

Catherine   She did, I remember it, oh God, give it here.

She takes the dress and begins to struggle out of her clothes.

Mary   Catherine, for Christ's sake –

Catherine   I'm wearing underwear. Anyway, he's a doctor, stop being such a pain –

There is a great cry of triumph from **Teresa**, *who has been rooting around in the pile.*

Teresa   Yes!

She brings out a wild pink dress, circa 1963.

This was her Alma Cogan phase. Which I think, on reflection, I prefer to the crimplene phase that followed it.

Mary   Teresa, are we sorting out these clothes or not because I've got better things to do at the moment?

Teresa   I mean, what *was* crimplene, was it a sort of by-product of Formica?

She is holding the dress up against her in front of the mirror.

Mary   Oh, this is ridiculous –

Teresa   Actually, margarine, you know, is a by-product of plastic. Or is it petrol?

Catherine *has got the dress on, and a hat.*

Catherine   What d'you think? Is it me?

Teresa *laughs with stoned hysteria. Even* **Mike** *laughs.*

Mary   And I don't know why you're laughing –

The room is in chaos. **Catherine** *and* **Teresa** *are unstoppable now.* **Catherine** *is trying on shoes, hats, lipstick. Earrings, anything.*

Teresa   Turn away, Mike, turn away –

She goes behind the wardrobe door.

Mary   I give up. Give that to me.

She takes the rubbish sack from **Mike** *and starts to stuff clothing into it.*

Mary   Who did it?

Mike   What?

Mary   The operation. Who did the operation?

Mike   Charlie Morgan. Why?

She starts to laugh.

Mary   Charlie Morgan?

Catherine   Who's Charlie Morgan? Oh, look, I've found a hairpiece from before the Boer War. Look at this –

Mike   Is there a problem with that?

Mary   No, no, no. Honestly.

Teresa *emerges from behind the wardrobe door, looks in the mirror.*

Teresa   Oh God, what do I look like?

Mike   So what's funny?

Mary   Charlie-whoops-I've-made-a-bit-of-a-hash-of-this-Morgan.

Mike Oh, for God's sake, that's a slanderous rumour, he's OK.

Mary He's in a clinic at the moment. Drying out.

Mike He did me years ago. He was steady as a rock.

Mary You didn't notice an overpowering smell of aftershave?

Mike Christ. He wasn't drinking it, was he?

Teresa (*scrabbling around in the bottom of the wardrobe*) Where're those pink shoes?

Mary He's about to be struck off –

Catherine Oh, look at this –

Mary Gross professional negligence, I think it was –

Catherine Mary, this is you –

She holds out the green dress which **Vi** *wore at the beginning of Act One.*

Teresa Oh, put it on –

Mike Are you sure?

Mary Give me some of that joint, Catherine – positive –

Teresa D'you think I need a handbag with this?

Mary I can't believe you went to Charlie Morgan. Did he give you a special price or something?

Mary *takes the dress and starts to struggle into it, giggling.*

Mike Are you making this up?

Catherine Go for it, Mary!

Mary Performing microsurgery when he was so drunk he had double vision.

Mike I think you're exaggerating a bit –

Mary I am not –

Catherine You need bigger hair. Big, crispy hair.

Teresa   Yes, you see, you didn't get shiny hair in those days, did you? Honestly, all that hairspray, think of the carcinogens. Now, d'you think this bag or this –

She holds up two. **Mary** *has got the frock on now.*

Mary   There. What d'you think?

Catherine   You look dead like Mum.

Momentary silence, before they realise, then screeches of appalled laughter. **Teresa** *and* **Catherine** *roll on the bed, clutch their sides. Wild, stoned hysteria, etc.* **Mary** *joins in. The door opens and* **Frank** *comes in, in his overcoat, carrying a suitcase.*

Frank   What the fuck . . . ?

Silence.

Teresa   Frank . . .

Frank   What are you doing?

Mary   We're sorting out Mum's clothes . . .

Pause.

Catherine   D'you think we're sick?

Frank *looks at his watch.*

Frank   It's taken me fourteen hours to get here from Düsseldorf. I spent six of those sitting next to a woman from Carlisle who runs a puppet theatre for the deaf. She'd maroon hair and drank an entire bottle of gin while telling me about her alcoholic father who once bit the head off a chicken. She was wearing a dress that looked like a candlewick bedspread and she'd been on a course in Cologne learning mime and North African devil dancing. I thought, take me back to sanity. And I walk in on this. Pan's bloody People.

Silence. The women suppress their hysteria.

Mike   I'm Mike. Hi.

Frank   How d'you do. And then I got diverted to East Midlands.

Mike   Goodness.

Frank   What is it with this country? It's too hot, it's too cold, there's leaves on the line, it's the wrong sort of snow –

Catherine   Frank, chill out, have some drugs –

They all begin to giggle uncontrollably.

Frank   How long have they been like this?

Mike   I think it's the grief, you know . . .

The women get more hysterical. They hold on to each other and look at themselves in the mirror. They scream with laughter.

Mary   Oh God, what do we look like.

Catherine   Where's my camera, where's my camera?

She goes to her bag and scrabbles around. Pulls out a camera.

Teresa   Oh yes, we've got to have a photo –

Frank   Don't be ridiculous –

Catherine   Frank, you take it –

She hands it to him. They all chant together like a football mob.

All   Photo, photo, photo –

Frank   OK, OK . . .

The women chant and pose and laugh hysterically.

Christ, they're a handful when they all get together. They just gang up, you'll get used to it . . . all right, all right, pull yourselves together . . . Where d'you want to be . . . ?

They all line up in front of the bed, linking arms and staggering and pushing each other.

Mary   OK, OK, smile everyone!

Catherine   I want to be in the middle!

They arrange and rearrange themselves. **Frank** *takes a photo. A flash.
Freeze frame: the women smiling in a row, arms linked. We realise there's
a fourth person in the line-up:* **Vi**, *smiling, cigarette held aloft, in her
green taffeta dress.*

Act Two

Scene One

Lights up on stage exactly as before. **Vi** *and* **Mary** *are alone.* **Vi** *gives her a long look.*

Vi   You look ridiculous in that.

Mary   The tin with the chrysanthemums on it. The one you don't remember. Where is it?

Vi   I told you. I've no idea.

Mary   What have you done with it?

Vi   You need a bit of colour on your face. You were always pasty.

Mary   Don't change the subject. Where's the tin?

Pause.

Vi   Have you tried the shed?

Mary   No.

Vi   It might be in the shed.

Mary   I'll look then.

Vi   Although it might not. It's been years since I saw that tin. It had toffees in it originally. From Torquay. I'd have liked to have gone there. They have palm trees. I've never seen a palm tree in real life. I expect you've seen dozens. You're probably sick to death of palm trees.

Mary *pulls on jeans and sweaters.*

Vi   I do wish you'd wear something a bit more feminine occasionally.

Mary   Apparently I look ridiculous. I'm going to look for the tin.

*She begins to go but **Vi** stops her.*

Vi   This patient. The one you've got all the books about. What's wrong with him?

Mary   He got hit on the head and lost his memory.

Vi gives a soft laugh.

Vi   So what's your prognosis? Doctor.

Mary   He'll recover. More or less intact. I think.

Vi   Intact. I like that word. Intact. Everything in order. In the bag. Right as ninepence. That's nice. Was he in a fight?

Mary   No, he opened a cupboard and a jar fell on him.

Vi   Must have been a big jar.

Mary   Pickled bell peppers.

Vi   You wouldn't get pickled bell peppers up here. Probably a good thing. They sound dangerous.

Mary   Can I go now?

Vi has taken a dress from the pile.

Vi   Look. D'you remember this?

Mary   No.

Vi   I loved this dress. It was the only dress your father ever bought me.

She begins to dance. It's slightly seductive and sensuous.

Saturday nights I used to wear this. The men loved me, you know. Oh yes. All the men loved me. And I loved the men. I never cared for the women. I never liked them. Once I got my first bra I couldn't be doing with them any more.

Mary   Pity you had three daughters really, isn't it?

Vi stops dancing.

Vi   You put words into my mouth. Every one of you does it, but you in particular, you mangle everything into something

else. My comedy mother. My stupid, bigoted, ignorant
mother.

Mary   Well, you shouldn't say such stupid things.

Vi   You lie in bed with your lovers and you tell stories about
me. None of them complimentary. Most of them complaining.
None of them true.

Mary   Excuse me. I'm going to look for that tin.

She turns to go.

Vi   Don't walk away from me! You've done that all your life.

Mary *turns round, like a guilty child.* **Vi** *picks up a book from the
bedside table and opens it at random.*

Vi (*reading*)   'A biological memory system differs from a
simple information storage device, by virtue of its
inherent ability to use information in the service of its own
survival . . . A library, for example, couldn't care less about
its own survival. The problem is not one of storage. The
problem is the difference between a dead and a living
system.'

She shuts it.

So there's a difference between a cat and a bookcase. I could
have told him that.

She looks at the price on the back of the book.

Twenty-five ninety-nine. My God.

Puts it down.

I don't know how this happened. I look at you and I think,
you've come out wrong, all of you. There's something not
quite right about how you've turned out. Not what I expected.

Mary   What a pity. After all your sterling efforts.

Vi   You seem like nice, personable people. I expect you are,
but I don't know what you've got to do with me. You're closed
off. I can't seem to get the hang of any of you. You don't tell

me anything. I tell you things. What I did, where I went. And you just look irritated. You've no patience with me. No tolerance. And I had years of patience with you. It's not fair. How dare you? That's what I feel. How dare you?

Mary   How dare I what?

Vi   Sometimes when I'm talking and I know you're not really listening, I could tear your heads from your bodies. I could tear you apart with my teeth. All of you. You behave as if I'd no hand in the making of you. I took you on picnics, I got up in the night for you. And you remember the things you didn't have. Holidays not gone on. Bicycles never got. A particular type of shoe. How was I to know? When are we going to be done with this? I hear you talking and I think your memories aren't the same as mine. I remember the time of your childhood, and it seems to me that you don't remember it because you weren't there –

Mary   Why are you doing this to me? Why don't you do it to Teresa or Catherine?

Vi   How d'you know I don't?

She strokes the clothes left on the bed.

All my lovely dresses.

Mary   I'm sorry. It's not as if you're going to be needing them.

She begins to stuff them into black bags.

Vi   You were in my bed with him.

Mary   He was cold. We didn't do anything.

Vi   You wanted to.

Mary   Has nothing changed? You used to read my diaries, you knew about every boyfriend I ever had. You used to poke about my room. I always knew you were doing it, I used to watch you.

Vi   I had good reason.

Mary   You did not. D'you understand? You did not. Ever.
Nothing gave you the right to sift through my life like that.

Vi   What is it you don't have? What's the word? Humility, is
that it? I've watched you being offered the world on a plate.
And all of it you've taken, without a backwards glance. Lovers,
sex. Exotic sex probably. Whatever that is. All tasted and
discarded. You take it in your stride, these trips to Paris, these
shoes from Milan, this bottle of wine and not that one, this
man and not that one. This choosing and refusing –

Mary   You know nothing –

Vi   I know different things. I know wanting and no choice.
That counts too. It's not nothing. Excitement was a delivery of
ornamental door knockers. You drink champagne because
you feel like it, you buy things with plastic cards. I've wanted
that. I've tasted bile in my mouth with wanting it. And you
carry it so lightly, you're not even grateful. I look at your
easiness with the world and I don't know how I spawned you.
But I started it. I taught you to speak properly, I saved you
from your own stupid mistakes –

Mary   It wasn't stupidity, it was ignorance, and for that I
blame you –

Vi   I made sure you'd get somewhere, I made sure of it –

Mary   Your idea of getting somewhere was marrying a
dentist in a sheepskin coat from the Rotary Club –

Vi   You invent these versions of me and I don't recognise
myself –

Mary   I'm not listening to you –

Vi   I'm proud of you and you're ashamed of me –

Mary   I am not –

Vi   I hear you say it all the time. I'm not like my mother, I'm
not, I'm not. I'm like my father. Look in the mirror. Why
can't you see it? Everyone else can. Look at the curve of your
cheek, look at your hands, the way they move. You're doing it

now. That's me. I got it from my mother. She got it from her
mother. And on it goes, so far back that we don't know who
began it or on what impulse, but we do it, we can't help it –

Mary   I've inherited some of your gestures. So what?

Vi   Don't try and reinvent yourself with me. I know who you
are.

Mary   You don't know anything.

Vi   I look at you and I see myself.

Mary   Have you finished?

Vi   Never.

Go to black.

Scene Two

Same place. **Catherine** *is praying to the telephone.*

Catherine   Ring ring ring, please God, make him ring.
Holy Mary Mother of God, I'll come back to the church, I'll
do anything, make him ring now. Xavier, listen to me, pick up
the fucking phone, please, I'm going off my head. I can't stand
this. Why are you doing this to me? It's not fair. I'm getting an
ulcer, you're making me ill. OK, I'm going to count to ten and
then I'm going to phone you. If you haven't phoned by the
time I've finished this joint I'm going to ring you, can you hear
me? Just pick up the phone and speak to me. You could be
dead for all I know, you could have had an accident or
anything. Xavier, this is killing me.

Mary *comes in.* **Catherine** *looks at her.*

Catherine   God, I hate him.

She picks up the phone and taps out a number.

Hola? Xavier, por favor . . . Oh, right . . . It's Catherine . . .
Catherine . . . I just wondered if he got my message because I
tried to leave a number but the line went dead . . . Oh, I see

. . . When? . . . Well, what time were you thinking he might
. . . OK, could you tell him then, just tell him that I called,
and if he could –

The line goes dead.

Hello? Hello?

Teresa *and* **Frank** *come in as she puts the phone down.*

Teresa   Did he call then?

Catherine   Yeah, yeah, he just rang, that was him –

Mary *turns and looks at her.* **Catherine** *refuses to catch her eye.*

Teresa   Where's Mike?

Mary   I've put him in a hot bath, he'd gone a bit blue.

Teresa   Look, we've got to sort these flowers out, just look
at the photos, will you? It'll take two minutes –

She hands the florist's book to **Mary**.

Catherine   Poor thing, he hasn't had a chance to get to the
phone, there's been a flood in the restaurant, all the furniture's
bobbing around in three feet of water, it's a disaster, but it'll
come off the insurance, I suppose. So that's all right. Luckily.

Teresa   Oh dear. Frank, take those bags out to the car.

Catherine   I just hope he can make the funeral, I mean I
hope it's all sorted out so he can get a flight tonight, otherwise,
well, he won't, will he? Make the funeral.

Frank *picks up an armful of black plastic.*

Frank   Had he ever met your mother?

Catherine   He'd talked to her on the phone. Anyway,
what's that supposed to mean? God, why does everyone in this
house have to be so oblique and sneery, why can't anyone say
what they mean?

Frank   Catherine, stop being so bloody paranoid –

Teresa   Frank. Bags. Car. Now.

Frank *puts the bags down.*

Frank   For Christ's sake, Teresa, I've only just thawed out.

Catherine   Mike's never met her either and no one's complaining about him coming –

Teresa   OK, OK, so what did he say?

Catherine   Nothing. He said he'd phone back as soon as he knew what was happening. That's what he said. Stop interrogating me, OK?

Mary   I'll have number seventeen B.

She hands the book back to **Teresa**.

Teresa (*looking at the photo*)   She was allergic to lilies of the valley, choose something else –

Mary   She's hardly going to start sneezing at her own funeral, is she?

She takes the book again. **Frank** *grapples with the bags, one of which bursts open.*

Frank   Oh, for fuck's sake!

Mike *comes in wrapped in a towel, clutching his clothes. He looks at the assembled crowd.*

Teresa   Sorry, Mike, d'you want to get dressed?

Mike   No, no, I'm fine really, don't mind me.

Catherine   I bet you've used all the water –

Mary (*handing the florist's book to* **Teresa**)   Twenty-seven A, not a lily in sight, absolutely no chance of impetigo, hives, or nervous eczema for either mourners or deceased. Catherine, you choose and then could you all leave us in peace for five minutes?

Catherine   Why are you always trying to get rid of me?

Teresa   Oh, don't start, Catherine. Choose your wreath, for heaven's sake –

She tries to give her the book.

Catherine   No, I always get this, 'Bugger off, Catherine, we don't want you here,' well, what am I supposed to do? Teresa's got Frank, you've got him, and what am I supposed to do on my own? I don't want to sit in the living-room on my own while everyone else has smoochy secret conversations, it's not fair, not at a time like this, but if that's what you want –

She gets into the wardrobe and shuts the door.

Frank   Have you ever thought of laying off the drugs for a while, Catherine?

Catherine   Who asked you?

The phone rings. She dives out of the wardrobe and grabs it.

Hello? Xavier . . . God, how are you, where've you been? Did you get my . . . Oh, right . . . Oh . . . What? . . . Oh. Well, couldn't you . . .

Long pause. She listens.

I don't think we should . . . maybe we should talk about this when I get back . . . OK, bye.

She puts the phone down. They all look at her. Awkward silence.

He can't come.

Teresa   Because of the flood?

Catherine   The what? Oh, no, well, yes, lots of things. Anyway, he's not coming.

Silence.

Mike   Are you all right?

Catherine   Yeah. Yeah. He said he'd ring back later.

She gets up.

So. What is there still to do? Shall we sort the drawers out? There's all the jewellery and stuff –

She goes to the dressing-table drawer and begins to rummage through it, taking things out haphazardly.

God, he's so funny sometimes, he's so apologetic. He was almost crying on the phone, you should have heard him. It's just a real drag he can't come, he's so lovely. Did I ever show you his photo? He's got beautiful teeth. I mean, he really, really wanted to come. It's just hopeless, you know, running a restaurant and everything, you never get any time off.

Mike   Maybe you'd like a cup of tea?

Catherine   I don't want any tea.

She takes a tin from the drawer and tries to open it.

Mike   Right. OK.

Mary   It's probably just as well he isn't coming. I mean, he wouldn't know anyone and it's a strange country and everything.

Catherine   Yes. It's probably just as well.

She hurls the tin across the room, narrowly missing **Frank**.

Frank (*ducking*)   Jesus –

Catherine   Fuck it!

Silence. She bursts into racking sobs.

I went to this counsellor – did I tell you this? – or a therapist or something and she said I had this problem and the problem was, I give too much, I just do too much for other people, I'm just a very giving person, and I never get any credit for any of it. I haven't even got any friends. I mean, I have but I don't like most of them, especially the women, and I try really hard, it's just I'm very sensitive and I get taken for a ride, nothing ever goes right, every time, I mean, every time it's the same – like with men. What is it with men? I mean, I don't have a problem with men or anything. I love men. I've been to bed with seventy-eight of them, I counted, so obviously there's not a problem or anything, it's just he didn't even apologise or anything and how can he say on the phone he doesn't want to see me any more? I mean, why now? Why couldn't he have waited? I don't know what to do, why does it always go wrong? I don't want to be on my own, I'm sick of people saying I'll be better off on my own, I'm not that sort of person, I can't do it. I did everything for him, I was patient and all the things you're supposed to be and people kept saying don't accept this from him, don't accept that, like, you know, when he stayed out all night, not very often, I mean once or twice, and everyone said tell him to fuck off, but how could I because what if he did? Because they all do, everyone I've ever met does, they all disappear and I don't know if it's me or what. I don't want to be on my own, I can't stand it, I know it's supposed to be great but I don't think it is. I can't help it, it's no good pretending, it's fucking lonely and I can't bear it.

She rushes out of the room. They look at each other. Silence. **Frank** *picks up the tin.*

Frank   She nearly had my head off.

Mary   Christ. I wonder what sort of therapist she went to. How could anyone in their right mind tell Catherine her problem was give give give?

She pours herself a whisky.

Mike   Actually, it is, in a weird kind of way, she's trying to give you something all the time. It's usually inappropriate, that's all. I mean, she's obviously got some kind of problem.

Teresa   Yes, we don't need you to tell us that, thank you –

Mike   Sorry, she's just, I mean, pretty miserable and not very stable –

Teresa   Thank you, doctor –

Frank   Teresa –

Teresa   Well, I'm sick of people feeling sorry for her. It's very easy the first time you meet her, but if you put up with her year in year out, you just want to kill her –

She takes the glass from **Mary**.

Teresa   Give me some of that.

Frank   Teresa, don't drink whisky, it makes you demented, you know that –

Teresa *knocks back the entire glass and grimaces.*

Teresa   Salt.

Frank   Don't drink it if it tastes of salt –

Teresa   I thought you were taking those bags to the car –

Mike   Maybe one of you should go and have a word with Catherine.

Teresa   How dare you walk in here and pontificate?

Frank   Put the bottle down, Teresa –

Mike   I just meant –

Mary   Don't get involved, Mike, please.

Mike   I'm just saying from an outsider's point of view, she gets a rough deal. I know you can't see it, because your tolerance has run out, but actually she's a mess and nobody really listens to her –

Teresa   Because she talks bollocks, that's why. I mean, this is rich, this is, coming from you, the man who's been two-timing his wife for the last five years telling us how to behave –

Frank   Teresa, what the hell's this got to do with anything? Stop it.

Teresa   No, why shouldn't I shout? Everyone else does in this house –

Frank   I never said you were shouting –

Teresa   Well, you're deaf then, because I am. Just answer me this, Mike –

Mary   Just ignore her –

Teresa   When are you going to do the decent thing? When are you going to leave your wife and marry my sister?

Frank   Oh, for Christ's sake, this is none of your business, Teresa –

Teresa   Well, it's about time someone asked –

Frank   But not you, and not now, OK?

Mike   It's very complicated.

Mary   You don't have to answer, Mike, it's OK. Teresa, can we stop this right here?

Mike   My wife's ill actually –

Teresa   Oh, very convenient.

Mary   She's got ME.

Teresa   ME my arse.

Frank   Teresa, I'm warning you –

Teresa   What sort of illness is that?

Mary   Stop it!

Teresa   The sort of illness where you lie on the sofa for six months with a bit of a headache. It's not a proper illness. It's not a brain tumour. It's not as if she's got both her legs in traction. Let me tell you something, Mike.

Frank   I don't think you should tell anybody anything right at this moment –

Teresa   There's nothing wrong with your wife, Mike.

Mike   Well, there is actually.

Teresa   No. She knows you're having an affair so she thinks if she's ill, you won't leave her.

Frank   Sorry about this, Mike, like you said, it's the grief, you know –

Mike   Don't worry about it. I'm sorry, I shouldn't have stuck my oar in –

Frank   Teresa, come on now, you're talking shite, come and have a lie-down.

Teresa   Actually, I'm not talking shite. Actually. I've done it. I've got ill so people would be nice to me. I used to do it to my ex-husband. Sometimes it's all that's left to you. You get ill for a reason. You do it so people won't go.

Frank   Teresa, I beg of you. Remember the last time. Three small gins, that's all. Took her bloody clothes off. In a car park.

Teresa   I was hot.

Mary   Give me the bottle. Now.

Teresa   Don't tell me what to do, and stop looking so bloody superior, because you've no cause –

Mary   His wife is ill. Genuinely ill. ME is real. It's not imaginary. OK?

Teresa   You see. We're our mother's daughters. Always take the man's side even when he's a complete pile of crap –

Frank   Teresa, that's enough –

Teresa   Just like with Dad.

Mary   Frank, get her out of here –

Teresa   Our father, Mike, hardly spoke at all during the forty-eight years he was married to our mother. D'you remember hearing him speak, Mary? D'you recall him ever uttering a word of encouragement, an endearment?

Mary   Teresa –

Teresa   He was like a professional mute. And fucking someone else for most of the time.

Frank   Right, that's it. Come on.

Teresa   D'you know what his last words were, Mike?

Mike   I don't, no.

Teresa   'Pass the mustard, Marjorie.'

Frank   That was George the Fifth –

Teresa   And she wasn't even called Marjorie. D'you understand?

Mary   For Christ's sake, this is all bollocks.

Teresa   Our mother's name was Violet and he said, 'Pass the mustard, Marjorie.' I think that just about sums him up.

Mary   This is pure invention –

Teresa   How do you know? You weren't there. As usual. Never there in a crisis, not even your own. It's always someone else does the clearing up. Always me and Mum.

Frank   Teresa –

Teresa   All those years she never said a word against him. Dad was always right, it was a perfect marriage. We've no secrets, she used to say. For heaven's sake. Who was she trying to kid?

Mary   Teresa, please, I'm exhausted with this –

Teresa   No! Who was she trying to kid? Tell me.

Mary   I don't know. Herself. She was trying to kid herself. OK?

Frank   Mike, believe me, I'm on your side –

Teresa   She dyed her hair red, d'you remember that? Dad didn't even notice. Didn't say a word. I mean, you could hardly miss it, it was a disaster, dogs ran away from her in the street –

Mary   He was being polite. He didn't want to hurt her –

Teresa   Stop putting a gloss on him, he didn't bloody care. We could have had three heads and he'd not have noticed. Our entire bloody lives spent making sure nothing ruffled his feathers. He used to laugh at the word stress. 'Stress,' he'd say, 'what a lot of rubbish.' He said he didn't know what it was. Of course he bloody didn't. We did it for him. We had the stress for him. We contorted ourselves. Literally, in your case –

Mary   I really don't want to get into this at the moment –

Teresa   I don't believe he didn't know. How could he not bloody know? I mean, he might have been mute but he wasn't blind for goodness' sake –

Mary   Yeah, well, it was a long time ago, let's just –

Teresa   No, let's not, let's not just pretend it never happened –

Mary   Nothing happened –

Teresa   Bloody hell, how can you not notice that someone's eight months pregnant?

Silence.

Frank   Who was eight months pregnant?

Silence.

Mary   Me.

Pause.

Teresa   She was fourteen.

Frank   Are you serious?

Mary   Yes. Anything else you'd like to know?

Mike   You never told me –

Mary   It was a long time ago. There's nothing to tell –

Teresa   What d'you mean, there's nothing to tell?

Mary   It's for me to tell or not. If I don't talk about it, that's my business. It didn't happen to you, it happened to me.

Teresa   Oh, typical solipsistic bollocks. No one exists but you. Have you any idea what Mum and I went through?

Mary   You went through nothing. What you went through was nothing, d'you understand me? No, I don't suppose you do, you stupid, unimaginative woman.

Frank   You're really excelling yourself today, Teresa. Although personally, I think your timing's a bit off. Much more effective if you'd waited till the funeral, and then got up and announced it to the congregation. You could have done it instead of the crappy Dylan Thomas poem. You'd have brought the house down.

Teresa   I'm tired of it. Why should she sail through her life getting pats on the back as if she'd never put a foot wrong?

Frank   It just strikes me as being a strange time to reveal it to the world, Teresa. I mean, it hardly qualifies as bereavement counselling –

Teresa   You don't know the half of it –

She picks up the bottle again.

Frank   If you take one more swig of that, your liver will explode –

Teresa   Hiding it all from Dad. It was ridiculous, but of course Mary was Goody Two Shoes, Snow White and Our Lady of Lourdes all rolled into one as far as he was concerned, and we couldn't disabuse him of that convenient fiction, could we?

Mary   This is a novel told entirely from your point of view –

Teresa   Mum had to arrange everything, poor woman, all those lies about peritonitis and hospitals and God knows what –

Mary   She put her hand over my mouth when the pains started. I bet you've forgotten that bit –

Teresa   She did not. She found a lovely, Catholic family who brought him up in the true faith, while you got on with your true vocation of being the best at everything. No questions asked, never mention it again, it never happened, even Catherine doesn't know. Poor bloody Catherine, she's always complaining no one tells her anything, and she's right, no one ever did, no one ever will –

Mike   So there's a grown-up son somewhere –

Teresa   Mary this, Mary that, Mary's bloody homework, Mary's bloody exams. We used to creep around on tiptoes in case her precious brain cells got thrown off-kilter by sudden exposure to pop music or someone slamming the front door. And all it's done is make her think she's immune, with her breathtaking fucking arrogance –

Mary   This is a fabrication, this is a complete distortion of the truth –

Teresa   And you still think you're unassailable, you still bloody do –

Mary   You're drunk, I'm not listening to this –

She walks out furiously. **Mike** *hurries after her.*

Mike   I'll just, er . . . Excuse me a minute – Mary –

Frank   D'you know something, Teresa, you're not just embarrassing, you're really quite repulsive, when you're drunk. I'm going to give Mike some friendly advice: don't leave your wife. You don't want to marry into this lot. It's worse than the Borgias.

Teresa   Oh, shut up.

She starts to cry. Long silence. Tears stream down her face.

I've wanted to cry for three days.

She takes another swig of whisky, sobbing.

The salt taste's gone.

Silence.

Say something, Frank.

Pause.

Frank   I've been awake for thirty-six hours.

Pause.

Teresa   You have a whole repertoire of silences, don't you?

Frank   Sorry?

Teresa   You've got a pissed-off one, and a resentful one, an I-hate-you-so-much-I'm-pretending-to-be-deaf one, and a worse one which is I-hate-you-so-much-I'm-pretending-to-be-foreign-and-I-don't-understand-anything-you're-saying. Your silences are the most eloquent thing about you. I can read them the way an Eskimo reads snow.

Frank   Inuit.

Teresa   What?

Frank   Inuit. That's what they're called now. They don't like being called Eskimos any more.

Teresa   How do you know? How many Eskimos have you ever met?

Frank   Teresa, I'm shattered –

Teresa   You're always shattered.

Frank   What's that supposed to mean?

Teresa   You come home, stare at the wall and pass out. You can fall asleep over a supermarket trolley, I've seen you, you can even do it with your eyes open so you look like you're awake –

Frank   It's because you keep sending me to these bloody conferences, sales junkets, glee clubs . . . Fuck, I don't know what they are most of the time, half the time I don't even know where I am –

Teresa   I do not send you –

Frank   Well, you bloody go. You spend a week living on goose fat and pickled cabbage in some emerging democracy. You try persuading people who haven't seen a banana for six months that what they need is royal fucking jelly. Then try it for six months of every year and see how you feel. You wouldn't even make it as far as the supermarket to fall asleep. You'd probably be dead.

Teresa   It's not my fault if Albanians haven't got bananas, it's not my fault –

Frank   I never said that –

Teresa *is very, very drunk.*

Teresa   Why is it all my fault?

Frank   Teresa, what is it that you want from me? I can't do a thing right. What is it that I'm doing wrong?

Silence.

Teresa   Why d'you do this to me?

Frank   Why do I do what?

Teresa   Oh he's so nice, Frank, isn't he, he's so good-natured. Well actually, I want to say, the minute he walks through his own front door, he's not nice, not remotely, he stops speaking in sentences, he just grunts, he's not the charming Frank you all think he is, he might as well be a hologram, it's a bloody nightmare, Frank, you're just like –

She stops. Pause.

Frank   Just like who?

Teresa   No one. Nothing.

She looks at him.

You said you were witty and entertaining. That's what you said.

Frank   Oh, don't start all this again –

Teresa   Witty and entertaining and five foot eleven. Hah!

Frank   You said you were twenty-nine.

Teresa   I did not say I was twenty-nine –

Frank   Excuse me, oh, excuse me –

He takes a piece of paper from his wallet and reads.

Thoughtful, sexy, vegetarian woman, coming up thirty –

Teresa   – seeks witty, entertaining man thirty to forty-five –

Frank   You weren't coming up thirty –

Teresa   And you weren't witty and entertaining.

Frank   You didn't argue at the time.

Teresa   Say something entertaining, then. Go on.

Frank   Oh, for fuck's sake –

Teresa   Well, say something interesting, then. Tell me something new.

Pause.

Frank   I hated *Hannah and Her Sisters*.

Teresa   What?

Frank   I hated it. I hate Woody Allen.

Teresa   *Hannah and Her Sisters* was our first date.

Frank   I know.

Teresa   You said you loved it.

Frank   I was lying. I didn't get it. It wasn't funny.

Teresa   There's that bit where the man won't buy the paintings because they don't match his sofa. That's funny.

Frank   It's not. It's perfectly reasonable. You wouldn't buy, say, a big green and purple painting if you had a red sofa, would you? You'd scream every time you went into the living-room. You'd get migraine.

Teresa   That's not the point of the joke.

Frank   So what is the point, then?

Teresa   You've been pretending to like Woody Allen all these years. You've been lying. I've been married to a stranger –

Pause. She looks at him unsteadily.

Frank.

Frank   What?

Teresa   Are you having an affair?

Frank   What?

Teresa   Just tell me.

Frank *is bewildered.*

Frank   I'm not having an affair.

Teresa   Are you sure?

Frank   Oh hang on, let me rack my brains, it might have slipped my mind –

Teresa   I'm serious –

Frank   I'm not having an affair. I haven't got the energy –

Teresa   But if you ever. I mean. If you ever did have an affair you'd tell me, wouldn't you?

Frank   I thought that was the whole point of having an affair. You don't tell.

Teresa *punches him in the stomach. He gasps.*

Frank   I was joking. I was joking.

Teresa   You've got a horrible sense of humour.

Frank   I'm sorry. Put the bottle down. Come on, you've had enough. Sit down.

She hands him the bottle, tearfully. Pause. **Frank** *takes a deep breath.*

Teresa. During the course of my spectacularly indirect journey here from Düsseldorf, in between bouts with the mime artist, I did a bit of thinking. Two and a half days at a health food convention being harassed by people who do vitamin therapy according to star signs reminded me of what deep down I've known for some time. We sell utter crap.

Teresa   Frank –

Frank   No, hang on, let me finish. I know you believe in it. I know you do. But just answer this. Were your parents happy running a hardware shop? Running a business together?

Teresa   No, of course not.

Frank   So why did you think you would be?

Teresa   It's got nothing to do with my parents.

Frank *looks at her.*

Frank   Maybe later, when the funeral's out of the way, we could, you know . . .

Teresa   What?

Frank   I don't know. Maybe you should run the business and I should go into something else.

Teresa   Like what?

Frank   The thing is, Teresa, I hate selling things. Or specifically, I hate selling things that people don't want and I don't believe in. I'm not cut out for it. I like a nice straightforward transaction, you know? 'Good evening, two pints of bitter, and a rum and Coke.' 'Certainly, sir, ice and lemon? That'll be five pounds fifty, thank you.' End of transaction. Not, 'Can I interest you in a double port while we're at it? No? Well, what about a set of toning tables, or cavity wall insulation?' I can't stand it, Teresa, it's driving me insane. I want to do something simple.

Teresa   Such as what?

Pause.

Frank   A pub. I want to run a pub.

Teresa   You want to run a pub?

Frank   I've seen one for sale just outside Ripon.

Teresa *staggers to her feet.*

Teresa   A pub! I don't believe you –

Catherine *walks in.*

Catherine   What's going on?

Frank   Nothing's going on, I'm trying to have a conversation with Teresa –

Teresa   I think I'm going to be sick. No, don't come near me. A pub, you must be out of your mind –

Frank   Teresa –

Teresa   Don't touch me. A pub, a pub for God's sake –

She goes out. Crashing noises from outside the room. Swearing. **Frank** *lies back on the bed, exhausted.*

Catherine   Oh God.

She jumps on to the bed next to **Frank**.

I'm so depressed.

Frank   Yeah, well, you know, it's a depressing business. Dying and whatnot.

Silence.

Catherine   Frank?

Frank   What?

Catherine   Am I unattractive?

Frank   I'm sorry?

Catherine   D'you think I'm pretty?

Frank   Of course you're pretty. Look, Catherine, I'm exhausted, I'm talked out, I'm sorry.

Pause.

Catherine   I'm very pretty. I'm good fun. I'm a very special person. That's what Carmen, my therapist, said. I'm a brilliant cook. So why did he leave me?

Frank   Jesus, Catherine, I don't know. People leave each other. You'll get over it. I have to go and talk to Teresa.

Catherine   She's probably being sick. That's what she usually does if she drinks. What am I going to do?

Frank   About what?

Catherine   Xavier.

Frank   Catherine, I've no advice to give you. I'm a middle-aged man with a health food business I don't believe in, and a normally teetotal wife who's taken to the bottle. I could say, have some ginseng tea, eat organic vegetables and learn to love yourself, but it's all a lot of bollocks.

Catherine   I have to get back to him, I can't bear it. I have to see him. I mean, this is the real thing, I know it is, so I can't just give in, can I? . . . I can't bear it –

She puts her head in his lap. He looks at her as if she's an unexploded bomb. He tries to move away. She puts her arms round him.

Frank   OK, OK, OK, that's enough, Catherine, take it easy –

Catherine   I need a hug.

He pats her awkwardly.

Frank   There you go.

Catherine   That's not a hug.

Frank   Teresa'll give you a hug.

Catherine   How can she, with her head down the toilet?

She grips him tightly.

Frank   Catherine, get off my leg –

Catherine   It's OK, you're family –

Frank   Exactly –

Catherine   Hold me, Frank, I'm so bloody lonely. What am I going to do? I just need a bit of a hug, that's all –

Frank   Catherine, I'm very flattered but steady on, eh, we don't want to –

She kisses him, immediately pulls away and jumps off the bed.

Catherine   I wasn't trying to seduce you or anything –

Frank   Catherine, you're a bit crazy at the moment, OK –

Catherine   Oh, typical –

Frank   No, I mean, it's understandable, look at Teresa. If I were you I'd phone this Pepe now, and tell him to eff off, just say, 'I'm sorry, Pepe, my mother's just died, I don't need this, take a hike –'

Catherine   He's not called Pepe –

Frank   Or whatever. Jose –

Catherine   Oh, for fuck's sake, all I wanted was a bit of affection. A bit of support. That's all I was asking for. I wasn't asking you to marry me and bear my children. What is it with men? Why d'you always have to misread the signals? God, you make me sick –

Mary *and* **Mike** *come in.* **Mary** *is carrying a tin box.*

Mary   I know you're drawn to this room like moths to a flame, but believe me, I've had enough of all of you. If anyone rings I'll let you know –

Catherine   I was going anyway –

She goes out. **Frank** *gets up.*

Frank   I'm worried about her. I'm serious – she needs six months in a secure unit, she's completely – anyway, I'd better go and sort Teresa out –

He goes. **Mary** *sits on the bed and opens the box. She sifts through papers.*

Mary   I'm putting my name on a register, so that if he's looking for me, he'll find me. I don't even know what he looks like. I have to make him up. I sit on tubes looking at twenty-five-year-old boys, and I think, maybe that's him. Ever since he went I've been looking for him, but he's like ether, I can't get hold of him.

She unfolds a piece of paper.

Oh, thank God. Thank God it's still here. Here he is. Oh, look. Patrick. Patrick James. My boy. I wanted to call him Heathcliff. I was fourteen. I still thought life was a novel. (*She reads.*) 'Sex: boy. Name: Patrick James. Weight: six pounds four ounces.' This is all I've got left of him.

She looks round the room.

This will all be gone soon. All this furniture, all this stuff. The room will go probably. It'll disappear into the sea. And this is all I want to take from the house. This is the only thing I want to salvage. So I can prove he's mine.

She puts the paper in her bag. Puts her hand on her stomach, and goes to the mirror. Looks at herself sideways.

It's a strange feeling being pregnant. You wake up one morning and you feel so absolutely other.

She looks at him.

Mike Mary, I think, you know, you're jumping the gun here –

Mary I need a real child, not a ghost one. What are you going to do? Are you sticking with me or walking away?

Mike If you are pregnant, *if* you are, of course, I mean, of course I won't walk away, I just don't think it's – look, I know Charlie Morgan's in the Betty Ford clinic –

Mary You could always sue him. Everyone else is.

Mike Look. I know you want a child, I accept that. I know you're furious with me for having a vasectomy –

Mary Five years and you never mentioned it, that's what I can't –

Mike I don't want a child, Mary! I don't want a child. I can't want one just because you do. Love and paternity aren't indivisible in my mind. When I say I love you it means I like you, I want to be with you, I want to go to bed with you, it means all sorts of things but it doesn't necessarily mean three children and Sainsbury's every Saturday for the next thirty years –

Mary   No, you've already got that –

Mike   I can't help what happened before I met you! You might not like what I'm telling you, but I can't lie to make you feel better. I never wanted kids in the first place. They happened and now I love them but I don't want any more. It's not because I'm cold or selfish – at least no more than anyone else is – it's that I feel sucked dry by what people need from me – patients, Chrissie, the children. You're where I come to be equal, I come to you because you're not asking to be healed. Some people aren't paternal. It's not a crime. I'm one of them. If you're a woman and you take care of your own fertility, nobody argues. Well, I've taken care of mine. I didn't have a vasectomy because Chrissie's ill, I had it for me.

Silence.

But obviously, you know, if you *are* pregnant, I'll stick by you.

Mary   Well, hey. That makes me feel a whole lot better.

Pause.

Jesus. Oh, Jesus, what a mess. Bring back the days when we had no choice in the matter.

Mike   Well, you did have a choice. You chose me.

Mary   Oh, choice shmoice. Have you seen what's on offer out there? Tiny little trainspotters in grey shoes, maniacs, alcoholics, men who wear their underpants for a week.

There's a knock at the door.

Go away.

Catherine *comes in.*

Catherine   D'you know what she's gone and done?

Mary   I don't know and I don't care.

Catherine   I'll kill her –

Frank *comes in.*

Frank   Look, I'm sorry, I know you're trying to get a bit of peace –

Mary   Oh, don't mind about us, please –

Frank   The thing is, Teresa's arranged for your mother to come back, that's all.

Mary   Sorry, I'm obviously in the grip of an aural hallucination. Say that again.

Catherine   The night before. She's coming back here. The night before the funeral. Tonight.

Mary   What, in her coffin?

Catherine   No she's coming on foot, what d'you think?

Mary   Apart from anything else, where are we going to put her?

Frank   In here, this is her room.

Mary   I'm sleeping in here. I can't sleep next to my dead mother. For Christ's sake.

Mike   We can go to a hotel –

Frank   You can have it open or closed, it's up to you.

Catherine   She's dead. I don't want to see her dead face.

Teresa *appears in the doorway, drunk and dishevelled.*

Teresa   You should see her, it's important, and then you'll know she's dead –

Catherine   She's been in a fridge for four days, of course she's bloody dead –

Teresa   Well, I'm sorry, she's coming home, I've arranged it and that's that and it's no good saying why didn't I ask you because you weren't here to ask. She's coming home to spend her last night in her own bedroom. And that's the end of the story. The end. Full stop. *Finito. La fin.*

She sways precariously.

Frank . . .

Frank   What?

Teresa   I've had far too much to drink . . .

Go to black.

Scene Three

Same room, early next morning. The coffin is there on a low trestle.
Teresa *is dressed for the funeral, talking on the phone.* **Catherine** *is*
sitting in her dressing gown, staring at the coffin.

Teresa   So when you say 'even later', you mean what? . . . I
see . . . No, of course . . . I understand . . . Could you ring as
soon as – thank you . . . Bye . . .

She looks at **Catherine***, looks at her watch.*

They must be snowed in.

Catherine   Who?

Teresa   The men who carry the coffin. Funeral operatives,
he calls them. They still haven't shown up for work. He's
trying to find some replacements. I wish I knew what he
meant, I mean, we don't want amateurs doing it. It's supposed
to be dignified. You can't just get anyone in.

Catherine *says nothing. She's staring at the coffin.*

Teresa   Why don't you get dressed, or are you thinking of
going like that?

Catherine   It's tiny, isn't it?

Teresa *looks.*

Teresa   She was only small.

Catherine   Not as small as that.

Teresa   She must have been. They don't fold them up.

Pause.

Catherine   D'you think they make them to measure?

Teresa   I suppose they must.

Catherine   I suppose so. Yeah. I mean babies' coffins are tiny, aren't they? They're about this big.

Teresa   They'd have to be. Otherwise they'd rattle around.

Catherine   Mmmm . . . Unless you used loads of bubble wrap.

Teresa   If you want to look at her, you just have to undo a little screw at the top. They gave me a wee screwdriver.

Silence.

I don't want to, do you?

Catherine   Not really, no.

Pause. She turns away from the coffin.

I'm so depressed. I can't change my flight.

Teresa   Forget him. He's a bastard.

Catherine   How do you know?

Teresa   You've never had a boyfriend who isn't. You don't go about it the right way.

Catherine   There was that nice Swiss one. He was all right. Did you ever meet him? He was gorgeous, I felt just like Heidi.

Teresa   I knew Frank was the right man for me straight away. Because I chose him. I got forty-seven replies. I whittled them down and chose the most compatible.

Catherine   Yeah, but the thing is . . .

Teresa   What?

Catherine   At the end of the day you still landed up with Frank.

Teresa   We're very, very happy actually. We're a perfect match. Because we went about it in the right way –

Catherine   D'you know who he reminds me of?

Teresa   Don't say it.

Catherine   He does though, doesn't he? It must be a bit depressing. You go through all the palaver of whittling out the dross and you end up married to your dad.

Mary *comes in, dressed for the funeral. She looks white and drawn.*

Teresa   Oh, there you are. You look lovely.

Pause. **Mary** *looks at the coffin.*

How was the hotel?

Mary   Fine.

Teresa *watches her looking at the coffin.*

Mary   Sorry. It's a bit of a shock. Brings you up a bit short, doesn't it . . . ?

Catherine   Everyone's snowed in. There's no one to carry it –

Teresa   That's no reason to still be in your dressing gown –

Catherine   OK, OK, I'll get dressed, I'm going, don't worry.

She goes out. **Mary** *looks round the room, obviously searching for something.*

Teresa   I'm sorry about yesterday.

Mary   Forget it.

Teresa   I shouldn't drink.

Mary   No. You shouldn't.

She sits on the bed and takes the green tin from underneath. Begins to look through it. **Teresa** *looks at her sharply.*

Teresa   Where did you find that?

Mary   At the back of the airing cupboard. Why?

Teresa When?

Mary Yesterday. I wanted the copy of his birth certificate.

Teresa *snatches the tin from her.*

Teresa It's not in here.

Mary *is bewildered.*

Mary I know it's not. I took it out. I was just wondering if there was anything else –

Teresa Like what?

Mary I've no idea, adoption papers. For goodness' sake, what's the matter with you?

Teresa It's just old gas bills and bus tickets, you know what she was like, she could never throw anything away –

Mary I just want to see if there's anything else about Patrick –

Teresa There's not, I've looked.

Mary Teresa, this is ridiculous, I'm not in the mood, give me the tin.

Teresa *holds on to it grimly, unable to think of a response.*

Mary Please.

Teresa I'll give it to you later. After the funeral. OK?

Mary Why can't I have it now?

Teresa We'll sort it out later, OK.

Mary Sort what out? Give me the tin, for goodness' sake –

She makes a grab for it. A tussle.

Teresa I told you, I'll give it to you later –

More tussling.

Mary What is it?

Teresa Nothing!

Tussle gets more violent.

Mary   Give me the bloody tin!

They fight. **Teresa** *manages to hang on. She sits down with the tin.*

Teresa, what the fuck is this about?!

Teresa   Nothing. Nothing. I'll tell you later –

Mary   Tell me now.

Teresa   I can't.

Pause.

Mary   It's about Patrick, isn't it?

Teresa *looks stricken. Pause.*

Teresa   There're some cuttings in here about him. Newspaper cuttings.

Mary   You know where he is?

Pause.

Where is he?

Pause.

Teresa   He's dead.

Silence.

I'm sorry. I wanted to tell you. I would have. I would have. I'm sorry. I told Mum, but she said no, and then . . . I mean, and then it was . . . I mean, the moment had passed –

Silence.

Mary   What happened to him?

Teresa   Some cliffs gave way. Just outside Whitby. Him and another boy. Father Michael told us.

Frank (*off*)   Teresa! What's happened to my trousers?

Teresa   I meant to tell you, but when? When could we have told you?

Mary   When it happened. Why didn't you tell me when it happened?

Teresa (*offering her the tin, gently*)   They're in an envelope marked medical cards. The cuttings.

Frank (*off*)   Teresa!

Mary   Go to him. Don't let him come in here.

Teresa   Mary, I'm sorry –

Mary   Go.

She goes. The lighting changes to the bluish-green glow. Faint sound of big band music in the distance. **Vi** *appears in the open doorway. Her hair is now completely white. She looks at the coffin.*

Vi   Open the box.

She goes over to the coffin. **Mary** *says nothing.*

It's open. Look.

She lifts the top section of the lid and looks.

A bloody old woman. I don't recognise her. A bloody old woman in green eyeshadow. Green. They call this dignity, apparently. Green frosted eyeshadow.

She shuts the lid. Closes her eyes and sways gently to the music.

I just want one last dance before I go . . .

Mary *watches her for a while. Empties the stuff out of the tin. Finds the envelope, takes out cuttings, looks at them in bewilderment.*

Mary   Nineteen eighty . . . Nineteen eighty . . . Why didn't you tell me?

Vi *stops dancing. Pause.*

Vi   It seemed right at the time. You were doing your finals.

Silence.

Mary   I've been waiting for him all these years. I've been waiting for him to turn up and claim me.

Vi   Don't become one of those women who blame. Don't be a victim. It's beneath you.

Mary   You made me give him away because it was embarrassing.

Vi   I wanted you to do well. I didn't want you to be trapped. I did it for you.

Mary   I look at this patient of mine. This twenty-year-old boy lying in a hospital bed, completely blank, no memory of anything at all, just an empty vessel. And all I see is Patrick. Full of memories that I didn't put there, that someone else filled him with. And I think, did I give him anything? Is there some part of him that's still mine? Maybe he smiles like me. Maybe he walks like me. Maybe he doesn't. You made me obsessed.

Vi   I thought nothing could shake you. I was wrong.

Pause.

Mary   Last night, I dreamt I was in a fishmonger's. On the slab, there was a box. It seemed to be full of chickens. Trussed. I couldn't be sure. 'Are they chickens?' I said. He pulled back the sacking and they weren't chickens but babies. Dead trussed babies, no bigger than my hand. When I woke up, blood. I'm not pregnant. I never was. Everything's dead. I can't bear it. I can't hold on to anything.

Vi   Despair is the last refuge of the ego.

Pause.

I got that out of the *Reader's Digest*.

Pause.

Mary   I'm in freefall. I opened a door and stepped out into thin air.

Vi   I never knew how you felt. I never knew how you felt about anything. You thought your feelings were too rarefied to share with me. You cut me out. You looked straight through me. You shared nothing with me, not a joke, not a smile that wasn't patronising, you never let me in, you never let me know you. This stony punishment all these years, wanting me to be better than I am, always your mother, always responsible, always to blame. How could I apologise, when you wouldn't give me the room?

Silence.

Mary I'm sorry.

Pause.

What was it like? The last few months?

Vi It's been a long time since you asked me a proper question. It's been a long time since you allowed me to know more than you.

Mary Tell me what it felt like.

Vi Like I had holes in my brain. Frightening. Huge rips. I'd not recognise people. You just think, where am I? What's going on? And then you don't know what you mean when you say 'I'. It doesn't seem to mean anything.

Mary You always still looked like you. Like essence of you. The way you moved your hands sometimes. Your laugh.

Vi Some things stay. Some things are in your bones. Songs. Babies. I was very keen on babies. Dogs. People's hair. Dancing. I wanted to dance. Usually in what Teresa called inappropriate places. Like the garden.

Mary But who did you feel like? Who are you if you take your memories away?

Vi I felt like I'd gone away. Like I'd broken up into islands and in between was just a terrible muddle of old songs and odd names drifting by, men I vaguely recognised. I felt like a cut-up thing. But sometimes the pieces would float to the surface, drift back together, and there I was, washed ashore from a pitch-black sea of nothing. Me. Still me. I'm still here.

Pause.

Forgiving someone's just like throwing a switch.

Mary   Is it?

Vi   It's just a decision. And afterwards you're free.

Pause.

I've done it.

Mary   Have you?

Vi   I forgave your father. And now I'll forgive you. But it's time I went.

She goes to the mirror and looks at herself.

Yes. I think it is.

Mary   Mum. Don't go just yet –

Vi *gives her one last look before she goes.* **Mary** *puts her head in her hands and cries.* **Teresa** *and* **Frank** *come in.*

Teresa   Frank, get the Rescue Remedy.

Frank   She needs a bloody drink.

Teresa *takes hold of her.*

Teresa   Mary, pull yourself together, you've got a funeral to go to. Frank, she needs Rescue Remedy, now –

Frank *goes out.*

Mary   I'm past rescuing –

Teresa   Take some of these –

She tries to give her some tablets.

Mary   What are they?

Teresa   Aconite, it's just a matter of –

Mary   It's not just a matter of anything, it's my life! Stop trying to make it little and solvable, stop trying to sort it out with vitamin pills!

Teresa   They're not vitamin pills –

Mary   There's no cure.

Frank *comes in with* **Mike**. **Mike** *goes to her.*

Frank   Rescue Remedy. Duty-free vodka. Take your pick.

Mike   Are you all right?

Mary   I'm tired, I didn't sleep.

Frank   I read somewhere the other day that if you eat a whole lettuce before you go to bed, it has pretty much the same effect as a Mogadon.

Mary   Well, I'm torn now. I don't know whether to have a Caesar salad or cut my throat.

She takes the Rescue Remedy from **Frank**, *and downs the lot.*

Teresa   No, no, you just need a few drops –

Mary   There you are, I feel better already. Suddenly life makes sense, suddenly my mother's not dead, I am actually pregnant, in fact it's triplets. Suddenly there is meaning where there was none before. Suddenly I'm Princess Michael of fucking Kent.

She sits down, exhausted. Silence.

Teresa   Pregnant?

Mary   A fantasy.

Mike   Sorry?

Mary   I thought I was pregnant, but I'm not. It was a phantom. You obviously caught Charlie Morgan on a good day.

Teresa (*desperately*)   Oh, why don't you two have a baby? Why don't you? Leave your wife and have a baby with Mary –

The door opens and **Catherine** *appears, in a very short skirt.*

Catherine   Hi. What d'you think?

They look at her in confusion.

Teresa   What?

Catherine   The outfit. What d'you think?

Frank   Sorry?

Catherine   Do I look all right?

Silence.

Frank   Very nice.

Teresa   It's halfway up your bottom.

Catherine   It's the only one I've got. Mary, d'you like it?

Mary   Apart from the fact you can see your ovaries, it's fine –

The phone rings and **Frank** *picks it up.*

Frank   Hello? . . . Oh, Jesus wept . . . And what? You've got what? . . . I don't believe this . . . Can we what? I beg your pardon? . . . I'm sorry? Well, I mean, I suppose if . . . Right, OK, OK, thanks, OK.

He puts the phone down.

He's on his way. He says, do we have any gentleman who can give him a hand? Taking the coffin out to the hearse.

Pause.

Mike   Fine, right, OK, no problem, absolutely.

Frank   I think he said it's a bit difficult for him because he's got a *plastic hand*. Is my hearing going or what?

Teresa   I'm afraid not, no.

Catherine *is staring at the coffin.*

Catherine   Did you open the lid?

Teresa   No.

Catherine   It's so weird.

Teresa   What is?

Catherine   It's weird she's in this box. I mean, I can't imagine it.

Frank   I don't think you're supposed to.

Teresa   You can't help it though, can you? Actually, if you think about it, it could be anyone in here. We'd never know the difference.

Catherine   We'll never see her again. And she's so close. She had such a nice face.

Pause.

I wish she wasn't dead.

Mike   Maybe we could all do with a drink.

He begins to pour whisky for everyone. **Teresa** *puts her arm round* **Catherine**.

Catherine   I'm all right. I'll be OK. I'll be OK. I will.

Mike *hands out drinks. Awkward silence.*

Frank   Whoops. Nearly said cheers.

Silence.

So. Here we are then.

He looks at his watch. Then at the coffin.

I presume it's a veneer, is it?

Teresa   What?

Frank   The coffin. Chipboard and veneer.

They all look at the coffin.

Mary   Well, you know, we were going for the jewel-encrusted mother-of-pearl but we thought this would burn better.

Silence.

Sorry.

Frank   You can get do-it-yourself coffins now, apparently. Made of cardboard.

Mary   Oh, good.

Mike   Something to do in the long winter evenings. Build your own coffin.

Sound of a car horn from outside. **Mary** *goes to the window.*

Mary   That'll be him.

Mike   Right. OK. Shall we, er . . . Frank?

Frank   God. Right. I'll take this end, shall I?

He takes one end of the coffin.

Mike   Keep your back straight –

They lift.

Frank   I'll go backwards, or would you rather?

Mike   No, no, I'm fine – can someone hold the door?

Teresa *does so. They manoeuvre the coffin.* **Catherine** *starts to laugh madly.*

Catherine   Poor Mum. Even her funeral's a cock-up.

Mike   Pull her round to the right a bit – the right –

Frank   Mind that bit of carpet – whoops, nearly . . . that's it . . .

They go out.

(*Off*) To me, to me –

The women pull on coats and gloves, etc.

Mary   Just check your phone's not in your bag, will you?

Teresa   I've checked.

Catherine   I look ridiculous, don't I?

Mary   You don't. You look fine.

Catherine   I didn't hate her really.

Mary   I know that. We all know that. She didn't hate you either.

Pause.

Catherine   D'you remember, when Dad was out sometimes, she used to get us up in the middle of the night and give us crisps and ice-cream soda?

Mary   And she'd have a Dubonnet and lemonade. God, I'd forgotten about that.

Teresa   She called it a girls' night in.

Catherine   We were all sleepy in our pyjamas, and she'd put on Nat King Cole.

Pause.

Mary   She must have been lonely. I never thought of that.

Silence.

Catherine   I put a hip flask in my bag in case we need it.

Teresa   I think I'll pass on that, if you don't mind.

Mary   Got tissues?

Teresa   Yes.

Frank *and* **Mike** *come in.*

Frank   Are we set?

Teresa   I think so. Shall we go, then? Are we ready?

Mary   You go on ahead. I'll be out in a minute.

Teresa   Come with us, Catherine. Come on.

Frank, **Teresa** *and* **Catherine** *go out.* **Teresa** *with her arm around* **Catherine**. *Silence.* **Mary** *and* **Mike** *look at each other.*

Mary   I think maybe that French guy was right.

Mike   Sorry?

Mary   The one who said water was like magnetic tape. My mother's the ghost in the machine. She goes through us like wine through water. Whether we like it or not. Nothing ends entirely.

Mike   What are you going to do?

Mary   Can you live a rich life without a child?

Mike   You know you can.

Pause.

Mary   Yes. I suppose so.

Pause.

I'm going to ask you something, Mike. I'm going to ask it once and I'll never ask it again. Leave your wife and come with me.

Pause.

Mike   I think . . . I don't think we should talk about this now. Maybe we should talk about it after the funeral . . .

Mary   I'm not asking you to talk about it. Take your chance, Mike.

Pause.

Mike (*almost a whisper*)   Maybe afterwards we could . . .

She goes to the window. He looks at her helplessly. She looks out of the window.

Mary   This snow's never going to stop. Everything frozen in its tracks. Everything cancelled.

Teresa (*off*)   Mary!

Mary   I've hated winter all my life. Ice on the windows, dark at three in the afternoon. Sea fret freezing the hairs in your nostrils. I've hated the stasis, the waiting for spring.

Teresa (*off*)   Mary!

She turns to **Mike**.

Mike   What are you going to do?

Mary   Learn to love the cold.

They go out. As they leave, the lights dim to gold and blue. The curtains billow into the room and a flurry of snow drifts in. Nat King Cole plays faintly in the distance.

Fade down lights.

Five Kinds of Silence

The stage version of *Five Kinds of Silence* was first performed at the Lyric Hammersmith, London, on 31 May 2000, with the following cast.

Billy	Tim Piggott-Smith
Susan	Gina McKee
Janet	Lizzy McInnerny
Mary	Linda Bassett
Policeman/Detective/	
Psychiatrist/Lawyer	Gary Whitaker
Police Inspector/	
Psychiatrist/Lawyer	Dione Inman

Directed by Ian Brown
Designed by Peter McKintosh
Lighting by Hugh Vanstone
Music by Barrington Pheloung
Produced by Out of the Blue Productions

Music. Lights up on **Billy**.

Billy   One night, I dreamt I was a dog. The moon was out, I could smell it. Ice-white metal smell. I could smell the paving stones, wet, sharp. The tarmac road made my dog teeth tingle, it was aniseed, rubber, and then the lamp-posts, studded with smells they were. Studded with jewels of wood, metal, meat. And the stars pierced my dog nose like silver wires. A woman came out of her house, sickly the smell of her, rotten, she smelt of armpits and babies and fish and a hundred other things screaming at me like a brass band. I knew what she'd had for her tea. I knew she was pregnant. I could smell it. She didn't look at me, just walked straight on by, thought I was just a dog. I laughed a quiet dog laugh: you think I'm a dog but I'm Billy, I'm me. The night smells of soot and frost and petrol and beer. I'm at my own door now. I don't need to see it, it comes to meet me, a cacophony, the smells are dancing towards me, the smells of home.

Lights up in the house. **Billy**'s *daughters* **Janet** *and* **Susan** *and* **Billy**'s *wife* **Mary** *stand around a single bed.*

I'm inside the house now. Hot citrus smell of electric light. My wife, my daughters, stand up as I come into the room. Oh, home, the smells I love, all the tiny shimmering background smells, and the two I love the most, the two smells that fill the room like a siren. One of them is fear: burning tyres, vinegar, piss. And the other one is the smell of blood, matted in Mary's hair. I gave her a good kicking before I went out.

Blackout. A TV cartoon programme tinkles. A shot rings out. Lights up: **Billy** *is sprawled on his back on the bed.* **Janet** *stands by.* **Susan** *is holding a rifle.*

Janet   Is he dead?

Susan   He's stopped moving, Janet.

Mary *comes in, bewildered.*

Janet   I'm frightened he's not dead.

Mary   What've you done, Susan?

Susan   We had to kill him, Mum.

Mary   Oh. I should have done that.

Janet   He's moving. I can see him moving.

Susan   He's dead.

Janet   Give me the gun. Best be sure.

Mary   What are you doing?

Janet   Don't want him to suffer.

Susan *reloads the rifle and hands it to* **Janet**.

Mary   Give it to me. I should do it.

Janet   No. No, Mum.

She fires at his chest. He bucks and subsides. They all stare at him fearful that he might suddenly revive. Dead **Billy**'s *voice comes out of nowhere. They don't hear it as they watch his body for signs of life.*

Billy   No need to do it twice. I was dead the first time. They got me when I was down, see. I didn't stand a chance. Bitches.

Janet   We should have done it years ago.

Pause.

Mary   I'll call the police then, shall I?

Susan   We need a drink.

Janet   We'll drink his whisky. We'll drink all of it.

Mary   Later we'll get the police.

Susan *gets whisky.* **Mary** *gets glasses.*

Mary   He looks nice like that. Lying there nice and still. In his red shirt.

Susan   It's blood. The shirt was white.

Mary   Still, he looks nice and neat. Nice and tidy. He'd be pleased. He never liked mess.

Janet   Why doesn't he close his eyes?

Mary   D'you think he looks a bit surprised?

Susan *hands out whisky.*

Susan   Drink.

They gulp it down in silence, the TV still tinkling in the background.

Janet   Susan?

Susan   What?

Janet   Is his eye flickering? Can you see it?

Susan   He's dead.

Janet   Look. There, there.

Susan   We killed him. We had to do it. Nothing's flickering.

Janet   If he comes back to life I'll top myself.

Music. Fade down light on women. Lights up on **Billy** *still in his bloodstained shirt.*

Billy   Washing day. Steam, wet sheets hanging, cold slapping against my face. I'm hiding. Suddenly someone's here. Big white arms. Big bony hands that do things I don't like. Punch me. Other stuff. What? What other stuff? She's big, huge. Veins in her white legs, like blue knotted ropes. Rotten cheese. Ugly, I hate looking at them. Muscles at the back of the knees, bulging, yellow skin on the heels. Clatter of what? Clogs on a hard floor. Noise that splits my head in two, hot metally taste in my mouth. Crack goes the bone of my head. Stars float, I'm laughing, ha ha, hit me again if you want, I won't cry. I never cry, me. Crack, I slip in the wet. Crack goes another bone, elbow maybe. The side of my head burns. Out of my mouth comes a noise like kittens make when you drown them. But no, I'm laughing, that's what I'm doing. I don't care me, if you cut off my arms and legs, if you hit me with the belt till my skin peels off I won't cry. I'd just laugh, right. But when I get bigger I'll bloody kill you.

Cross-fade to the women, sitting at the table, with a **Policeman** *standing and taking notes.* **Billy** *exits.*

Mary   Can I get you a cut of tea, Officer?

Pause.

Susan   We did it. My sister and I did it. Mum was in the other room.

Mary   I was there.

Janet   No, she wasn't. We did it.

Policeman   You two shot your father?

Mary   Is he dead?

Policeman   They're taking him away now.

Susan   But is he dead?

Janet   We shot him twice. Was that enough?

Susan   Will we go to prison.

Policeman   Was it an accident?

Janet   We don't mind if we go to prison. Do we, Susan?

Susan   We don't mind. No.

Mary   If you could just tell us if he's dead, Officer.

Policeman   It seems that way.

Susan   Are you sure?

Policeman   I'm not qualified to say.

Janet   I told you, I saw his eye flickering.

Policeman   Was there a reason for shooting him? You must have had a reason.

All   We don't want to talk about that.

Mary   If you don't mind.

Pause.

Policeman   Something's gone on, hasn't it?

Mary   Things have been . . . quite tense recently.

Susan   Tense, yes.

Janet   What with his fits.

Mary   Six a day sometimes.

Susan   Our nerves have been bad.

Mary   Never knew when a fit would take him.

Policeman   He was having fits so you shot him? Is that what you're saying?

Billy *enters the room in a white shirt.*

Mary   He wasn't – he wasn't an easy man.

Susan   He was a difficult man.

Policeman   And that's your reason, is it?

Silence.

Is it?

Janet   We don't want to talk about it. If you don't mind.

Music. Fade down lights. Lights up on **Billy** *as the others exit.*

Billy   I'm in bed, it's pitch dark, I'm holding my knees up to my chest. Icy, icy cold, you can't sleep for it, not even with your coat on and your boots. There's shouting along the landing, banging, same as every night, Dad's drunk. She's screaming at him: You bastard you useless bloody bastard, you're no bloody good to me, and he's roaring like a bull in an abattoir, no words, too drunk for that. Under the covers now, me, stop it stop it but I can hear them, I know them. I've seen them biting and tearing and heads banged off walls teeth fly blood spurts. You stupid drunk pig! They're staggering, three steps this way, three steps that, one two three, one two three. Wood splinters. You stupid drunk blind fuck pig! I hear them fall, feel his bones, his blind head hits each stair, sinews tear and snap. She says get out, you're no good to anyone. I'm out of bed now, running downstairs. The front door's open, she's trying to throw him into the street but she's holding him round the throat and she screams like this arrgghh, like a banshee. I don't want my mother to make noises like that so I kick her, I don't know why, but I do. He's on his hands and knees in the street, there's frost on the ground, glittering. He gets up and falls over because he's drunk and he's blind, and his hands are stretched out, he wants someone to help him. Sounds come from him, there's snot and tears. Bitch, he says, bitch. Stupid blind bastard, stop it, stop crying, Dad, you mustn't ever cry, I don't like looking at you when you do that, I don't like hearing you. I'm glad when she slams the door. She punches my head, bang, what are you doing up? It's cold upstairs, Mum, it's pitch-black dark, it's like being blind I don't want to go blind like my dad I don't want to go blind. She pulls me by my arm, twists with both hands like she's wringing out washing. Don't be so bloody soft, don't be so bloody soft. I don't like to think about him out there in the dark, banging into things. I don't like to think about it. So I don't.

Cross-fade lights as **Janet** *and* **Policeman** *enter the police cell.* **Billy** *exits.*

Janet   Is this a cell?

Policeman   Yes.

Janet   It's beautiful.

Policeman   You should try and get some sleep now, Janet.

She sits on the single bed.

Janet   I could live here.

Policeman   I'll take your belt.

He takes her belt.

Janet   You're not to lock the door.

Policeman   I know.

Janet   I'm on antidepressants.

Policeman   I know.

Janet   I've never slept on my own.

Policeman   How old are you, Janet?

Janet   Thirty-four. I've always slept with my sister.

Policeman   Even when you went on holiday?

Janet   We've never been on holiday. We've never been anywhere.

Policeman   The door will be open. I'll be right outside.

Janet   We had to do it, you know.

Policeman   I'll be right outside.

Janet   You don't know what it's been like. Your life's normal. We come from a different world.

Policeman *exits as there is a cross-fade to downstage as* **Mary** *and a* **Police Inspector** (*female*) *enter.*

Mary   I walked into the room, I picked up the gun and I shot him.

Inspector   We know you didn't, Mary. Your prints aren't on the weapon.

Mary   Pardon?

Inspector   The fingerprints aren't yours. We know the girls did it. They told us.

A beat.

Mary   Oh.

Inspector   Why?

Mary   Why what?

Inspector   Why did they shoot their father?

Pause.

Mary   I think something – burst.

They exit. Cross-fade to **Susan**, *talking to male* **Detective**. **Janet** *remains in semi-darkness on the bed.*

Detective   I'm just trying to imagine what led you to do it, Susan.

Susan   He was fitting. We shot him.

Detective   What did he do to you?

Susan   Nothing.

Detective   How old are you, Susan?

Susan   Thirty-six.

Detective   Ever had a boyfriend?

Susan   No.

Detective   What about your sister?

Susan   No.

Detective   Never?

Susan   We were very close as a family. We didn't need that sort of thing.

Detective   Most girls have boyfriends at some time in their lives. Why not you?

Susan   We – had each other.

Detective   Did he knock you about?

Pause.

Susan   Sometimes . . .

Detective   Your mother? Your sister?

Susan   Sometimes.

Detective   Badly?

Susan   He had – quite a temper. Sometimes.

Detective   What got him in a temper?

Pause.

Susan   Things.

Detective   Such as?

Pause.

Susan   We weren't to make a noise when we clicked on the light switch. Plates clattering. That wasn't allowed.

Pause.

Sometimes we buttered his toast wrong.

Detective   Sometimes you buttered his toast wrong?

Susan   In the wrong direction. The butter in the wrong direction.

Detective   I see.

Susan   No you don't. How could you see? You couldn't begin.

Detective   Tell me then. Explain. Then maybe I will see.

Susan   I'm tired. I'm very tired. Don't ask my anything else, I just want to sleep now. I just want to sleep for a very long time. I think I'm coming down with something.

Detective   You haven't told me everything, Susan

Susan   I'm sorry. I'm tired. I'm not well.

Pause.

Detective   Did he sleep with you?

Billy *enters.*

Susan   What? I think I've got a temperature. I'm burning. My face is burning. Is the room tilting?

Detective   Did he do anything sexual to you?

Susan   I'm sorry, you must think I'm drunk. Is it me or is it the room skewed like this? My head's in flames. I need aspirins. I need a doctor. I'm coming down with something.

Detective   Your sister's told us he did. She told us he slept with both of you.

Susan   Oh. Oh.

Billy *leans calmly in the doorway.*

Billy   Gather your thoughts, say nothing, take your time, there's still time. Laugh at him, go on. Laugh. She's a bloody liar that Janet. Tell him she's mental.

Susan   I've a dry mouth.

Detective   He did, didn't he? Since you were thirteen years old.

Silence. **Susan** *speaks in a quiet, cracked voice.*

Susan   Yes.

Billy   You bloody bitch, you've done it now. You said the thing that should never be said.

Detective   Can I get you a drink of water?

Billy   Snatch the yes back, take it back, go on. Shout no, no, I didn't meant that –

Susan   I –

Billy   You're opening your mouth, go on, speak –

Detective   I'll fetch you some water.

He exits.

Susan   I –

Billy   Just shout no, you stupid bitch –

Susan   I . . . I'm very sorry –

She gets up and her legs give way.

Billy   They've tricked you, Susan, I'm not dead, not dead at all, and soon I'll burst through the window and kill you. Water streaming down her leg. Her eyes streaming. The dam is breached, the walls have collapsed.
Get up off the floor, you stupid bitch – Get up off the floor!

Music. She scrambles to her feet and runs from the room. **Mary** *and female* **Inspector** *enter.*

Inspector   I need some help here, Mary. I'm in the dark.
Can you tell me a little about yourself maybe?

Mary   There's nothing to tell.

Inspector   I'll fetch you a cup of tea. Would that help?

Mary   That'd be nice, love. Thank you. Not too much
milk –

Inspector *goes out.*

Mary   I'm six years old, walking home from school. There's
deep snow crunching on the ground and my feet are tingling
cold. I have on wellingtons and green woollen mittens
threaded through my sleeves with elastic. I get to my street,
and before I can get to our house Auntie Ruby comes out of it
in a black fur hat, and hurries me away. Oh the mite, she says,
oh the mite. In my head it muddles with Almighty God whose
son suffered and died because He loved us. Imagine the nails,
Mary. Imagine the nails, Sister Bridget says, being driven into
Our Lord's beautiful hands. Think of the pain, Mary, think of
the blood, as the nail is driven through sinew and bone and
soft, soft flesh. He suffered this because he loved us so much.
I'm thinking this all the way to Auntie Ruby's. I'm thinking let
the dark thing not happen, I will dwell upon the suffering of
Our Lord, I will drive nails into my own hands only let it not
happen. Ruby's house is dark and cold and something terrible
is wrong, the praying didn't work. My food congeals on the
plate, my heart is lodged in my throat like a stone. Why can't I
go home, but I know the world has ended. Your poor mother.
Your poor mother, is what they say. That chop will be put in
front of you at every meal until you eat it. But my throat is
closed. I will never eat again. Days pass, there are carols on
the wireless, I feed the chop to the dog and my mother is not
coming back. They've put her in the ground, they say. But
won't she be cold? How will she breathe? How will she eat?
Won't she be lonely? It is Christmas, and my poor mother is
deep in the ground, up by the moor. I go back to my home.
No point lighting a fire, says my father. We won't be having a
tree. On Christmas Day I sit hunched in my coat, longing for

my mother to come up out of the lonely cold ground, watching my father drink a bottle of whisky. I am mad with grief, he says, forgive me. I don't know what grief is but I start to cry anyway. I cry louder and louder but my mother never comes and my father doesn't wake. Through the wall, I can hear the neighbours having a sing-song.

The **Inspector** *returns with a polystyrene cup of tea.*

Inspector   Ready to tell me anything?

Mary   We thought any day now he'll kill us all and then shoot himself. And no one will ever know what went on. It's a form of torture to think that no one will ever know, isn't it?

Cross-fade to **Susan** *and* **Janet**. *They are sitting on the bed. They talk together.*

Susan/Janet   Dear Mum, we are in a lovely place with gardens and a small pond –

Janet   – with fish,

Susan   – and it is beautiful here.

Janet   Last night we had baths –

Susan/Janet   – with as much water as we wanted and it was as close to heaven as we've ever been. Everyone is kind, and our rooms are warm, people say the rules are strict but we just laugh –

Susan   – Janet and me. Sometimes we talk to lawyers.

Janet   They are very nice.

Susan/Janet   This is the first time we've been free in the whole of our lives, which is really funny when you think about it because a remand centre is actually a sort of prison, isn't it?

Janet   Thinking of you often.

Susan   Your loving daughters, Susan –

Janet   – and Janet.

Music. Cross-fade to **Mary** *with* **Psychiatrist 1** (*male*). **Billy**'s *face can be seen at the window.*

Psychiatrist 1   Are you sleeping now, Mary?

Mary   In the night he comes back to accuse me.

Psychiatrist 1   Of what?

Mary   Betrayal. He says you let them kill me, now I'll have to kill you.

Psychiatrist 1   He can't harm you any more.

Mary   You don't get it, do you, love?

Psychiatrist 1   Explain it to me, can you?

Mary   I love you, he said. Practically straight away. I believed him. I was twenty. I knew nothing. I was lonely and he was handsome. And now he'll never leave. It'll never be over, it'll never end. Every time I look in the mirror, he's there. Scars. That was the time he did this or that, here is where he broke my fingers, my nose, my wrist. When he comes into my dreams I think my heart will stop. That's how he'll kill me. That's how he'll get me. I'll die of fright.

Music. They exit. **Janet** *enters with* **Lawyer 1** (*female*). *Dialogue between * and * overlaps.*

Lawyer 1   * We're trying to prepare a case for the defence –

Janet   – I had clinical depression. That's what they called it. The doctors kept saying, Why, Janet, why are you like this?

Lawyer 1   – so if you can tell us everything you can about what happened –

Janet   Every morning, wake up crying. It made him mad, he wanted me to smile, go on, take that look off your, smile, Janet, smile, or people might catch on –

Lawyer 1   – I think we may be able to provide a very strong case –

Janet   I couldn't do it any more, the muscles in my face stopped functioning. I just wanted whisky and tablets and sleep.

Lawyer 1   – citing mitigation, over a period of years.

Janet   He'd shout, You lot've got everything, you want for nothing.

Lawyer 1   Perhaps you'd like a cup of tea –*

Janet   Every time I went to the hospital, is there anything you want to tell us? No, nothing, no. Because what could I say? Where would I start? And if I did, I knew he'd kill us all. Mum, then Susan, then me. In that order. Then himself. I knew he would because he told me.

Lawyer 1   What did you feel when you'd shot him?

Janet   Pardon me?

Lawyer 1   When you shot him, what were your feelings?

Janet   What did you feel here, what did you feel there? Where did the intercourse take place? What difference does it make? The pictures in my head are mine, and giving them to you won't wipe them out.

Lawyer 1   Janet? Are you listening.

Janet   I felt nothing.

Lawyer 1   You must have felt something?

Janet   No, I don't remember. We drank a lot of whisky.

Lawyer 1   Did you feel relieved, elated?

Janet   You think he's gone now he's dead. But the dead don't go anywhere, they dance in your head, they come to you at night. The dead don't die, I know that now.

Lawyer 1   Did you love him?

Janet   Of course we did. He was our father.

Music. Cross-fade to **Billy**.

Billy   I don't remember pain, I don't remember pleasure. I was born aged six with teeth and a black, black heart. I'm what, eight? She has a new man now, a soft milky thing, no match for my lost blind dad. He winds wool for her with his limp fish hands. A voice like gruel. Boneless he is. And yet. And yet – Dark . . . feet like blocks of ice, heart bumping against my throat. Voices burbling in the blackness, Is anybody there? Is anybody there? They got a drowned man once, he spoke with weeds tangled in his throat, I heard him. He opens his mouth and it's not his voice come out it's dead people. Not frightened, me, I'm just cold, that's what that banging noise is in my chest. Dry tongue. Stupid bastards don't know I'm here. Stupid bastards. There's someone coming through, he says, there's someone coming through, it's a man. Stupid bastards, I don't believe them, I wish someone would put the light on the skin's going tight on the top of my head I think I'm having a heart attack, MAM! Billy? Is that you? Let me stay, I want to stay, I won't make no noise. I told you, bloody bugger, I told you. She's pulling me, dragging me upstairs, I'm fighting back, bloody get off me, bloody get off. No don't shut me up in the dark, it's black in there, the black gets in my nose and mouth and eyes, I can't breathe. She says get in the cupboard, you'll have no light, you don't deserve it. Bloody bugger bastard, I shout, bloody damn bugger. Crack. She hits me. Crack. Keep your fury, Billy, she says, you'll need it out there, but never cry, or I'll send the devil to you. No, no, I won't cry, don't send him, I don't want to see him, don't shut the door, what if he comes, Mam, what if he comes? But she slams the door anyway. I won't cry, I shout, I bloody won't. Bastards . . . bloody damn blast shit bastards . . . don't send the devil to me, I don't want to see him . . . bloody bugger pig devil, I bloody am not I bloody am not I bloody am not frightened you buggers – you pig buggers.

Billy *exits. Lights up on* **Susan** *talking to* **Psychiatrist 2** (*female*). **Mary** *stands at the window, looking out, listening.* **Janet** *is lying on her bed.*

Psychiatrist 2   You must feel very angry, Susan.

Susan   Pardon me?

Psychiatrist 2   With your mother. She let it happen all those years.

Susan   They said we could go home now. They said unconditional bail.

Psychiatrist 2   Your mother was there all the time, and she did nothing to stop it, did she?

Susan   We don't think of it like that.

Psychiatrist 2   Why?

Susan   Why what?

Psychiatrist 2   Do you sometimes feel resentful towards her perhaps?

Susan   Why?

Psychiatrist 2   Why d'you think?

Susan   We love her. She's our mother. Why d'you want us to be angry?

Psychiatrist 2   I wonder if sometimes you deny what you feel. I think it's understandable.

Susan   I think we live on different planets.

Pause.

I'm sorry, that was rude.

Psychiatrist 2   You must be rude if that's how you feel.

Susan   Most of what you say we don't understand.

Psychiatrist 2   You said yesterday you didn't mind going to prison. Did you mean that?

Susan   We killed him. He's dead. We feel better now. There's nothing you can do about any of it.

Psychiatrist 2   Let us try.

A beat.

Susan   This getting angry, this feeling this and feeling that. It's not for us. It's not really our sort of thing. It's too late now. You think you can understand it but you can't see the size of it. If you had to live inside our heads for five minutes you'd go mad and die. Best we deal with it ourselves.

They exit. Lights up on **Billy**, *standing high above the set.*

Billy   Our town is full of soldiers. There's a war on. I like the shine on their boots, I like the sound they make on the cobbles, harsh and strong, it sets my teeth tingling. They are polished and trim and neat these men, belted and tucked and ready for action. Already I'm hooked. I follow them to their barracks, oh, the neatness of it, the rows of bunks, the order, I'm beside myself with longing. Each bed tight made, corners neat and parcelled, no gaps, no mistakes, there's method in this. The air smells of carbolic and boot polish and engine grease. One of them shows me his kit, his boots gleaming under his bunk, placed just so, at just such an angle, the precision of it makes me feel faint and then a quivery ripple shivers across my groin. I am at home here. I am in paradise here. They take me to show me the storerooms. Miles of shelving, stacked to the roof with supplies. I say the word under my breath. Supplies. In case of. In the event of. Supplies. This is organisation. Nothing can go wrong here. Everything, every last thing labelled everything in its place. The soldier talks to me in his strange accent, London or Scotland or somewhere, says you have to be organised, see, because if anything's out of place, if ever there's an emergency, think of the chaos then. He shows me the order books, the requisition pads, cancellation forms, goods in, goods out, pink for in, green for out, and things are dancing inside my head, I'm practically singing. He lets me hold his gun. I imagine shooting all the people in our street, pop, pop, pop. I shoot them because they shouldn't be in here, messing everything up, throwing the system into disarray. I imagine the look on their faces, stupid, caught by surprise. Pop. Astonishment, pain, fear, twisted mouths, some of them even cry. I am laughing, shivers run up and down my spine, my feet are going like Fred Astaire. I feel the most pleasure I've ever felt. I think, there, there. See what it feels like. The soldier takes the gun. There's no bullets in it anyway.

Billy *exits. Cross-fade to* **Mary** *and* **Psychiatrist 1**.

Psychiatrist 1   You could have left him.

Mary   I did once. I went to my father's. Took the girls and ran. My father said: You made your bed. Now lie in it. Marriage is a sacrament. Marriage is for life.

Psychiatrist 1   Tell me more about your father.

Pause.

Mary   I remember this time I made supper for him, a struggle, heaving boiling kettles as big as myself, setting out the glass milk jug, just so, standing on a chair to slice bread. Baked beans it was. The battle with the tin, burning my fingers on the stove. And then the waiting. Look how good I have been, look, Dad, look. Midnight he comes in. It's cold, is all he says, and my heart shrivels. Later, he wakes me, and says, I'm sorry, Mary, forgive me, and that one thing makes me leap for joy inside, because it means he loves me. Doesn't it?

Psychiatrist 1   Did Billy ever say, I'm sorry, Mary?

Mary   When he came to get me from my dad's that time, he gave me a kiss and said, I'm sorry, let's make up. And there was a bit of the old Billy there, the one I loved. I wanted to believe him and so I went home. When we got in the door he broke my ribs. Jumped on them. I never went again. He said if I did he'd find us and kill us.

Psychiatrist 1   You mentioned the old Billy. What does that mean?

Mary   When I met him he was gentle. Walked me to my door. Said you're the one for me. Said he'd known straight away. I wish I had a lad like that they all said. Polite and quiet and handsome. His mother said: If you marry our Billy, he'll put you through the eye of a needle. I didn't know what she meant. I do now. I was soft and shy, not the sort to argue. I was lonely. I was a bit of a wallflower. He must have seen me coming.

Music. **Mary** *moves to the bed. Lights up on* **Billy**.

Billy Tarts. Primping and powdering and giving you the
eye, wouldn't mind if they meant it but no, half the time
they'd hardly give you a feel, not that I'd want one. Not that
I'd want one. Other fish to fry, me. They don't know, see.
They can't see the rays coming off me. No idea, any of them.
I'd wipe the smiles off their faces, I'd knock their bloody
blocks off, I'd have them on their knees begging, they'd be.
On their backs, begging. I'm tanked up, a bursting thing. I can
feel the blood pounding in my head. I'm thinking how when I
get like this I do things. Dark, jittery things, I'm thinking how I
killed next door's cat to see how it felt. Better, I felt better for a
while, seeing it squirm and cry, it was better than feeling up
one of those tarts. There's a look I like to see, fear is it, face
twists, mouth pleads. I fizz and burn, my insides leap. Then
after, nothing, dead is what I feel. It reminds me of something.
I can't remember what. I'm just thinking this when I see her.
Sitting quiet like a rabbit, none of the lipstick, none of the
flash. She looks up at me.

Mary *looks up. He goes to her.*

Billy I know I'll marry her. This is the woman. This is the
woman. This is the one. I see my life mapped out before me, I
see her, I see children, I see a world. In a flash it comes
together. I'm a pioneer. I'm in enemy territory, I'm going to
knock it into shape, impose a bit of order. Carve something
out for myself.

Band music plays.

I dance in my heart. The world is black and cold but I'm
taking her with me.

He offers his hand. They dance.

She smiles. I feel like I did in the army barracks. It's better
than killing the cat. Although, somehow, that's muddled in
with it too.

They exit, separately. Cross-fade to **Janet** *as she sits up on the bed.*

Janet I can't sleep, Mum, I can't sleep on my own, the bed's
too big, things creak, footsteps on the stair, out in the corridor.

I think it's him, every time I think it's him. They say he's dead
but what if he's not? The golden glow's gone. Euphoria, they
said, hysteria. Small dreams I had then, a glimpse of him, a
hand here, a breath there, but quick to go. He's shrinking, I
thought, death has shrivelled him. He's back now, the whole
of him, his breath on my face, his hands in my hair, pulling
me to places I want to forget. I'm not strong like Susan, soon I
will die of this. Big dreams now, huge dreams. Close my eyes
and I'm trapped in the film of our life. Snap. Another photo.
Snap. Smile, Janet, smile. What will they make of these happy
family snaps, our sandals and frocks, our arms entwined, a
rabbit eating grass at our feet. And we're smiling smiling
smiling for our lives but at the back of my head I say please
someone read this secret sign, I'm sending you a message,
read it read it please. This is not real, this is not true, can't you
see it in my eye. He kicks us where it can't be seen, under our
hair, under our clothes, he boots us across the room. I want to
tear off my dress and shout look look look look look. I look at
the photo and where is the message, the sign in my eye? I look
at the photo and we're just smiling.

Exit. Enter **Mary** *and* **Lawyer 2** (*male*). *They are in the house.*

Mary   This is where we slept, Billy and I. He had the bed by
the window. He was frightened of upstairs. All his life. Never
slept up there.

Lawyer 2   Is this the – ?

Mary   This is where he died, yes. He did look peaceful.
You'd never think to look at him he'd been shot.

Lawyer 2 *looks at the bed, trying to fathom the situation.*

Lawyer 2   Why did you put up with it so long, Mary?

Mary   And this is his medication list.

She hands him a piece of paper.

Lawyer 2   Dad: 4 phenytoin, 1 sun, 1 royal jelly, 1 vitamin.
Mum: 1 sun, 1 royal jelly, 1 vitamin, 1 blood pressure, 1 anti-
sickness.

Mary So there wouldn't be any mistakes.

Lawyer 2 I'll put it in the file. We can use it in court.

Mary He liked to have it down on paper. Always best to have things in writing.

Lawyer 2 Like what?

Mary Oh, most things really. Rules. Lists. Because, you see, if we didn't there was always a risk.

Lawyer 2 Of what?

Mary That something might go wrong.

Lawyer 2 Why did you tolerate this?

Mary *turns away.*

Lawyer 2 D'you mind if I look upstairs?

Mary No. Go on.

He goes. **Mary** *sits on the bed.* **Billy** *is in the shadows behind her.*

Mary A flickering memory I have, of warmth and light, a wireless playing when I come home from school, but this is long ago, before they put my mother in the ground. After that, nothing. Every night I come home, nobody. No fire, he even sold the wireless. It's not his fault. It's not his fault, I won't have that, my dad loves me, and I love him so hard my chest hurts, but there's drink and a great sadness and I'm so small I can't help. The first winter, I think it's the first, freezing fog and my heart like lead, I'm waiting in the parlour for him. Waiting, and aching, like a dog, every footstep in the street, every fleeting sound, my head cocked. Is he coming? Is he coming? He never does. Long past dark he stumbles in the door with a bag of chips or a bottle of pop, I'm sorry, Mary, forgive me, and he lies on the floor or the stairs or sometimes he might make the chair, and sleeps like a dead man. All those nights waiting for him, nothing stirring, just me and silence and a world going on outside. As cold and unreachable as the grave, like the place they've put my mother. Sometimes I make a mewling noise, like a cat, to see what it sounds like, to remind myself I'm still here. The noise gets louder and louder, until eventually I'm howling, howling into the darkness: come home, you fucker, come home or I will howl my throat to shreds and then you'll be sorry for what you've done. He doesn't come. After a while I stop howling. No one ever comes. I think perhaps I have died, like my mother, and so I cut my arm, a big slice, with the carving knife and the pain is a good thing because it's real, a sharp true thing that skitters the stone away from my tomb. The blood flows down my arm and through my fingers, brightest flowing red. And now I know I'm not dead. The next night I do the other arm and I think of Jesus and what he suffered for love of us, and as the knife draws a ruby ribbon from shoulder to elbow I'm thinking of my father as much as the pain. I don't know why, but I am.

Susan *and* **Janet** *join her on the bed.* **Billy** *comes out of the shadows.*

Billy   I love my family. They're mine. I love them. What's different about me, see, is that I love them more than what you might call normal. Don't ever say I don't love them because I do. I do. I've everything I want. A wife. Two girls. Glad they're girls. Nice balance. Nice sense of proportion. Me and them. Them and me. No one else. We don't need it. We don't want it. The house shipshape, it's all under control. Lay my hand on anything any time I want it. Blindfold.

The girls leave.

Mary   When you walked into that dance hall, you handed me a port and lemon, and I recognised you, as if I'd known you all my life. I looked into your eyes and my heart welled up. Oh, I will save you, I will, I will save you.

She looks at **Billy**, *surprised.*

Lawyer 2 (*off*)   Mary?

Mary *gets up.* **Billy** *follows her as lights come up on* **Lawyer 2** *and shelving.*

Lawyer 2   What is all this?

Mary   Billy did the shelving. It took him three weeks. It's arranged alphabetically, d'you see?

Lawyer 2   Brown polish, budgie food, bullets spare, bullets spent, curtain rings, dried peas and beans . . .

Billy   I've got rules. I've got a system.

Mary   Pulses are in a separate section under P.

Lawyer 2   Emergency supplies, firelighters. You don't have any open fires.

Mary   No. They were just in case.

Lawyer 2   Of what?

Billy   What I say goes.

Mary   He liked to cover all eventualities. He made the rules.

They walk along the shelving, **Lawyer 2** *taking notes.*

Billy   Glasses! Five inches from edge of table.

Mary   Each item to be no more than five inches apart and no less than two.

Lawyer 2   What happened if you got it wrong?

Mary   Sometimes a broken nose. Sometimes he just went into the shed and chopped up bones for soup.

Billy   Spoons!

Mary   You could never tell. So we tried never to make mistakes.

Billy   Bowls down when you drain them.

Mary   Which is difficult when the rules keep changing.

Billy   That blue china cat, I like that cat. Three inches from fruit bowl. Not four not two but three.

Mary   It's quite tiring really.

Billy   What I say goes.

Lawyer 2   Garden implements, hand cream, knives, macaroni, pest poison, razor blades, rope . . .

Mary   Susan and Janet did the labels. They've a very neat hand, haven't they?

Billy   You can't take a breath without me. Don't even try.

Lawyer 2   Did he ever explain the purpose of all this?

Mary   It's just spare items. Just in case.

Lawyer 2   Of what?

Billy   Can't take any chances, can't take any risks.

Mary   That's all he said.

Lawyer 2   But didn't you ever ask?

Mary   I think he was expecting a siege. Or a war. An explosion of some sort.

Billy   I'm the one who has to go out there.

Mary   He wanted to make sure we'd survive. Just the four of us.

Billy   In the cold. In the dark.

Mary   He made us do the football pools.

Billy   You lot don't know you're born.

Billy *exits*.

Mary   He said if we won, he'd buy a desert island, and we'd all go and live there and never come back. That was his dream.
It was our nightmare.
We must have been the only family in England praying not to win.

Exit **Mary** *and* **Lawyer 2**. *Cross-fade to* **Susan** *and* **Lawyer 1**. **Billy** *stands above the set, listening*.

Lawyer 1   It's not enough, Susan. You have to tell us everything. We're trying to construct a defence.

Susan   I've told you.

Lawyer 1   When did he first start having intercourse with you.

Susan   I can't remember. I was quite young. Sixteen.

Lawyer 1   Yesterday you said thirteen.

Susan   It was a long time ago. I can't remember.

Lawyer 1   Sixteen or thirteen, which?

Susan   I was probably younger than sixteen. I don't know. Maybe I was thirteen.

Lawyer 1   And how did it happen?

Susan   Pardon me?

Lawyer 1   What were the events which led up to it?

Susan   He just said. He just said. You know.

Pause.

Lawyer 1   What?

Susan   I was in the shed. He was chopping bones. And he just. You know.

Lawyer 1   In the shed?

Susan   Pardon me?

Lawyer 1   It happened in the shed?

Susan   No. He told me in the shed.

Lawyer 1   Told you what?

Susan   He said, Susan, you know I have sex with your mother, well, now I want it with you too.

Lawyer 1   And what did you say?

Susan   I just – I wasn't – I didn't know what it was. I knew it was bad.

Pause.

Could I have a glass of water please?

Lawyer 2 *pours water.* **Susan** *drinks.*

Susan So I just said, I don't want to, Dad, I think it's wrong. And he said what he always said which is what I say goes.

Lawyer 1 And?

Susan And what?

Lawyer 1 What happened then?

Susan Nothing for a couple of weeks. I felt sick. I didn't know what was going to happen. I didn't know what to expect. One day he sent Mum and Janet out to a jumble sale. And that's when he did it.

Lawyer 1 Did you tell your mother?

Susan Yes.

Lawyer 1 And she did nothing?

Susan There was nothing she could do. He bought a gun.

Lawyer 1 Did it happen regularly?

Susan Every Friday. Other times in between.

Pause.

We were trapped. Stop looking at me like that. You don't understand. There was nothing we could do. He could have done it to you. Even someone like you. It's easy. You don't fight. You don't know how to. You keep going. You survive.

Pause.

You think we're freaks, don't you?

Lawyer 1 No.

Susan Your mother couldn't have saved you either. You're all in it together. You're all locked up together. And you don't tell anyone . . . because it's . . . because it's private.

Lawyer 1 Would you like a cup of tea?

Susan I'm sorry for shouting.

Lawyer 1 You weren't shouting.

Susan I'm sorry. Can I stop now?

They exit. **Janet** *enters.* **Billy** *watches.*

Janet Dear Dad, I'm writing this because the psychiatrist says I should. I'm to tell you what I feel. They ask us all the time. How does this make you feel, how does that, what did you feel at this time, what did you feel at that? We know how to do it now. We say what they want. We felt vulnerable, we felt frightened, we felt terrified. What I feel is embarrassed. Words words words. Useless, every one. You were our father and we killed you. We're glad you're dead but sad you weren't nicer because then we wouldn't have had to shoot you. Once, when I was seven or eight, I came in and you were at the sink playing with our goldfish you'd tipped it from its bowl. You were watching it flap and gasp, with a strange dreamy look in your eye. No colour in them, all black. The corners of your mouth turned up. That's how you looked after you hit Mum. That's all I know about you. That look. I can't write this any more. I don't understand the point. We tell them this bit and that bit, but for them it's just some horrible incidents. A case history. Sometimes I think I'll never be free of you. Sometimes I want to come into your grave and shoot you again. And again and again and again. Just to make sure.

Cross-fade to **Susan** *and* **Psychiatrist 2** *as* **Janet** *exits.*

Susan Is there a drug you can get to stop you dreaming?

Psychiatrist 2 Why?

Susan I'd like one.

Psychiatrist 2 What are your dreams about?

Susan Stuff. Is there a drug then? Tablets or something?

Psychiatrist 2 Dreams can be important.

Susan They're not. They're just rubbish.

Psychiatrist 2   Sometimes dreams tell us how we really feel.

Susan   That's not true.

Psychiatrist 2   Tell me about them.

Pause.

Susan   I can't.

Psychiatrist 2   Why can't you? Do they make you feel violent? Angry?

Susan   No.

Psychiatrist 2   What then?

Susan   I wish I'd never said it now.

Psychiatrist 2   You'd like the dreams to stop?

Susan   They're killing me. I can't live with them.

Psychiatrist 2   Try and tell me about them.

Long pause.

Susan   I dream that – I can't say it. I'm sorry.

Psychiatrist 2   Could you write it?

Susan   I can't say it. I can't write it. I can't get rid of it. I'm burning up with it.

Psychiatrist 2   With what?

Susan *begins to cry, in a choked, reluctant way.*

Psychiatrist 2   If you tell me, I'll help you carry it. I won't be shocked.

Susan   I can never tell the worst. I can never tell.

Psychiatrist 2   Is your father in these dreams?

Susan   Of course he is.

Psychiatrist 2   And what is he doing?

Susan   I can't tell you –

Psychiatrist 2   You can, you know.

Pause.

Susan   He's having sex with me. He's having sex with me and I'm – and I'm . . .

She breaks off.

Psychiatrist 2   And you're what?

Susan   I'm enjoying it.

Fade down lights. **Psychiatrist 2** *goes. One light on* **Susan.**

She said try writing it, so I'm writing it. You come into the room. I can't see your face. It's dark. I'm lying on the bed and I've no clothes on. You kiss me a lover's kiss. You put your tongue inside my mouth and you tell me that you love me. I say, I love you too. That's what lovers say, isn't it. I love you too, Dad. I say, I love you too, Dad. I can't write this. She said the dreams will fade if I write it down. She says it's normal. These feelings are normal. I say, they're not my feelings they're my dreams. You touch me. I want you to. It's you and it's not you. I ask you to touch me again. And you do. I look at your face above me, and you look so sad, and I'm not your daughter I'm your lover. Except I'm lying now because I know I'm your daughter and that's what makes it so special, and secret. You look so sad and I will make everything better for you. I don't want you to stop. You're the only lover I've ever had. I pull you down towards me. I wake up. I'm sick over the side of the bed. How could you do this to me, Dad? How could you do this?

Cross-fade as **Janet** *and* **Mary** *enter.*

Janet   We can come home next week. Until the trial.

Mary   That's very kind of them.

Janet   We're not a danger to society.

Mary   Of course you're not.

Susan *comes in.*

Susan   They've given Janet a tape.

Janet   A relaxation tape. I listen to it on a Walkman.

Mary   Does it help?

Janet   No.

Susan   She's not doing it right.

Janet   You have to concentrate. He keeps getting in the way.

Mary   It'll be better when we're all back together.

Janet   I'll sleep in your bed.

Mary   Yes.

Janet   Until the dreams stop.

Susan   What's it like without him, Mum?

Mary   I had mushrooms on toast yesterday. I haven't had that since I was a girl.

Susan   We went shopping yesterday. With Deirdre.

Janet   She's one of the staff.

Susan   Very kind.

Janet   We didn't know what to buy.

Susan   We felt a bit light-headed.

Janet   We felt a bit sick.

Susan   It was a hypermarket. We had ten pounds each.

Janet   We bought some Shredded Wheat.

Susan   And three packets of biscuits.

Janet   Deirdre laughed. She said, Is that all you want?

Susan   But we'd never had Shredded Wheat.

Janet   We'd seen it on the telly.

Susan   She said, You two are weird.

Janet   The weren't very nice actually. The Shredded Wheat. But I expect we'll get used to them.

Cross-fade to **Billy** *with a rifle. The women are wearing matching red jackets.*

Billy   The girls are grown now, I've got them taped, I've got them tabbed, don't let them out of my sight. Dress them the same, them and their mother, three red jackets so I can see them coming. My little army, my little crew. There's men on the streets, men on the corners. I've seen them, I know what they want. Right, I say, right, no talking to men, no talking to boys, not now, not ever, d'you hear me. Point my gun, that always gets them, never argue with a gun, I taught them that. Oh yes Dad no Dad three bags full Dad, but they're bloody lying just like their mother, saying one thing, mean another, don't know why they bother, I know everything. I know you, you say one word, you flash one look, we don't, Dad, we don't, but they're taking the piss.

Cross-fade to **Susan** *and* **Janet** *as the two* **Lawyers** *take notes.*

Susan   He bought us rings.

Janet   Wedding rings.

Susan   We went to the jewellers and chose them ourselves.

Janet   Mine was patterned.

Susan   Mine was plain.

Janet   The jeweller was delighted, he said to Dad –

Susan   – oh, a double wedding –

Janet   – and Dad said –

Billy   Yes. A double wedding.

Susan   In his special voice. His outside voice.

Billy   Yes. They'll both be wives.

Janet   And we put our rings on and left the shop.

Susan   He said it was to keep us safe.

Janet   To keep the men at bay.

Susan   But when we got home –

Mary *joins them. They cower at the table.*

Billy   You talk to men and this is what I'll do –

He points the rifle at the audience.

Bang, bang, bang!
I fire at the wall and they jump and cower, so I do it again,
I'm tingling and racing, there's holes in the wall. I fire at their
feet to make them dance, oh, I'm laughing now –

Janet *starts to cry quietly.*

Billy   – and then she spoils it, she bloody spoils it. She starts
to cry. I've told you, I've told you, no bloody tears in this
house, no bloody tears. She keeps on, she keeps on, get her out
of here, get her out before the room explodes. She doesn't go.
So I do, I go.

He is in the garden in the rain.

I lie in the garden face down in the wet grass, gun sleeping
soft beside me. Rain patters and splashes around me. I could
sleep for a year. I wish I was dead. I don't know why, but I
do.

Lights up on **Mary**, **Susan** *and* **Janet**. **Billy** *stands by the bed in
shadow.*

Susan   He wasn't a bad man.

Janet   In his own way.

Susan   But he needed to be put down.

Janet   The way you do with dogs.

Susan   You put them out of their misery.

Janet   Sometimes he'd lie on the floor and shout.

Billy   I don't want to live, I want out, I want out.

Susan   So really we did him a favour.

Janet   Either he went, or we all did.

Susan   It was just a matter of time.

Mary   He wouldn't let us leave.

Susan   We couldn't let him live. Sometimes he kissed us in the street, not a father's kiss. People were nearby, people we knew, and nobody said a word. No one said nothing. Janet, me, Mum, Dad. And no one else did either. But they knew, they saw. All that silence. Five kinds of silence. Each of ours and the world outside. Cars passed, people shopped, drinks were bought in pubs, and we slipped through it all like ghosts. This man is my father, I wanted to shout. I was banging on the glass but it made no noise, I was opening my mouth but no voice came. He was sucking away at our lives, soon we'd be gone and the dust would settle. As if we'd never been. This, most frightening of all: as if we'd never been. We felt the waters closing over us. He was dragging us down to unmourned graves, and with one last gasp, we made for the surface where we saw the light, threw ourselves on the mercy of the air. One square of light. A promise of breathing unaided, and we saw our chance in the darkness. There was no option, d'you see that? When you're drowning, you snatch at life. We came out of the dark and into the light. We are newborn babies and we are learning to walk.

Fade down. Lights up on **Billy** *alone. Gradually, the family appear around the bed.*

Billy   I'm standing at the sink. Fizz, crack, there's a ripple in my head, a burning smell, my brain shattering into fragments, hundreds and thousands of coloured glass. I am dissolving. The room turns magenta pink. When I come to I'm on the bed.

Mary *pats the unseen* **Billy**'s *hand.*

Billy   Epilepsy, they say. Fits. Bring me my gun, I shout, and no one moves a muscle. They're smiling and patting my hand. And then I realise I'm not actually talking, I'm not even moving my mouth. God damn you bastards and this last word

like a roar bursts from my lungs and smashes them in the face.
Oh, they can hear me now all right.

Mary   Billy?

Billy   Let's get this place shipshape, I'm not out for the
count yet.

Mary   No, Billy, the doctor says –

Billy   Sod the bloody doctor, I hope he rots in hell, bring me
my gun. Crack. A noise.

Mary   Billy?

Billy   Where did that come from? Is it outside or in my
head? I say nothing. I don't let on.

Mary   Billy? D'you think he can hear me?

Janet *starts to cry.*

Billy   Bring the gun, let's have a party, I'm feeling on top of
the world. Tell Janet to stop crying, tell her to shut her bloody
face. Let's all have a whisky, let's get this show on the road.
Crack. Someone's popping something in my head. What's
wrong with you lot, what are you gawping at?

Mary   You've had a fit, Billy, calm down.

Billy   She says I've had a fit, but she's just saying it. What I
think is some bastard spiked my drink.

Billy *exits.*

Susan   The fits got worse.

Janet   They took him to hospital.

Mary   And that was the happiest time of our lives.

Janet   It was lovely waking up in the morning knowing he
wasn't there.

Susan   We could eat what we wanted.

Mary   Read magazines.

Susan   The bruises began to fade.

Janet   That's when we knew. We got a taste of forbidden fruit.

Susan   We understood what we didn't have. He was sunk from then on, really.

Billy *enters. He is wearing his bloodstained shirt. He sprawls on the bed.*

Mary   When he first came home he seemed different.

Janet   Weak as a kitten. Quiet as a lamb.

Susan   We were walking on air.

Mary   But it didn't last.

Janet   That last weekend was like being in hell.

The television comes on, a tinkling cartoon programme.

Billy   Another little whisky. Everything's under control. More crackling in my head last night, I didn't say a word. Give them an inch and they'll take a mile. A bird in the hand is worth two in the bush. What I say goes, what I say goes. Somebody come up here, I'm on my own in the dark. Mary, Susan, Janet, somebody come and do something. Stop bloody crying, Janet, you live the life of Riley, you don't want for nothing. Any more tears and I'll break your neck. Another little whisky. Crack. Sparks fly. Bright phosphorescence. My brain hisses and fizzes. Crack. Oh. Oh. I am hurtling through black sky on a sea of pungent scent. I can smell the colours of my own mind, I can smell this television programme, I'm back to my dog self, back to the dream. Metal, I smell metal and wood and cordite.

Mary *exits.* **Janet** *and* **Susan** *come close to the bed.*

Billy   Janet's tears, Susan's breasts, I smell something blinding white and relentless. I smell things I can't control. Piss, my piss, something between my teeth.

Janet   I can't go on, get the gun.

Susan *picks up the gun and aims it at* **Billy**'*s chest.*

Billy   Oh, burning tyres, spent diesel, an overtone of brass, stinging nettles, cold sweat, I love that smell so why don't I love it now. My body bucking, the room is rank with it, my eyes stream with it, my fear is filling the room. Bang. Bang. Bang.

Fade down lights on **Billy**. **Mary**, **Janet** *and* **Susan** *walk into the light.*

Mary   Let it end here. Let it end with us. I don't want grandchildren. Let the blight end here.

Susan/Janet   When the judge told us we weren't going to prison, we wanted to say thank you but nothing came out. She said, you've suffered enough. That was very kind of her, we thought.

Susan   We can start a new life now.

Janet   We've got a maisonette.

Mary   We plan to have pink carpets.

Susan   And a dog.

Janet   We've got four bedrooms.

Mary   One for each of us.

Susan   And one for spare items.

Janet   We've already bought the shelving.

Music. Fade down lights.

An Experiment With An Air Pump

An Experiment With An Air Pump was first performed at the
Royal Exchange Theatre, Manchester, on 12 February 1998.
The cast was as follows:

Fenwick/Tom	David Horovitch
Susannah/Ellen	Dearbhla Molloy
Harriet/Kate	Louise Yates
Maria	Sarah Howe
Roget	Tom Smith
Armstrong/Phil	Tom Mannion
Isobel	Pauline Lockhart

Directed by Matthew Lloyd
Designed by Julian McGowan
Lighting by Peter Mumford

An Experiment With An Air Pump received its United States
premiere at the Manhattan Theatre Club in New York City
on 5 October, 1999. The cast was as follows:

Fenwick/Tom	Daniel Gerroll
Susannah/Ellen	Linda Emond
Harriet/Kate	Ana Reeder
Maria	Clea Lewis
Roget	Christopher Duva
Armstrong/Phil	Jason Butler Harner
Isobel	Seana Kofoed

Directed by Doug Hughes
Set design by John Lee Beatty
Costume design by Catherine Zuber
Sound design by David Van Tiegham

Characters

1799

Joseph Fenwick, *physician, scientist, radical, fifty-five.*
Susannah Fenwick, *his wife, forty.*
Harriet, ⎫
Maria, ⎭ *their twin daughters, twenty.*
Peter Mark Roget, *physician, scientist, later of Thesauraus fame, twenty-one.*
Thomas Armstrong, *scientist, physician, twenties.*
Isobel Bridie, *a Scots servant with a twisted spine, twenty-five.*

1999

Ellen, *a scientist, forty. Doubles with Susannah.*
Tom, *an English lecturer, fifty-five. Doubles with Fenwick.*
Phil, *a Geordie builder, twenties. Doubles with Armstrong.*
Kate, *a scientist, friend of Ellen, twenty-five-ish. Doubles with Harriet.*

Act One

Prologue

*Chiaroscuro lighting up on slow revolve tableau involving the whole cast (except **Susannah/Ellen**), which suggests Joseph Wright's painting,* An Experiment on a Bird in the Air Pump. **Fenwick** *takes the role of the scientific demonstrator. Revolve continues slowly throughout this scene. The bird flutters in the glass dome. Strategically placed above the audience are four large projections of Wright's painting.* **Ellen**, *dressed casually in loose trousers, T-shirt, deck shoes, is looking up at them. Two dressers come on with her costume, wig, shoes, etc., for the part of* **Susannah**.

Ellen   I've loved this painting since I was thirteen years old. I've loved it because it has a scientist at the heart of it, a scientist where you usually find God. Here, centre stage, is not a saint or an archangel, but a man. Look at his face, bathed in celestial light, here is a man beatified by his search for truth. As a child enraptured by the possibilities of science, this painting set my heart racing, it made the blood tingle in my veins: I wanted to be this scientist; I wanted to be up there in the thick of it, all eyes drawn to me, frontiers tumbling before my merciless deconstruction. I was thirteen. Other girls wanted to marry Marc Bolan. I had smaller ambitions. I wanted to be God.

The dressers hook her into a tight corset over her T-shirt.

This painting described the world to me. The two small girls on the right are terrified he's going to kill their pet dove. The young scientist on the left is captivated, fascinated, his watch primed, he doesn't care whether the dove dies or not. For him, what matters is the process of experiment and the intoxication of discovery. The two young lovers next to him don't give a damn about any of it.

The dressers help her into her dress and shoes, put on her wig.

But the elderly man in the chair is worried about what it all means. He's worried about the ethics of dabbling with life and death. I think he's wondering where it's all going to end. He's the dead hand of caution. He bears the weight of all the old certainties and he knows they're slipping away from him, and from his kind. But when I was thirteen, what held me more than anything, was the drama at the centre of it all, the clouds scudding across a stage-set moon, the candle-light dipping and flickering. Who would not want to be caught up in this world? Who could resist the power of light over darkness?

The dressers hand her a fan and leave. The lights change, the projections fade, and as **Susannah**, *she joins the tableau.*

Maria   Will he die, Papa?

Fenwick   We'll see, won't we?

Maria   I don't want him to die.

Armstrong   It's only a bird.

Harriet   It's Maria's pet.

Armstrong   The world is bursting with birds, she can get another –

Maria *bursts into tears.*

Maria   I don't want another one. I want this one! I named him for my fiancé.

Harriet   They do have a similar intellectual capacity.

Susannah   Don't start, Harriet.

Roget   Perhaps we could use a different bird . . .

Armstrong   D'you happen to have one on you?

Roget   Well, I could – I'm sure we could find one –

Susannah   Mr Roget, there's really no need to go trampling round the garden with a net, I'm afraid Maria is being a dreadful baby.

Maria   I don't want Edward to die, Papa –

Susannah   Maria, show a little faith, your father would never conduct an experiment unless he was quite sure of the outcome, isn't that so?

Fenwick   You haven't quite grasped the subtlety of the word 'experiment', Susannah –

Maria   He's going to kill Edward!

Armstrong   This goes to prove the point I made earlier, sir: Keep infants away from the fireplace and women away from science.

Fenwick *gives him a long look.*

Fenwick   How old are you now, Armstrong?

Armstrong   I'm about to be twenty-six, sir.

Fenwick   You're an awful prig, has anyone ever told you that?

He performs the experiment. Gasps. The bird flutters out, unharmed.
Maria *gives a cry of delight, general clapping, laughter. Blackout.*

Scene One

Sounds of rioting going on outside – breaking glass, a baying mob, crashes, screams, etc. A chandelier descends from the ceiling and throws out scattered, shimmering light.

A bewildering variety of stuffed birds, animals and reptiles are suspended on strings, mounted on plinths, displayed in cases. A large cluttered desk, piled up with books, a microscope, a skull, bits of bodies and organs pickled in jars, nearby a telescope. Various bits of machinery.

Fenwick *sits at his desk, writing calmly, ignoring the tumult outside.*

Susannah *sits at a small card table endlessly playing patience, drinking brandy, and growing steadily more intoxicated.*

Roget *hovers anxiously, wincing at some of the more alarming crashes. Occasionally he peers through the telescope.* **Armstrong** *is agitated, glancing at his pocket watch.*

Armstrong D'you think we're trapped?

Roget *looks through the telescope.*

Roget I can't see a thing. Apart from smoke.

Fenwick (*not looking up*) Stop fretting for God's sake.

Susannah That's right, Mr Armstrong. Stop fretting. It's merely a crazed mob, mad on drink and wild for blood. Nothing to fret about.

Fenwick Any more proposals for the New Year lectures?

Susannah We could all be burnt in our beds. Probably will be. Hey ho. (*Turns over a card.*) Excellent. Three of spades.

Armstrong (*very agitated*) I have an appointment.

Fenwick I'd advise you to forget it. What about these proposals, Roget?

Roget *rummages around in his pockets and produces some sheets of paper. He looks through them.*

Roget A marked preoccupation with all things dental.

A roar from the crowd outside. He winces at the sound of a huge crash.

Armstrong Someone ought to put a stop to this.

Roget Go on then.

Fenwick Stop agitating and sit down, Armstrong, you're not going anywhere at present –

Armstrong I was expected ten minutes ago!

Fenwick *turns round to look at him.*

Fenwick What's the nature of this pressing appointment?

Armstrong *is hesitant. He glances at* **Susannah**.

Armstrong Dr Farleigh is . . . a demonstration.

Pause. **Fenwick** *gives him a long look.*

Fenwick I see. Well, I'm sure there'll be others.

Armstrong   This is a particularly interesting one.

Susannah   A particularly interesting what?

Armstrong   It's an unusual – it's a very um, singular . . . case, anatomically speaking . . . woman of thirty years, enormously malformed skull –

Fenwick (*briskly*)   Well, it can't be helped. Unless you want to risk your neck out there. Roget, where were we?

Roget   Mr Matthews is offering 'Notes on the Development of Wisdom Teeth' and Mr Devenish offers 'On the Early Failure of Pairs of Grinding Molars'.

Armstrong *is still in a state of agitation, pacing up and down, glancing at his watch, and then through the telescope.*

Fenwick   God save us. What else? Oh, sit down, Armstrong, for God's sake. You've missed your appointment and that's the end of it. There's no need to make us all suffer for it.

Armstrong *sits down, furiously.*

Armstrong   This is a bitter disappointment.

Susannah   All life's a bitter disappointment, Mr Armstrong. Take it from me.

Roget   Moving on from teeth, Mr Percy Fellowes would like to offer a learned paper on 'Left leggedness'. He points out that 'The rule in nature seems to be to bear to the right, and this phenomenon would seem to be universal.'

Fenwick   When Kant said we were living in an age of enlightenment he reckoned without the existence of Percy Fellowes.

Susannah   A very dreary man. Last year he delivered a lecture on pimples, Mr Roget. Unsavoury and quite unnecessary.

Roget   The piece comprises twenty-three pages and comes complete with illustrations 'which may be passed amongst the audience'.

Susannah　Fortunately his last offering came without supporting diagrams.

Fenwick　Tell him to go hang himself. Perhaps he could produce a learned paper on the universal rules of that particular phenomenon. Give us all some peace.

Roget (*checking off his list*)　Then I take it that's a no to the teeth, and a no to the legs –

Susannah　– I do hope so –

Roget　– moving on, in that case, to the next sub-section, what about Reverend Jessop's offer? 'On the Fundamental Laws of Vegetable Bodies, Whether Plants Have A Principle Of Self Preservation, And The Irritability Of Plants In General.'

Fenwick *turns round.*

Fenwick　We're talking about New Year's Eve for God's sake. The last night of the century. Has this fact bypassed these people? We want something worthy of the past and fired by visions of the future. We want to excite the audience, exhilarate them, we want to celebrate the intellect, march towards a New Jerusalem with all our banners flying. We discussed all this at the last meeting. What did we say our aim was? 'A lively ferment of minds producing a radical vision for the new century.' And what do we get? A botany lesson.

Armstrong　I think botany does come within the brief of Literary and Philosophical, Dr Fenwick –

Fenwick　Bugger it. Bugger botany –

Susannah　He's quite foul-mouthed when he's riled, have you noticed, Mr Armstrong –

Roget　To be fair, sir, I think you'll find the paper neither dull nor irrelevant, in fact it seems to me quite stimulating –

Fenwick　– bugger constipated, dull-as-ditch-water musings –

Susannah　– it's almost a nervous twitch –

Fenwick – from a bunch of retired curates. They should all be shot.

Roget   – I'll put that down as a possible then –

Fenwick   Have you ever met the Reverend Jessop? A milky, self-righteous, insipid little mannikin with a handshake like a dead fish. The man has piss where his blood should be –

Susannah   Now there I must agree with you.

Fenwick   If he's to lead us into the new century we're all doomed.

Armstrong   With respect, I think you confuse a personal antipathy towards Reverend Jessop with the quality of his proposed lecture.

Fenwick   Rubbish, one look at the man is enough to tell you he's a complete fool. He sets out with a premise and trims the world to fit it. What he practises is not science, but a branch of theology.

Armstrong   Objectivity is paramount in these things, you said so yourself, sir. One set of prejudices is as dangerous as another, I think that's how you put it.

Roget   And besides, you've not read the paper. I think you'll find there's not a mention of God in it anywhere –

Fenwick   Very well, very well, you've proved your point. I concede defeat. Passionate aversion has indeed muddied my strict impartiality. I admit it, I make no excuses for it. And I still won't give the man house room. Next.

Armstrong   It's a lost cause, Roget.

Roget   On a lighter note there's Mr Charlton's paper on 'Suffocation and Resuscitation from Apparent Death'. Very popular with the ladies according to the author.

Susannah   Then that's the man for me. Hire him immediately.

Roget   Or Mr Cowgill's on 'The Cunning Ways In Which Animals Conceal Themselves From Their Enemies'?

Fenwick   For God's sake, we want to storm into the next century not doze through it –

Roget (*scanning his list*)   'The French Revolution. Success Or Failure? Its Lessons For The New Century.' Dr Cavendish. Or Dr Farleigh: 'Is Progress an Illusion and The Past a Myth?' Now that sounds tremendously interesting –

Fenwick   Better. Depressing, and hardly a celebration, but better.

Roget   A good point for debate though, surely you must admit –

Susannah   Speaking personally, I'd rather have Reverend Jessop and his legs.

Fenwick   What else?

Roget   But, sir, I do think the notion of a mythological past –

Fenwick   Yes yes yes, Roget, stop whimpering, we'll come back to it later. What else?

Roget   'A History of the Flute from Roman Times to the Present Day', I don't think so . . . 'Whelks and their Habitat' . . . I think that fails on the visionary count . . . 'A History Of Northumberland in Watercolours', no . . . 'The Colour Green and Why it is So Generally Diffused in the Plant Kingdom' –

Fenwick   Reverend Jessop?

Roget   I'm afraid so. That seems to be it.

Fenwick   What a collection of dismal drips –

There is an enormous explosion. **Susannah** *stops playing cards.*

Susannah   This is past a joke.

Fenwick   I love a good explosion, don't you? The best tonic in the world is the sound of institutions tumbling. If I could bottle it I'd take a draught every day and live to a hundred. Though, sadly, this is merely a lot of noise signalling nothing whatsoever. Tomorrow morning the only thing to have changed will be the price of fish. If they're lucky.

He turns back to his desk with a sigh.

Armstrong, when you see Farleigh, ask him to call in. There might be something in his gloomy little sermon. And try and find a few more radical offers, can you, Roget? I don't think we could stomach an entire evening listening to that other rot.

He concentrates once again on his work.

Roget I was wondering, sir, if I might –

Susannah (*peering at the card table*) Can you see a ten of clubs anywhere, Mr Roget, or am I going blind?

Roget I'm sorry?

Fenwick (*not looking up*) Wondering what?

Roget Well, whilst I was cataloguing your collection, it occurred to me that a cross-referencing system might render it more accessible. A link perhaps, not only between the artefacts, but between categories, in accordance with their differing provenance and varying uses, both real and symbolic. Egyptian amulets, for example, of which you have several, might be located under the heading Egypt – obviously – but also under Religion, or Votive Objects, or indeed Insects in the case of scarabs –

Fenwick Are you volunteering for this thankless task, Roget?

Roget Well, I –

Harriet, **Maria** and **Isobel** *come in, breathlessly.* **Harriet** *is dressed as Britannia,* **Maria** *as a shepherdess, with crook, etc. A reluctant* **Isobel** *brings up the rear dressed as a sheep.*

Harriet They've just put a brick through the greenhouses, Papa.

Fenwick *doesn't look up.*

Fenwick I'm sure they didn't mean it.

Susannah   Take a leaf out of your father's book, Harriet. View it with sublime equanimity. You see in his eyes, it is not a brick, not at all, but more a sort of proletarian calling card.

Maria   They're setting carts on fire. The poor horses are screeching with panic.

Fenwick   It will all blow over presently, Maria.

Harriet   Papa, for goodness sake. They'll tear the house down around our heads.

Fenwick   They wouldn't dream of such a thing, I can assure you –

Harriet   Can't you do something?

Susannah   Yes, Joseph, do something, why don't you –

There is an almighty crash in the distance, and a roar from the mob.

Fenwick   What do you suggest?

Harriet   I don't know. Talk to them. They'll listen to you. Calm them before they burn the house down.

Fenwick   They know I'm on their side, they won't touch us.

Susannah   All this hoo-hah about corn –

Fenwick   Fish. Corn was last week.

Susannah   Always on the side of the mob, I don't understand it. It's pure, what's the word I'm looking for –

Fenwick   Perhaps you'd prefer them to burn the house down.

Susannah   Pure affectation, don't you think so, Mr Armstrong?

Fenwick *puts down his pen.*

Fenwick   We are trying to work, Susannah. Do you mind?

Susannah   Good God. I have your attention. What did I do?

Harriet   Accused him of affectation and you know how he loathes that.

There is another roar and a crash.

Maria   Go and talk to them, Father, please!

Fenwick   Maria. A riot is like a play. Action, reversal, climax, catharsis and we all go home. A relief, generally speaking, in a play. Disappointing in a riot, but true nevertheless.

The noise dies down slightly.

Isobel   I think they're moving off, sir.

They all listen. Another crash of glass, another louder roar.

Susannah   There go the cucumber frames.

Fenwick   Let us hope that's the catharsis. They'll all trail home soon, tired but happy. Twopence off fish and that's all they want. We demand our rights as Englishmen, we demand that herrings be less expensive. Universal suffrage? Not interested. Revolution? Bugger it. We demand fish. No one dreams of taking over the fishmongers. Not a revolutionary amongst them.

Susannah   Thank God.

He turns back to his desk.

Harriet   You said you wanted to see a rehearsal of our play, Papa. And I'd rather like to get it over with.

Fenwick (*reading*)   'Gentlemen of the Newcastle Literary and Philosophical Society, Ladies, we stand on the cusp' – (*He pauses, considers, scratches out and replaces words.*) 'threshold' – 'the very brink' – no, that sounds ominous. Cusp or threshold then, which d'you prefer?

Harriet   I don't know, cusp. So can we show you our play? Mama says we would benefit from your advice and criticism.

Fenwick   When have you ever taken my advice, Harriet? And as for criticism, the last time I dared to utter mild dissent you threw a pot of tea at me.

Fenwick *turns back to his desk.* **Maria** *gives a twirl.*

Maria   What do you think, Mr Roget?

Roget   Sorry? Oh, I see, very, yes, most . . . affecting.

Fenwick   Cusp? Doesn't sound right to me somehow.

Maria   I'm playing an Arcadian Idyll.

Armstrong   We guessed immediately.

Harriet   It's metaphorical.

Armstrong   Oh, obviously.

Maria   It was Harriet's idea.

Susannah   Harriet is an uncommon genius, Mr Armstrong, to read her poetry is to be reminded of, oh, Milton, Shakespeare, Southey, that other fellow, you name it, you must show the gentlemen your poems, Harriet, no point in them languishing in a drawer –

Harriet   Mama, please –

Susannah   But they're such pretty little verses, dear –

Harriet   Do we have to talk about them, Mama?

Roget   I'm sure they're very fine, but perhaps Miss Fenwick prefers to hide her light at present. Very understandable.

Harriet   Thank you, Mr Roget.

Armstrong   What's the plot to this entertainment then?

Maria   I'm sorry?

Armstrong   Your play. Is it comedy or tragedy?

Maria   How would you describe the plot to our play, Harriet?

Harriet   It's a hymn to progress.

Roget   How apt.

Maria   Of course when we say hymn, we don't mean it literally –

Harriet   They're not completely stupid, Maria –

Maria   Because in any case Harriet has rejected established religion, haven't you, Harriet –

Armstrong   Very wise.

Harriet   Maria represents the past, and I represent the future.

Roget   Arcadia meets Britannia, very neat.

Harriet   I am Empire, Industry, Science, Wealth and Reason.

Maria   For the most part I sit on a hillock and wave at my flock. According to Harriet, this suggests Pastoral Innocence –

Harriet   I think the gentlemen have grasped the general principle, Maria –

Maria   I must say it's terribly dull, I don't know how those poor shepherdesses stood it.

Harriet   I plan to have a sort of chimney, here, as a headpiece, but the steam is proving a little complicated at present.

Roget   I see. We look forward to that. But tell me, I'm interested in your idea of pastoral innocence. Where does it come from?

Harriet   I don't quite catch your drift.

Roget   Shepherding's a harsh trade. Living in this region you cannot fail to have noticed that. Bo Peep might freeze to death on these hillsides. Drifts ten feet deep on the Cheviots last year, and no sign of spring until May. Hardly an Arcadian Idyll.

Harriet   Maria represents an ideal. That's what idyll means, Mr Roget.

Roget   Of course. But is this ideal based on truth? Does an idyll have its basis in reality?

Harriet   Yes. No. You are being very difficult.

Armstrong   Leave her alone, Roget.

Harriet   It's a fable. Our play is a fable. And that's a sort of universal truth.

Armstrong   Of course it is.

Harriet   You're even more irritating than Mr Roget. He at least resists the temptation to patronise.

Armstrong   I'm sorry. Forgive me. No doubt all will be revealed when we see the performance.

Harriet   Exactly.

Susannah   It's best not to cross her, Mr Armstrong. She's as stubborn as her father.

Armstrong   Yes, I can see that.

Susannah   But sweet, sweet –

Harriet *glares*.

Roget   So. Anyway. I'm sure the play will be a delight. Isobel, you're obviously playing . . . what?

Isobel   A sheep, sir.

Roget   Of course. A sheep. Yes.

Isobel   I've the wrong ears.

Harriet   Oh, for goodness sake, stop complaining about your wretched ears –

Isobel   Sheep don't have ears like this.

Susannah   She's right of course, they don't.

Maria   They're perfectly adequate for a small, unimportant part. No one will notice them, Isobel.

Isobel   To my mind, if you'll excuse me, it's a very low sort of play –

Maria   No one's interested in your mind, dear –

Isobel   – for a start, sheep don't speak.

Harriet   That's the magic of theatre, Isobel. Anything is possible.

Susannah   I had a pet lamb once. Judith. She was a Welsh ewe, and one would almost swear she could speak. Such a plaintive little bleat, of course she's cutlets now, poor thing. Do you bleat, Isobel?

Isobel   My lines are ridiculous. They're infantile. Why can't I say something of consequence?

Harriet   Primarily because you're playing a sheep. And besides, some people are not meant to say anything of consequence. As in life, so in a play. Certain rules must be obeyed. And one of them is you stick to your own lines. You can't swap them round as it takes your fancy. Think of the chaos. Think of the audience.

Fenwick   What do you think, Isobel? Cusp or threshold?

Isobel   It depends on the context, sir. In this instance I think threshold is the word you want. Cusp is too poetic, and also imprecise.

Silence. They all stare at **Isobel**.

Fenwick (*reads*) . . . . we stand on the threshold of a new century, we stand at the gates of a New Jerusalem . . . ' Thank you, Isobel.

Harriet   Now you've established that, Papa, would you like to see our play or not?

Fenwick   I will see it, but not now, Harriet.

Harriet   You are impossible, Papa. How many times have we sat through your experiments, your visiting speakers droning endlessly about combustible gases and electricity?

Fenwick   You enjoyed every moment of it –

Harriet   That's not the point! We've spent hours labelling every piece of your useless bric-a-brac, arranging in alphabetical order your rhinoceros horn, your dried walrus flipper, tooth of hippopotamus, pointless chunks of volcanic lava, even the hair balls of an ox –

Fenwick   Calculi they're known as –

Maria   He even made us attend the dissection of a dear little spaniel –

Fenwick   Which was quite dead, I assure you, gentlemen –

Maria   – because he said it would be illuminating –

Susannah   You got quite sick, didn't you, dear –

Harriet   But you see, Papa, how d'you know our play is not equally illuminating?

Fenwick   I've told you, I will watch it, Harriet, but not now –

Harriet *stamps her foot.*

Harriet   We have rehearsed and rehearsed the wretched thing because you told us you'd look at it now –

Fenwick   Then I'm afraid I must disappoint you.

Harriet   You're selfish and cruel and you think of nothing but your own concerns. I hate you.

She storms out.

Susannah   Such an awkward age. They can move from sweet docility to murderous rage in the course of a sentence. It's quite unsettling. But just a phase –

Maria   It's got nothing to do with her age, Mama. She has a ferocious temper, always has had. I'm not given to rages at all. I'm the quiet one, gentlemen, which is why I have a fiancé and Harriet has not. Excuse me. Harriet, dear . . .

She hurries after **Harriet**.

Isobel   Will that be all, sir?

Fenwick   Stay a moment, Isobel. Sit down.

Isobel   I'd rather not, sir.

Fenwick   I'm sorry?

Isobel   My back. I cannot sit.

Fenwick   You must sit sometimes, surely?

Isobel   Yes, sir, but there are occasions when it is painful. And then it is better that I stand.

Armstrong *goes to her and looks at her twisted back. Takes hold of her.*

Armstrong   Is it getting worse? By that I mean, is the degree of malformation increasingly pronounced?

Isobel   It is a long time since I looked in a glass. But I imagine it is more severe. It feels to be. My clothes twist and pull more.

Armstrong *feels her shoulders and back.*

Armstrong   Does that hurt?

Isobel   The pain is not in my back. It is in my hip.

He moves his hands to her hips, and she jerks away.

There's nothing you can do about it, sir.

Susannah   Quite right, Isobel. They're all quacks. A quart of brandy's what you need for pain, whatever noxious remedy they might prescribe.

Fenwick   Susannah –

Susannah   And don't tell me I'm drunk because I'm not. I'm merely pointing out that physicians never cure anything. That's a well-established fact. None of you know what you're talking about –

Fenwick   And you do I suppose –

Susannah   I don't pretend to –

Fenwick   Can we discuss this later, Susannah –

Susannah   A discussion? With me? How novel. D'you think I'm up to it? Goodness, what shall we have as our topic? 'One Shakespeare is worth ten Isaac Newtons. Discuss.' My dear, I'm in a lather of expectation.

Fenwick   Not half as much as me, I can assure you.

He turns away from her.

I'm sorry you're in pain, Isobel. Are we working you too hard?

Isobel   No, sir. The work is not burdensome.

Fenwick   You like words, don't you? I've noticed it before.

Isobel   I suppose I do, sir.

Fenwick   Can you read?

Isobel   All Scots can read, sir.

Fenwick   I wasn't aware of that.

Isobel   It's generally the case, sir.

Armstrong   All Scots are born literate, is that what you're saying?

Isobel   All Scots learn to read. Most of them anyway.

Fenwick   But the English are ignorant?

Isobel   I wouldn't go so far as that, sir. Of course I wouldn't.

Fenwick   Don't worry, we're not angry with you. But I'm interested in your opinion of the English.

Isobel   I don't have any opinion, sir.

Fenwick   Be as bold as you please. Is there something you dislike?

Isobel   I never said I disliked the English, I merely said that the Scots read a lot of books.

Armstrong   You must have some feelings on the subject surely.

Isobel   It's hard to say, sir.

Fenwick   In what sense?

Isobel   I'm not sure what 'English' means. In Scots we have a word for it and it's 'Sassenach'. But they tell me that means only 'Saxon'. And as I'm a lowland Scot, and therefore a Saxon, it seems that I too am a Sassenach.

Roget   So the word has two meanings. The literal and the commonly understood. Perhaps in time, the latter may come to supersede the former, d'you agree?

Isobel   Perhaps, sir. Unfortunately.

Roget   Would you call me English?

Isobel   Yes, sir.

Roget   Even though my father was Swiss?

Susannah   My mother was French and my father grew up in Leitrim. What does that make me?

Fenwick   Isobel?

Isobel   The English are hard to place. Englishness is difficult to pin down. It is like a tide which swallows up everything in its wake, and whilst altered in its constituents, appears outwardly little changed.

Armstrong   Bravo. Who told you that?

Isobel Why do you assume that I was told it, sir?

Fenwick   So the English are infinitely adaptable and mindlessly rapacious. That's interesting. Are you aware of any other qualities by which we may be identified?

Isobel   Not especially, sir.

Fenwick   None?

Isobel   I only know words, sir. Words are what interest me.

Fenwick   And?

Isobel   The English have a single word, sir, nursery, for the place where both children and plants are raised. Perhaps that is telling. Apart from that, I only know that I am a Scot, sir. I am not one of you.

Fenwick   Might that not be class, rather than race, Isobel?

Isobel   I'm sorry, sir, but I find this discussion very difficult.

Fenwick   Why is that?

Isobel   Because I'm wearing these ears. You cannot take me seriously whilst I am disguised as a sheep.

Susannah   I think 'disguised' is overstating the case, Isobel.

Fenwick   I'd quite forgotten about the ears actually.

Susannah   You see how much attention he pays to a woman's appearance, gentlemen? Sometimes I think it hardly worth dressing in the morning.

Harriet *comes in.*

Harriet   Papa, there are some men in the kitchen. The cook has let them in. They say they'd like to 'hide' for a while.

Susannah *gets up unsteadily.*

Susannah   That cook's been drinking again. She opens the house to anyone after a bottle of brandy. Last week it was a woman with two pigs, I found them asleep in the library. I've warned her it must stop. Leave this to me.

She goes. **Fenwick** *gets up.*

Fenwick   Susannah, let me deal with this please – excuse me, gentlemen –

He hurries out after her, followed by **Harriet**.

Harriet (*as she goes*)   The men seem quite docile, Papa, but one of them has a badly sliced head . . .

Isobel *is left with* **Roget** *and* **Armstrong**.

Isobel   May I go now?

Roget   Of course, Isobel.

Armstrong   No, stay a while. Tell us about yourself.

Isobel   I'm sorry, sir?

Armstrong   Tell us about your life.

Isobel   Why would you want me to do that, sir?

Armstrong   It might be interesting.

Isobel   It's not.

Roget   Let her go, Armstrong.

Armstrong   You're rather pretty, d'you know that, Isobel?

Roget   Armstrong –

Armstrong   I don't suppose anyone's ever told you that before, have they, Isobel?

Isobel   Only a blind man or a liar would say such a thing, sir.

Armstrong   You think me a liar?

Isobel   I won't tell you what I think of you.

Armstrong   You're a pretty woman, accept the fact.

Isobel   I know what I am. I am a serving girl, a waiting woman, a maid, hireling, drudge and skivvy. I am a lackey, an underling, a menial and a minion. I am all these things but I am not pretty.

Roget   A general factotum.

Isobel   A slave.

Roget   A retainer perhaps?

Isobel   A dogsbody.

Roget *laughs.*

Isobel   I know twenty-seven words for what I am, sir. And none of them corresponds to pretty.

Roget   Twenty-seven words for servant, that's remarkable, but yes I suppose it's possible –

Armstrong　Beauty is more complex than mere appearance, Isobel.

Roget　And of course there are different catagories of servant, aren't there? What about amanuensis? Slightly more democratic but certainly a possibility – I presume you're only counting the female variants, are you –

Armstrong　I wish you'd take me seriously, Isobel.

Roget　We're trying to have a discussion, Armstrong –

Isobel　I believe you're making fun of me, sir.

Armstrong　I swear on my life, I am not –

Isobel　And I would ask you to stop –

Armstrong　Very well. It seems I can't persuade you. I wish I could.

Isobel　May I go now, sir?

Roget　Of course you may, and please believe me, Mr Armstrong means no harm, I can assure you – What about scullion – did you count that?

Isobel　I did, sir. Thank you, sir. If that's all, I will go now.

She hurries out.

Roget　Pretty?

Armstrong　She loves it. Every woman loves a compliment. Especially a plain one.

Roget　You're toying with her. It's cruel beyond belief.

Armstrong　No, I'm not actually. I don't find her plain at all. I find her quite fascinating.

He pours himself a glass of brandy.

A strange little thing, isn't she? I wonder . . .

Roget　What?

Armstrong　I wonder what caused the hump . . .

He sips his brandy thoughtfully. Blackout.

Fade up dim lightiug. English pastoral music in background. **Maria**
enters during the scene change, and reads out a letter from **Edward**.

Maria   'My dear Maria, A chapati is a sort of thin, flapping
bread, since you ask. This morning on rising, I found a fierce
boil beneath my ear, the size of a gull's egg. The boy wanted
to apply some sort of dung to it, but as he was loathe to
divulge which animal it might originate from I declined his
offer. I am in great agony. Yesterday one of our bearers was
crushed by an elephant. His head popped open like a
pomegranate. So now we are one bearer short, and the
remaining are in a very sullen mood. We visited some of their
temples on Saturday, and were all agreed that many of the
statues are quite disgraceful. The Collector said it makes one
wonder what sort of jinks they get up to when they are out of
our jurisdiction. A Miss Cholmondely, out on a visit from
Yorkshire, quite fainted away from shock at the sight of one
of them. We had done our utmost to preserve her from the
spectacle, but she would insist. Whereas gentlemen are able
to appreciate the instructional aspect of such things, women,
for the most part, are merely affronted, or, as in the case of
Miss Cholmondely, quite prostrated. Afterwards, she
remembered nothing of the incident, or indeed the statues,
which is a blessing. The natives seemed to find the episode
faintly entertaining. Their temperament is generally placid, I
find, but not in the English manner. An Englishman has a
modesty of demeanour, a judicious thoughtfulness and an
equanimity of temperament which makes him a stranger to
passionate outbursts. The native composure is altogether
different. One might almost feel that they were hiding
something. Please write soon. Your affectionate servant,
Edward.'

Scene Two

Lights up. Same room, 1999.

The stage is now almost bare apart from the desk, now free of its clutter, and from a one-bar electric fire which glows weakly. A single electric light bulb casts a thin light. Tea chests are scattered round the room, some full, some still in the process of being packed. Piles of books and clothes.
Ellen *is sorting through stuff and packing it up.* **Kate**, *wearing scarves and a coat, is talking on her mobile phone.*

Kate   . . . No, she's sitting here in front of me . . . yes I'll tell her . . . she hasn't had time to sit down and think about it, that's all . . . no honestly, I don't foresee any problems at all . . . OK . . . bye, Mike.

She clicks off the phone.

He says they have to know by New Year's Eve.

Ellen *carries on packing.*

Ellen   Yes, OK.

Kate   I just think it's a wonderful opportunity, that's all.

Ellen   Yes. I know.

Pause.

Kate   So have you talked to Tom about it?

Ellen   Sort of. Look, I'll sort it out, OK –

Phil *comes in carring clipboards, tape measures etc.*

Phil   D'you mind if I take a few measurements in here?

Ellen   No, no of course not. Kate, this is Phil, he's doing a building survey.

Kate   I think I'll go and make some tea, it's bloody freezing in here.

She goes out. **Phil** *looks slightly awkward.*

Phil   Did I interrupt something?

Ellen   Not at all. Kate's an old colleague of mine. She's staying with us for New Year but I think the cold's getting to her.

Phil *takes out his tape measure and looks round the room.*

Phil   By, it's a canny size, this place.

Ellen   That's why we have to sell it. It's crippling us. I got it from my mum. Her parents had it before her. But we can't afford it so that's that.

She looks at her watch.

What exactly is Tom doing in the basement?

Phil   Showing us where the pipes run under the floors. They've got to come up. Most of them are lead. I'm surprised you've not been poisoned. You wouldn't believe what you find when you start poking around the foundations of some of these old houses. We were sorting out a place in Corbridge last year and we found a Roman bathhouse. Well, they said it was Roman. Which was a bit of a blow, like, because I fancied a few of the tiles for our kitchen, but with it being that old they slapped a preservation order on it.

Ellen   What's the plan for this room, then?

Phil   Corporate hospitality. Private bar in here, private conference facilities through there, private gym. Private sauna for the Scandinavians. Good views of the park, handy for the miniature railway in case any of them are steam train enthusiasts –

Ellen   A miniature railway?

Phil   Actually, they call it a heritage railway.

Ellen   They told us they just wanted to restore it to its former glory.

Phil   Aye, but everything has to be on a heritage trail now and you can't be on a heritage trail unless you've got attractions. I mean, this is a nice enough house and that, but it's not got much going for it in your commercial sense. People like to feel they're getting their money's worth. I think they want to reopen one of the mines down the road as well. You know. Employ some ex-miners to dress up as miners and pretend to dig coal and then charge people a tenner to go down and experience life at the coal face.

Ellen   You're not serious?

Phil   Well, why not? They've Disneyfied everything else, why should the miners get off scot-free?

Ellen   It's such . . . what's the word I'm looking for.

Phil   Shite.

Ellen   I mean, why fill it with ersatz history when it's already got a proper history? It doesn't need to be ponsified and half-timbered. The Newcastle Lit and Phil had its first meetings in this room, did you know that?

Phil   I didn't, no –

Ellen   Lavoisier visited this house. Tom Paine was given secret readings in this very room. It's a big, plain, solid house, it's not quaint or charming. The history of this house is the history of radicalism and dissent and intellectual enquiry, and they're going to turn it into a tin of souvenir biscuits.

Phil   Well, don't sell it then.

Ellen   I told you. We can't afford it. Tom's been made redundant, and it just eats up money –

Phil   Is he in the same line of business as you then?

Kate   No. He's an English lecturer.

Phil   Actually, I meant to ask you something, seeing as I'm here like. My seven-year-old daughter, we think she's allergic to jam. Big red hives on her arms every time she eats it. And I wondered if it was common, like. A jam allergy.

Ellen   I've no idea. I would have thought it was some additive rather than the jam itself.

Phil   You don't see many cases of it then?

Ellen   Oh, I see, no, I'm sorry, I'm not a medical doctor, I'm a research scientist.

Phil   So you're not a doctor?

Ellen   Yes. But not a medical one.

Phil   Oh.

Pause.

So you don't know anything about medicine then?

Ellen   No.

Phil   What, nothing at all?

Ellen   Not in any helpful way, no. I'm sorry.

Phil   You must know a bit, like, being a scientist.

Ellen   I don't actually.

Phil   I bet you do really.

Ellen   No I don't, honestly.

Phil   So what d'you do then?

Ellen   I'm sorry?

Phil   What d'you research?

Ellen   Oh, it's boring.

Phil   Why d'you do it then?

Ellen   Well, not to me. It's not boring to me.

He taps the floor, gets down on his knees, jots notes down on his clipboard.

Phil   I tell you something, black holes, I like the sound of them, it's like the bloody *X-Files*. Apparently, light goes into them, right, but it never comes out again, and if you're hanging around on the edge of one, time slows down until you get to the horizon and then it stops altogether. They're like sort of wormholes, right, and if we could go down one of these wormholes we'd come out in a different universe. Incredible.

Now I wouldn't mind researching them. Mind you, I suppose you'd need the qualifications.

Ellen   I don't know much about any of that, I'm afraid. Not really my area.

Phil   So what is your area then?

Ellen   I'm doing . . . well, I work in genetics, that sort of thing.

She looks at her watch again.

I wish Tom'd hurry up, he's been down there for ages.

Phil   Cloning, is that the sort of thing?

Ellen   No no, nothing like that.

Phil   I bet it is.

Ellen   No, it's not.

Phil   Actually, I've always wanted to ask a scientist this: what d'you make of spontaneous combustion?

Ellen   I'm sorry?

Phil   Because a mate of mine said a friend of his found the lad next door fried to crisp, well, a pile of ashes actually, apart from his slippers, which he said were just sitting there, smouldering. With the feet still in them. Not a mark on them, he said. Apparently it's very common.

Ellen   It is?

Phil   So what d'you make of that then?

Ellen   Well, I'm not sure. I think it's probably an urban myth.

Phil   You see, that's the sort of science that interests me. The tricky stuff.

Ellen   Well, it's certainly . . . that . . .

Phil   What about alien invasions then? D'you think we're being visited by extraterrestrials?

Ellen Er, I don't think so, no.

Phil Now, no disrespect, don't get me wrong, but that's what I hate about scientists. Closed minds.

Ellen Oh. Sorry.

Phil So why don't you believe in them?

Ellen It's not a matter of belief. It's a matter of evidence, and I don't have any that persuades me they exist.

Phil I don't know how you can be so sure –

Ellen I'm not sure. If someone can present me with compelling evidence of their existence, I'll accept it –

Phil Well, a friend of mine, right, said him and his wife were followed home from the races one day by a lozenge-shaped thing, a bit like a Victory V but green, sort of hovering and swooping, just above the hedge. Followed them for twenty mile. And then shot off in the direction of the power station. And this lad works for the council, so you couldn't call him a nutter.

Ellen Is this the same one who found the smouldering slippers?

Phil No, that was his mate. So you see, you say you've got no evidence and I've just given you two very compelling bits of it if you ask me.

Ellen Anecdotal doesn't count. They could be making it up. Or elaborating something much more explicable.

Phil Why would they want to do that?

Ellen Because people like telling stories. They like sitting around and telling tales for which there's no rational explanation. Like ghost stories. And crop circles. And being a reincarnation of Marie Antoinette. I'm not entirely sure why. You'd need to ask a psychologist.

Phil Well, I know what I think, and I think we'll have to agree to disagree on this one.

Ellen   Fair enough.

Phil   Mind you. This cloning lark. I bet that could get a bit out of hand, couldn't it?

Ellen   In what way?

Phil   Well, it'll be people next, everyone knows that, I mean, they say it won't but it will. And what worries me is, well, can you imagine, I mean, say if, I don't know, William Hague decided to clone himself. There'd be two of him then. Or hundreds even. Imagine that.

Ellen   I can't see why he'd want to clone himself. What's in it for him? And even if he did, you wouldn't get hundreds of William Hagues. They'd be genetically identical, but culturally and socially and chronologically completely different.

Phil   Well, you say that . . .

Ellen   It's true –

Phil   No, but just imagine it for a minute. William Hague looks like something that needs to be put back in the oven, right?

Ellen   No he doesn't –

Phil   He does, man. He looks like he's not cooked properly. D'you remember Pilsbury Dough men? You got them in little tins. He looks like one of them. And if there was hundreds of him, quite apart from the politics, which'd be very fucking scary, it'd be like a science-fiction film, *Invasion of the Pastry People*.

Ellen   Yes, well, that's science fiction, not science –

Phil   Well, the whole thing's very dodgy, you don't know what you're dabbling in, if you ask me. I think I'll stick to rewiring. That's as far as my technological know-how goes.

Ellen   Probably just as useful as what I do.

Phil   You still haven't told me exactly what that is.

Ellen   Foetal diagnostics. Detecting genetic abnormalities in the foetus. Well, attempting to, anyway.

Phil   I thought you said it was nothing to do with cloning?

Ellen   It isn't –

Phil   It's as close as makes no difference –

Ellen   It's very complicated –

Phil   Oh aye.

Ellen   I'm sorry. I'm not used to talking about my work, OK? People get the wrong end of the stick. They jump to insane conclusions and accuse me of all sorts of things. Creating monsters that are half man, half muffin, secretly cloning Dan Quayle, single-handedly destroying the family, you name it. The fact that they have only the haziest idea about any of this stuff doesn't seem to hinder them at all.

Kate *appears with a tray of tea and a bottle of whiskey.*

Kate   Hi. Hot toddies all round, and if you think it's cold in here, try the kitchen. I don't know how you live here.

Ellen   You get used to it.

Phil   So what's your opinion on spontaneous combustion then, Kate?

Kate   I'm sorry?

Ellen   Phil has a friend of a friend of a friend who burst into flames.

Kate   Oh, that. Absolute bollocks. Are you having your tea straight or with a shot of this?

Phil *looks at his watch.*

Phil   Well . . .

She slugs whiskey into his mug and hands it to him.

Kate   It's after five, and it's starting to snow out there. Give yourself a break. Ellen?

Phil   What d'you mean it's bollocks? It's very well
documented actually –

Ellen   Did you know they want to turn the house into a
theme park?

Kate   So don't let them. Don't sell it. You don't have to.

Ellen   If it were that straightforward –

Kate   It is.

She hands her a mug of tea. Pause.

Ellen   Kate's company is offering me a job, Phil, which will
pay me a great deal of money, which might even mean we can
pull out of selling the house, and I'm not sure whether to take
it.

Phil   So what's the problem?

Kate   That's what I keep saying.

Ellen   Well, firstly, it's not just my decision, it's Tom's too –

Kate   It hasn't got anything to do with Tom.

Ellen   He's my husband, that's one consideration. It means
moving two hundred miles away –

Kate   But what exactly is he objecting to apart from that?

Ellen   Nothing. He's not objecting to anything. He just . . .
he has a problem with some aspects of the research, that's all.

Kate   Like what? Anyway, he won't be doing the research,
you will.

Ellen   Yes, but . . . oh never mind. You won't understand
what I'm talking about.

Kate   What's that supposed to mean?

Ellen   You're fifteen years younger than me and nothing
frightens you. You still want to be God.

Kate   Christ, you do talk shite sometimes.

Ellen   You're still in love with the work –

Kate   So are you –

Ellen   But with me it's been a long marriage and some of the romance has worn off –

Phil   If you don't mind me asking, what is this job?

Kate   Ellen is a very brilliant scientist, did she tell you that?

Phil   I'm sure she is. In her own field.

Ellen   Phil believes in flying saucers.

Phil   That's not what I said actually. But you're being very cagey about this job. You see, that's why people don't trust scientists. They're always up to something.

Ellen   I'm having an ethical crisis, Phil –

Phil   What did I tell you? I knew it was dodgy –

Tom (*off*)   Ellen?

Ellen   We're up here.

Kate   Ethical crisis, for fuck's sake –

Ellen   The fact that you've never had a moral qualm in your life doesn't mean you have superior reasoning power, it just means you have a limited imagination. One of the difficult areas, not for me, but for some people –

Kate   Like Tom –

Ellen   – OK, like Tom, is the idea of research using embryos –

Kate   – pre-embryos –

Ellen   In my mind they're embryos, OK?

Kate   It's a fourteen-day-old bunch of cells. It's not a foetus, it's a cluster.

Ellen   You can call it what you like, he's still uneasy with it –

Phil   I don't blame him.

Kate   Have you got children, Phil?

Phil   Two. Boy and a girl.

Kate   If, very very early in your wife's pregnancy, you were able to discover in your child the gene for, say, Alzheimer's disease, or asthma, or maybe something more alarming like schizophrenia, would you be grateful for that information?

Phil   Er . . . I'm not sure . . .

Kate   Ellen's team have perfected a technique that does this. It's completely safe, and it can be done very very early. And the most important thing is it's non-invasive, so there's no risk to the foetus. And I just want to point out that this is pretty radical stuff. Now, wouldn't you say this was a good thing?

Phil   Aye, I suppose so. Where do the pre-embryos come in?

Kate   We use them in our research. They're left over from in-vitro fertilisation.

Phil   What d'you mean, left over?

Kate   Sometimes too many eggs are fertilised and the mother doesn't need them all –

Phil   Bloody hell.

Kate   Anyway, my company wants Ellen to come and work for us because we can invest a lot of money in development of her technique, so that eventually it'll be available to a mass-market. Everyone benefits, nobody suffers.

Phil   Apart from the pre-embryo.

Kate   Which, as I've explained, is nothing more than a mass of cells. Now. Can you see a problem with that, Phil?

Phil   I can actually.

Ellen   Forget the embryos for a minute.

Phil   Aye, OK. What's the point of any of it?

Kate   Well, you might want to terminate the pregnancy, for example.

Phil   What, because the kid might get asthma?

Kate   Well, not for something like that, obviously. But eventually we'll be able to apply gene therapy in the womb. We'll be able to eradicate all sorts of things. Schizophrenia, manic-depression –

Phil   My uncle Stan was manic-depressive and he was magic. He built us a tree house covered in shells and bits of coloured glass. He used to play the Northumbrian pipes.

Ellen   We're mapping the human gene system at the moment. There's something called the Human Genome Project. Have you heard of it?

Phil   You what?

Kate   It's like a new map of humanity, every element described and understood. It's breathtaking –

Phil   Oh aye.

Kate   We'll be able to pinpoint genes for particular types of cancer, for neurological disorders, for all sorts of things, some of them benign, some of them not, but what it really means is we'll understand the shape and complexity of a human being, we'll be able to say this is a man, this is exactly who he is, this is his potential, these are his possible limitations. And manic-depression is genetic. We'll pin it down soon.

Phil   And then what? No more Uncle Stans.

Kate   How is your uncle Stan these days?

Phil   Dead.

Kate   What happened to him?

Phil   He killed himself.

Kate   I rest my case.

Phil   You never met him. You don't know anything about what went on in his life, or what things meant to him –

Kate   I'm just saying manic-depression can be fatal –

Phil   Bollocks, man, you don't know what you're talking about –

Tom *comes in, in thick outdoor clothes. He looks white and shaky.*
Kate *beams at him.*

Kate   Tom. Hi. D'you want whiskey with your tea?

Tom   What? Oh . . . um . . . yes . . . yes, please . . .

Ellen   Is something wrong?

Tom   Yes . . . yes, I suppose there is . . . .

Ellen   Well what?

Tom   We've found something a bit odd underneath one of the kitchen cupboards. In the extension.

Phil   If it's the electrics, I could have told you that. Whoever did your wiring was a bloody menace.

Tom   No, no. It's a box of um . . . it's a box of bones.

Blackout. Music.

Maria *comes on with a letter which she reads in a pool of light during the scene change.*

Maria   'My dear Maria, I hope you are well. My neck has subsided, but now my gums feel all wrong. They are white at the edges and bleed when I eat. Please send one bottle Daffy's Elixir and two of Spilsbury's Efficacious Drops by return of post. Yesterday the Collector's horse was bitten by a snake, and one of our party beat it to death with an ivory club. The snake, not the horse. It was an enormous size, and the sight of it made me long quite childishly for our own gentle land, where one can walk a country road without being threatened by vicious nature on all sides. Do English animals kill? I can think of none. One never feels apprehensive about sheep, for instance, or cattle. Bulls can be unpredictable, of course. I dream of England, and yet I must own that my dreams are strangely imprecise. I cannot place the images at all, yet I know that I dream of home. The mere word "England" conjures up a landscape in my head, and although this picture is familiar, it is not a place I have ever visited, but rather, *almost* such a place.

It is unbearably hot here, and though I stay indoors a great deal, I cannot think such extremes are good for one's general health. I think of you often, in the cooler, gentler climes of home, and I am glad that you are safe and far from harm and strife.

Your most affectionate servant, Edward.'

Scene Three

Lights up. 1799. One day later.

The dining-room. A large table centre stage. Chairs around it. Chandelier.

Isobel *is polishing the table.* **Roget** *comes in, wrapped up in coats and scarves.*

Roget   Isobel?

Isobel *turns. She looks disappointed.*

Roget   I was looking for Dr Fenwick.

Isobel   He's not here, sir.

Roget   No.

Uneasy pause.

I was wondering, Isobel, whether you'd care to take a stroll with me later today.

Isobel   No thank you, sir.

Roget   Oh.

Awkward pause.

Perhaps I'll just wait here for Dr Fenwick then.

He goes to the window.

Awful weather.

Pause.

Isobel   Yes, sir.

Roget   I'm afraid I can't get used to the northern climate. Can't seem to get warm. In Edinburgh I was chilled to the marrow, even in summer. That terrible wind off the sea. And the same here. Relentless, unforgiving cold. All year round.

Isobel   Perhaps you should go back to London if you can't stand the climate.

Roget *looks at her.*

Isobel   I didn't mean to offend you, sir.

Roget   No offence taken. Slavey. I thought of that in the night.

She looks at him.

Another word for servant.

Isobel   I counted that.

Roget   Did you count Scots dialect words?

Isobel   Some. D'you have a particular interest in the word servant, sir?

Roget   It's not the word itself that interests me. I just like lists. How are we to understand the world unless we organise it coherently? The world is a web of connections and affinities, don't you think? I have a systematic mind. I get it from my mother. You should see her household accounts. The cross-referencing would stump a mathematician. I'm a good physician because I'm methodical and intermittently inspired.

Isobel *is silent.*

Roget   Have you tried laughing gas?

Isobel   No, sir.

Roget   I thought Dr Fenwick may have offered you some.
We once thought it might cure consumption but it all proved
rather inconclusive. It has a remarkably pleasant effect
though, I can thoroughly recommend it as a tonic –

Fenwick *comes in, with* **Susannah**.

Fenwick   What are you doing, Roget?

Roget   Waiting for you, sir.

Susannah   Isobel, the table is quite polished enough. We
don't want to be blinded over supper.

Isobel   Yes, madam.

She goes. **Susannah** *settles down to some needlework.*

Fenwick   Not putting ideas in her head, were you?

Roget   What about?

Fenwick   I don't know. You tell me.

Roget   We were talking about words.

Fenwick   I've seen girls like her ruined, that's all. Taken
advantage of. Men think they're game for anything because
no one will marry them. And I don't want her ruined, I don't
want her heart broken, d'you understand me?

Susannah   So noble of you.

Roget   I had no intention of ruining her.

Fenwick   We have an enlightened view of servants in this
household. We think of them as family –

Susannah   Of course you don't, Joseph, you like to think
that, but you don't really –

Fenwick (*ignoring her*)   – and you don't fuck your family.
Whatever they might do in some of the more remote areas.
Now, to the point. I want you to look out of this window.
What do you see?

Roget *goes and looks, uncertain of what is required of him.*

Roget   Um . . . A view . . . A vista? . . . A prospect?

Fenwick   Specifically, Roget, specifically.

Roget   A city landscape . . . An urban panorama?

Fenwick   It's not a word game, Roget. An urban panorama composed of what?

Roget *looks again.*

Roget   Oh. I see. Banks running down to the Tyne, sir. The bridge. Smoke curling into the frozen air. Ships. Coal barges.

Fenwick   D'you know what I see? Bridges. Plural. Can you imagine?

Roget   Bridges, plural . . . Well, yes, I think I can imagine that.

Fenwick   Huge, graceful bridges. Triumphs of engineering. Hymns to invention and the conquest of nature.

Roget   I see.

Fenwick   You don't sound inspired.

Susannah   That's because he's not, Joseph.

Roget   Well, yes, bridges. There's no doubt, that would be a very good thing.

Fenwick   This is a great city, Roget. It could be the Athens of the North.

Roget   I understand Edinburgh has already claimed that particular title, sir.

Fenwick   Bugger Edinburgh. You know who lived here in the sixties? You know who chose to make Newcastle his home? No less a man than –

Roget/Susannah (*together*)   – Jean Paul Marat –

Roget   You told me.

Fenwick   Of course what he was doing practising as a vet is beyond me. No feel for it at all. Could kill a creature just by looking at it.

Susannah   That's one skill he took back with him to France then.

Fenwick   He was great man, Roget. An inspiration. A terrible vet but a great republican.

Roget   Of course it hasn't been huge success in France. Republicanism.

Fenwick   They got rid of the king. That's what the word means for God's sake.

Roget   But at what cost, sir?

Susannah   My husband doesn't like to sully himself with such vulgarities as cost, Roget –

Fenwick   We'll do it differently here. It may take longer, but I guarantee you, one hundred years from now, there will be no monarchy in England –

Susannah   Take my advice, Mr Roget, and stop him before he starts –

Fenwick (*ignoring her*)   – and how will we get there? By the relentless, irresistible advance of science and the consequent wider dissemination of knowledge.

Roget   Dr Guillotine managed to dispatch the king quite effectively purely by the application of science. Are you planning something similar here?

Fenwick   The monarchy will disappear, Roget, it's inevitable. Logic demands it. Science is inextricably linked with democracy. Once people are released from their ignorance, they will demand universal suffrage, and once we have it, it follows as night follows day that we will vote the monarchy out of existence.

Roget   How do you propose to achieve this spectacular release from bondage?

Fenwick   By the end of the nineteenth century everyone
will understand how the world works. By the end of the
following century, if you can imagine that far, every man or
woman in the street will understand more than we can ever
dream of. Electricity, the stars, the composition of the blood,
complexities beyond our imagination, will be as easily
understood as the alphabet. Magic and superstition won't
come into it. And it stands to reason, any citizen with the facts
at his disposal could not tolerate a monarchical system unless
he was mentally impaired or wilfully resistant to reality.

Roget   It seems to be a condition of existence to resist an
idea of reality when it threatens a tradition of mystery.

Fenwick   What?

Roget   People like the monarchy because it's got nothing to
do with reality.

Fenwick   Oh, they bang on and on about our mystical,
pageant-filled past, and I say bugger it, it's a myth. The British
monarchy doesn't bear too much close scrutiny, Roget, let me
tell you.

Susannah   I feel sorry them, poor creatures. So much
responsibility, so much money, and so badly dressed. The last
time I saw the queen she looked like a catastrophe in a cake
shop –

Fenwick   Susannah, what exactly are you doing here?

Susannah   I'm sewing.

Fenwick   Is there any need for you to do it here? Why are
you following me around the house?

Susannah   For the simple reason that if I didn't, you'd
forget I existed.

Fenwick   Don't be ridiculous –

Susannah   He doesn't listen to me, have you noticed, Mr
Roget? I said, Joseph, that I pitied the king and queen. They
are mere mortals, like the rest of us.

Fenwick The Hanoverians are, to a man, philistine, dull and profoundly stupid, not to mention vulgar.

Susannah Exactly. Just like the rest of us. That's precisely why they're popular, Joseph.

Fenwick If they're just like us, why don't they live like us? Why are we keeping them in palaces? Our people cannot afford to feed themselves adequately, our children sleep in the streets, with vermin for company, and we still think it reasonable to fund a drab family of feuding Germans who do nothing more than wave at us from their carriages occasionally. Ask yourself this simple question, Roget. Are we all mad?

Susannah Note, again, Mr Roget, how he addresses his question to you, rather than to me –

Fenwick Susannah, in God's name, stop interrupting me –

Susannah I'm sorry if I exasperate you, Joseph, but I prefer it to being ignored. Excuse me.

She throws down her needlework and goes out, furious. Silence.

Fenwick Sorry about that, Roget. She's er, very highly strung.

Roget Perhaps she feels – perhaps you –

Fenwick What?

Roget Nothing, sir . . . These things are clearly . . . not my affair . . .

Awkward pause.

Fenwick Where were we?

Roget You were being dangerously seditious.

Fenwick Not that you'd dream of turning me in.

Roget So science is what, as far as you're concerned? A sort of philanthropic odyssey? Its sole purpose to rescue people from ignorance and dissolve the state?

Fenwick   We're scientists because we want to change the world.

Roget   We're scientists because we want to understand the world.

Fenwick   We're scientists because we want to change the conditions under which people live.

Roget *says nothing.*

Fenwick   Well. Go on. Argue with me.

Pause.

Roget   Well. I er, I don't think Armstrong would agree with that at all . . . sir.

Fenwick   Fuck Armstrong. What about you?

Roget   I . . . I reserve judgement, sir. I take no ethical position. I do what I do because it fascinates me. I don't question its purpose.

Fenwick   Piddling niggler.

Pause.

I'm not very keen on Armstrong. I don't suppose that's slipped your notice, has it? Only got him here because Farleigh asked me to take him on for three months. Clear eye, sharp brain, ruthless logician. In short, a clever young bastard, but cold of heart.

Roget   Does good science require a warm heart?

Fenwick   I like to think so, Roget. In fact, I suspect pure objectivity is an arrogant fallacy. When we conduct an experiment we bring to bear on it all our human frailties, and all our prejudices, much as we might wish it to be otherwise. I like to think that good science requires us to utilise every aspect of ourselves in pursuit of truth. And sometimes the heart comes into it.

Pause.

I'd better go and find my wife. Excuse me, will you?

Roget   Of course.

He goes out. **Roget** *picks up the needlework from the floor and follows him. As they leave by one exit, Isobel comes in by another, followed by* **Armstrong**. *He takes her hand. She pulls away.*

Armstrong   I know you thought my behaviour a little forward yesterday, and I apologise for it, Isobel.

Isobel   I accept your apologies, sir. For the third time. Please, no more.

Armstrong   However, I must point out that I meant every word. I do think you're very pretty. Is that so odd?

Isobel   It is unusual, sir, that's all.

Armstrong *takes a book from his pocket.*

Armstrong   Will you at least accept this small gift from me?

Isobel   That is not . . . it is not necessary, sir.

Armstrong   Oh, reason not the need, Isobel.

Isobel   *King Lear.*

Armstrong   Really? Please, take it, will you?

He tries to hand her the book. She refuses.

So you refuse my present?

Pause. **Isobel** *is confused.*

Isobel   I've never had a gift before, sir.

Armstrong   What, never?

Isobel   I have never, to my recollection, inspired material generosity in others.

Armstrong   Well, in that case, let this be the first time –

He thrusts the book at her. She looks at it.

Isobel   Shakespeare's Sonnets . . . . Oh, sir . . . I am most . . . thank you, sir.

They stand, quietly looking at the book and frozen in time as **Tom** *comes on, wrapped up in outdoor clothes over pyjamas, heavy boots. He has a pair of shears in his heads and an armful of cuttings from the garden.* **Ellen** *enters, dishevelled, in her dressing-gown.*

Ellen   There you are. Where have you been? I woke up and you'd gone.

He doesn't turn round.

Tom   I was just getting some air.

Pause.

I took a few cuttings from the garden. I thought we could plant them in the new one. Lavender. Honeysuckle. Some of the old white roses. Otherwise it'll all disappear under a car park or something. Roses are all hybrids now. You don't get them like this any more. These ones are older than the century. We should save them.

Ellen   What?

Tom   The roses. I'm going to have a lot of time for gardening now.

Ellen   You'll get another job.

Tom   No I won't. You know I won't. I'm too old, I'm too expensive and I don't give a fuck about post-modernism.

Pause. He starts trimming the cuttings.

Ellen   I have to give Kate an answer by tomorrow.

Tom   So give her one.

Ellen   That's what I've been trying to talk to you about.

Tom   I know.

Ellen   So talk to me.

Tom   What is there to say?

Ellen   Tom, look, I know you're depressed –

Tom   I'm not depressed. I'm redundant. And there's a dead body under the kitchen sink.

Ellen   It's not a dead body –

Tom   That's what it started out as –

Ellen   A long time ago –

Tom   So what's the difference? At what stage does it stop being disturbing and start being archaeology?

Ellen   What did the coroner say?

Tom   The skeleton's small, so she's quite young.

Ellen   She?

Tom   It's a young girl. She's been there since at least the First World War, which is when they extended the kitchen. Where we found her was part of the garden originally. And that's all they told me. You'd think you'd sense something. You'd think something like that would taint the place somehow. I've never felt anything, have you?

Ellen   No, but people don't –

Tom   I do. Remember the house in Coldstream?

Ellen   Yes, but that was just – well, I mean, I don't know, you were in a weird mood.

Tom   No I wasn't. I couldn't go across the threshold because I felt chilled to the marrow. The hairs stood up on the back of my neck.

Ellen   No one else felt that.

Tom   The dog did.

Ellen   So what are you trying to say?

Pause.

Tom   That we've lived with a dead girl under the floor for twenty years. And I find that disturbing. It makes me feel strange. That's all.

Pause.

Ellen   OK. But to return to more practical matters. The job. Shall I take it or not?

Tom   I can't make the decision for you.

Ellen   You could try and make it with me. We'll be moving away. That involves you too.

Pause.

Tom   I feel responsible somehow.

Ellen   Sorry?

Tom   For the girl. Now that we've found her.

Ellen   Tom, she's dead, she's been there for years and we've no idea who she is. How can we be responsible for her?

Tom   She was in our house.

Ellen   But we didn't put her there.

Tom   She was a person, she had a name.

Ellen   I know, I'm sorry, look, the thing about the job, they're now offering me even more money. We need it –

Tom   Rub it in, why don't you –

He sweeps the trimmings into a plastic bag.

Ellen   – but how can I possibly take it if you're going to freeze me out with this prim, disapproval thing?

Tom   I'm sure you'll manage somehow.

Ellen   Oh, for Christ's sake. I feel like I'm walking on eggshells. Half the time I'm frightened to bring the subject up because . . . because . . .

Tom   Because what?

Ellen   In case it offends your self-esteem. Because you've lost your job. And I'm being offered one.

Tom   It's got nothing to do with that. Nothing at all.

Ellen   OK, listen, I have some qualms about the job myself – not the same as yours, but qualms nevertheless. But I don't have a problem working with pre-embryos. I'm sorry but I don't. What I do have a problem with is you thinking I'm some sort of murderess because of that.

Tom   I never mentioned the word murder.

Pause.

I just want to remind you of something, that's all.

Ellen   What?

Tom   How many times have you been pregnant?

Ellen   Oh don't start this, Tom.

Tom   How many times?

Ellen   Five.

Tom   Six.

Ellen   OK, five, six, what difference does it make?

Tom   D'you remember how you felt every time?

Ellen   I try not to think about it actually.

Tom   Ecstatic. From the very first moment.

Ellen   Thank you for reminding me.

Tom   On at least two occasions, when it was no more than what you now refer to as 'a cluster of cells' you called it a pregnancy. You knew from the very moment of conception. You knew it was a potential person.

Ellen   Potential. That's the key word, Tom. I mean, you know, I might just as well have flushed them down the toilet because in my particular case they never got beyond the most minimal potentiality. Any of them.

Tom   I just wonder, that's all. When you're poking at these cells in a Petri dish –

Ellen   – which is just the stupidest way of describing what I do –

Tom   – d'you not think about who they might have become?

Ellen   They were never going to become anyone, Tom, because if we didn't use them, they'd be discarded.

Tom   Discarded. You see, that word doesn't really get it for me.

Ellen   I'm sorry. I can't help that.

Tom   Look, I'm not saying don't take this job, truly I'd never say that to you –

Ellen   You could have fooled me –

Tom   It just unsettles me, I couldn't do it, something in me rebels against it, and I don't know why it doesn't unsettle you –

Ellen   Because it just doesn't.

Tom   And the other thing is, what are you doing these experiments *for*?

Ellen   You know why –

Tom   I mean, for whose benefit?

Ellen   Everybody's.

Tom   It's a totally commercial operation. Kate's firm exists to make money above and beyond anything else.

Ellen   That's the nature of the world we live in, Tom –

Tom   I mean, where's it all leading? If you can eventually determine the genetic code of any given foetus, all I know is that's going to lead to trouble. Can you imagine what insurance companies will do with that information? Mortgage companies? Health insurers? As soon as you put this stuff into the market place –

Ellen   Oh for God's sake, Tom, d'you think I don't worry about these things? Every scientist is aware of the implications, but we all live in the market place. Even you. I want to do the job I love and unfortunately funding is a prerequisite. At the moment, I don't have enough. It's easy to have rarefied ethics if all your job involves is decoding bits of Shakespeare. It's not so bloody easy if you're trying to move genetics into the twenty-first century. All you have is moral principles, Tom. You don't have any solutions.

Tom   I know. I'm just saying you don't either.

He clears up the rest of the mess.

Did I tell you there was a tiny gold chain there?

Ellen   Sorry?

Tom   With the body. The coroner found it.

He picks up his cuttings and bag.

Right. Rooting powder. I bet we haven't got any.

He goes out. She's left, brooding. Exits other side of stage. **Isobel** *shuts the book.*

Isobel   I'll take great care of it, sir. It's beautiful.

Armstrong   Why did you agree to meet me today?

Isobel   I'm not sure. I think perhaps it was the novelty. No man has ever asked such a thing of me.

Armstrong   Surely that can't be true. What about at home, in Scotland?

Isobel   Do not ask me to talk about myself.

Armstrong   Why not?

Isobel   I'm unused to answering questions. When I talk about myself my face feels hot. When I talk about myself I feel that I am lying.

Armstrong   Are you?

Isobel   I'm not sure. I try not to. But we all lie about ourselves.

Armstrong   Do we?

Isobel   We don't mean to but we do.

Armstrong   Do you lie in general?

Isobel   No. Do you?

Armstrong   Inconsequentially.

He kisses her. She is taken by surprise, and pulls away.

Armstrong   Don't you trust me?

Isobel   I do not know you, sir.

Armstrong   You've allowed me to kiss you. What does that mean?

Isobel   That I am susceptible to flattery.

Armstrong   So you don't trust me?

Isobel   No, sir.

Armstrong   Don't call me sir.

Isobel   I would prefer to.

Armstrong   My name is Thomas.

Isobel   I know that

Armstrong   I kiss you, call you pretty, I give you a book of sonnets. What could be my motive other than genuine affection?

Isobel   I have no idea, sir. That is what bothers me. I am confused. Men do not, in general, show such interest in me.

Armstrong   You must have been wooed from time to time.

Isobel   Once. By an old man with a face like a goat. Perhaps he thought the fact of my hump cancelled out the fact of his face.

Armstrong   Will you trust me in time?

Isobel   I cannot say, sir.

Armstrong   Nevertheless, your face did light up when I appeared in the hallway.

Isobel   I was not aware of that.

Armstrong   You know it did. You gave me a ravishing smile.

Isobel   Now you are most definitely making fun of me.

Armstrong   But it is a most beautiful, transforming smile, like sunlight on a glacier –

Isobel   Stop it, please. I am not used to such remarks. They do not make me happy, as you no doubt believe, they make me confused –

He takes hold of her, turns her round, covers her twisted back with kisses and caresses, fascinated and bewitched by it.

Armstrong   Isobel –

She pulls away, confused.

Isobel   Go, sir, you . . . muddle me . . . Leave me, please –

Pause.

Armstrong   Very well. If that's what you wish. I'm sorry if I've offended you. My feelings ran away with me. Forgive me. May we meet tomorrow? Please say yes, please.

Isobel   Perhaps. I don't know. Perhaps.

He kisses her hand.

Armstrong   Till tomorrow then. I have taken the liberty of marking some lines in your book. Look at them, won't you? Page seventy-three.

He goes. **Isobel** *sits down at the table, opens the book at the marked page.*

Isobel (*reading*)   'All days are nights to see till I see thee, All nights bright days when dreams do show me thee.' . . . He thinks my smile ravishing. He thinks it transforming . . . like sunlight on a glacier . . . His name is Thomas . . . Thomas . . .

She stretches round to feel her twisted back. Lights fade.

Act Two

Scene One

Some room as Act One, Scene One.

Maria *comes on in her shepherdess outfit.*

Maria (*reading*)   'My dear Maria, Miss Cholmondely has invited several of us to a party to celebrate the New Year, and I have decided to attend. She plays the harpsichord with great skill, and I hear there is to be dancing. Strangely, after all my homesickness, I now feel apprehensive about my return. I know that it is winter in England, and although the heat is oppressive here, one is forced to admit that there is little to recommend a northern English January. Chilblains hold no romance for me. I like the thought of home, but I shiver at what I know to be reality. Last year, two of our lads died of cold, do you remember? We found them in the top meadow, frozen, rigid as stone, clinging together like babes, and were quite unable to prise them apart until we had thawed their corpses before a fire. This memory oppresses me every time I think of England. However, I long to see you, and that is what sustains me. I dream of your soft blue eyes –' (*She breaks off.*) Blue? My soft blue eyes? Oh, Edward. What are you talking about?

Harriet *and* **Isobel** *come on dressed for their play, clutching pieces of paper on which the script is written.* **Harriet** *begins to move furniture, sets out four chairs.* **Isobel** *and* **Maria** *watch mutely.*

Harriet   I hope you've made a start on your lines, Maria. Isobel, for goodness sake, lend a hand, don't just stand there like a, like a –

Isobel   – sheep. (*She picks up a chair.*) Where d'you want these?

Harriet   Over here, thank you –

Maria   Harriet, dear, what colour would you call my eyes?

Harriet   I'm sorry?

Maria   Would you call them blue at all?

Harriet   Only if I was utterly unfamiliar with the word. Your eyes are a pronounced and definite brown, Maria. Like mine.

Maria   Are there any conditions of lighting, any curious atmospheric distortions under which they might show themselves to be azure?

Harriet   They are very pleasing as they are, Maria. They will never be blue, and you mustn't wish it.

Maria   Have they ever looked blue to you, Isobel?

Harriet   Oh, for goodness sake –

Isobel   They've never looked blue to me.

Maria   They have always looked brown?

Isobel   Most markedly. It is not a thing one would forget.

Maria   Exactly. That's what I thought.

Fenwick *and* **Susannah** *come in.*

Harriet   No! No! We're not ready –

Fenwick   Oh. Sorry –

Isobel   We're as ready as we're ever going to be.

Susannah   I thought it was just a rehearsal, dear?

Harriet   Oh, very well, come in, sit down, no not there! Here, look where we've set out the chairs.

Maria   I don't think I can perform today. I'm sorry.

Harriet   What?

Maria   I'm afraid I'm not in the humour.

Harriet   Excuse me a moment. Maria –

She takes hold of **Maria***'s arm and drags her out, passing* **Armstrong** *and* **Roget***, who enter as they leave.*

Roget Oh. Have we missed it?

Fenwick Unfortunately, no.

Isobel *looks awkward.*

Susannah Still the same ears, I see, Isobel.

Isobel Yes, madam.

Armstrong I think they're very fetching.

Fenwick You're to sit here, I think.

Roget *and* **Armstrong** *sit down next to him.*

Armstrong What's happening?

Susannah One of the actresses is temporarily indisposed.

Fenwick But the actor manager is placating her with the promise of her name appearing most prominently on the handbill, and a solemn vow that Wakefield will not be included in the tour.

Maria *returns, followed by* **Harriet**.

Maria Papa –

Harriet Maria –

Maria Papa, Edward thinks my eyes are blue, he said so in a letter, and Harriet says this is because he's a complete fool and that she never liked him anyway, but I think, perhaps he has a tropical fever and his mind is wandering or perhaps he meant brown but wrote blue –

Fenwick Perhaps he has an inability to distinguish one colour from another. It is not so rare.

Harriet He cannot tell brown from blue? Don't be ridiculous.

Fenwick It's possible, Harriet, can we simply say that it's possible –

Harriet   Edward's problem is that he's awash with milky sentiments lapped up from bowls of cheap poetry. In which of course the heroine's eyes are always blue –

Maria   Harriet –

Harriet   And I lay money on it, were you to cut his heart out, you would find it indistinguishable from tripe –

Maria   Oh. How dare you! Poor Edward –

Susannah   I think you've made your point, Harriet –

Maria   You're jealous of me.

Harriet   Of course I'm not jealous –

Susannah   Girls, girls –

Maria   Because he asked me to marry him and not you –

Harriet   Why would I want to marry Edward? I don't want to marry anyone!

Susannah   Don't be silly, Harriet, of course you do –

Harriet   I do not –

Susannah   Now look what you've started, Joseph!

Fenwick   Me?

Susannah   Your daughter doesn't want to marry. Who put that idea into her head?

Fenwick   As far as I recollect, I suggested that Edward might have a problem with recognising colours. Harriet's marriage plans were not mentioned –

Susannah   Not in this instance perhaps –

Roget   Any chance of seeing the play?

Maria   I don't want to be in her wretched play.

Roget   Oh.

Harriet   You may not be given to rages, Maria, but you are most expert at sulking –

Armstrong   This is as good a play as I've ever seen. Carry on, do.

Susannah   Girls, girls, now come along, make up and apologise to each other, and, Harriet, stop making foolish pronouncements.

Harriet   It's not foolish, I mean it, I never want to marry –

Susannah   You're overexcited, dear, perhaps it's stage fright –

Harriet   I am not overexcited!!!

Fenwick *rises up.*

Fenwick   For God's sake, stop it, all of you!

Silence.

We have guests.

Awkward silence.

Now. When we've all calmed down, we might begin the entertainment. Perhaps you could bring everyone a glass of wine, Isobel.

Isohel   Yes, sir.

She goes to pour wine.

Susannah   Harriet, Maria, kiss and make up.

Harriet *and* **Maria** *kiss each other on the cheek reluctantly.*

Maria   Forgive me, dearest Harriet.

Harriet   Forgive me, dearest Maria.

They both look at **Susannah**.

Maria/Harriet (*together*)   There.

Isobel *hands out wine.*

Susannah   Excellent.

Silence as **Isobel** *puts the tray back on the table. She goes to join*

Harriet *and* **Maria** *They search for scripts and fiddle with them sullenly. The audience sip their wine and wait expectantly.*

Susannah   Well?

Harriet   All right. It won't be very good. I'm Britannia, she's Arcadia –

Susannah   Yes yes yes, we know that. Get on with it.

Harriet *takes a deep breath, coughs, rustles her script.*

Harriet   Well, first of all there'll just be me on stage and I'll he reading a Brief Prologue, but I haven't written that yet, and then possibly a song, which we'll all sing –

Maria   Which one?

Harriet   I don't know yet. One which we all know.

Susannah   'Greensleeves' perhaps.

Maria   Or a hymn. I like a hymn.

Harriet   It's not important at the moment –

Maria   What sort of atmosphere must this song provoke?

Susannah   D'you want a happy song or a sad song?

Harriet   For heaven's sake, I don't know yet, I wish I'd never mentioned the wretched thing.

Pause.

Maria   Sorry.

Harriet   Anyway, then we all come on dressed more or less like this –

Susannah   I do hope you'll be doing something about Isobel's ears –

Harriet   – and I will have some steam coming out of a chimney here, at least I hope so –

Maria   I think perhaps you should start, Harriet.

Harriet   I'm trying to start!

Maria   Sorry, sorry.

Pause.

Harriet   So. I'm Britannia.

She clears her throat, looks at her script.

I am Britannia, spirit of our age, champion of our nation. Fair play and enterprise are my guiding lights, industry and endeavour are my saviours.

She coughs.

> I stand atop these lonely hills, from whence
> This land I view, all sage, soft gold spread out.
> The slate-grey sea, the dry stone walls I know,
> The shepherdess, her flock –

Isobel   Baaa.

Harriet   – the frisking lambs.

Maria
> But lo, on the horizon now we see –
> What can this be, what towers are rising here,
> What lights that burn so late into the night?
> That smoke that billows forth, what fires are these?

Harriet
> The future's ours, these chimneys belch out hope,
> These furnaces forge dreams as well as wealth.
> Great minds conspire to cast an Eden here
> From Iron, and steam bends nature to our will –

Maria
> The future is as new Jerusalem –

Isobel
> But not for sheep, for sheep it's looking grim.

The audience can contain their laughter no longer. **Maria** *throws down her script.*

Maria   That line ruins the entire piece, Harriet –

Isobel   I told you this yesterday. I don't know why you want sheep in it anyway –

Harriet   The line won't work if you say it like that –

Isobel   – unless it's just an exercise in humiliation. That strikes me as a distinct possibility –

Fenwick   Harriet, perhaps you should –

Harriet   You're the audience, shut up –

The audience roar.

Armstrong   This should transfer to Drury Lane immediately –

Harriet   It wasn't my idea in the first place! You made me write it, Mama. I don't want to write plays! I don't want to write anything! Why will you insist that I am a poet? I am nothing of the sort –

Susannah   Oh, come come, Harriet –

Harriet   I have no talent for it whatsoever. You might wish me to be a poet, but I am not. I cannot bend words to my will, I don't want to be a poet –

Susannah   We heard you the first time, dear –

Harriet   I want to be a physician, like papa –

She throws down her script and storms out. Silence.

Susannah   Did I hear her correctly? Did she say physician? Has she taken leave of her senses? Harriet?

She goes after her. **Maria** *follows.*

Maria   Oh lord . . . Harriet, dear . . .

Fenwick *gets up.*

Fenwick   Well, that's that. House full of madwomen. What about a stroll, gentlemen? Let's take a little wander down to the river –

Roget   There's a blizzard out there –

Fenwick   Nonsense, Roget, you've never seen a blizzard, we call this bracing, come along –

He strides off and **Roget** *follows him.* **Isobel** *is left alone with* **Armstrong**. *She goes over to the table and begins to pull off her ears.* **Armstrong** *comes over and helps her.*

Armstrong   Oh, Isobel, Isobel, let me . . .

He nuzzles her. She is embarrassed. Pushes him away.

Isobel   Sir, this is not the place . . .

He looks at her, pulls her into his arms, kisses her passionately before she can resist.

Armstrong   If I give you a guinea, will you let me see you naked?

Isobel *pulls away, horrified.*

Isobel   What?

Armstrong   A joke, a joke, and a very bad one at that –

Isobel   I am bewildered at such a jest, sir –

Armstrong   Isobel, surely you did not take me seriously? Oh God, I am mortified, why did I say that? I'm sorry. I am most truly sorry and ashamed. It's a thing I do.

Isobel   What is?

Armstrong   I make inappropriate remarks in certain situations.

Isobel   What sort of situations?

Armstrong   Those in which . . . I find myself in the grip of bewildering and powerful feelings.

He goes to the desk and sits down.

When my mother died I made jests at the funeral. Can you imagine? My mother whom I loved beyond anything, whom I nursed through the most wretched agony of her final illness. I don't know why I behaved as I did. I can only say that it was at odds with how I felt.

Isobel   I'm sorry for your trouble, sir.

Armstrong   Don't you see, Isobel, that I am beside myself with longing for you? I dream of you, your imprint is stamped upon my mind indelibly, I cannot help myself. Forgive me, I beg of you, and I will go, and never trouble you again.

Pause.

Isobel   There is nothing to forgive, sir.

He goes to her, kisses her hand.

Armstrong   But can you love me, Isobel?

Isobel *looks away.*

Isobel   Can you love me, sir? Surely that is more to the point.

Armstrong (*tremulously*)   I do, Isobel . . . I do.

He dashes from the room. **Isobel** *hugs herself: delight, bewilderment and uncertainty battling for supremacy. Lights fade.*

Scene Two

Lights up. Main room. 1999.

Still full of packing cases, etc. **Phil** *is sitting at the top of a ladder, dressed in overalls, covered in dust. He's drinking a mug of tea.* **Tom** *is sorting through books, papers, old photos, general junk, and packing it into boxes.*

Phil   The whole ceiling'll have to come down.

Tom   Yeah, well, wait till we've moved out, will you?

Phil   Have you heard anything else about the body?

Tom   I've just spoken to the coroner's office. They've done a preliminary report. Female Caucasian, between twenty and thirty, probably been there a couple of hundred years. Much longer than they thought at first. And the skeleton's incomplete.

Phil   How d'you mean?

Tom   Some of it's missing.

Phil   Poor lass. I wonder what happened to her. That's if she is a lass of course.

Tom   What d'you mean?

Phil   Well, there's some strange things go on round here. Friend of mine says they found a body up by Holy Island that's not human and it's not animal. They've never seen anything like it apparently.

Tom   Who's 'they'?

Phil   The authorities, man. They don't want to cause mass panic so they like to keep these things quiet.

Tom   Phil, they were human remains. Female human remains.

Phil   Well, they say that –

Tom   They are. I saw them. They're not Venusian or extraterrestrial in any way.

Phil   OK. Fair enough . . . D'you think she was murdered then?

Tom   The bones cut clean through, they said, with a knife or a cleaver. And crammed into a hole any old how.

Phil   In that case . . .

Phil *comes down the ladder. He goes to his tool bag and rummages around. Brings out a candle.*

Tom   What are you doing?

Phil   Emergency supplies. In case all else fails.

He sticks the candle in a piece of putty, sets it on the floor, and lights it.

Tom   What's that for?

Phil   For her soul.

Tom   Oh.

Phil   It's about time somebody did it if she's been there that long.

Tom   Oh. Right . . . Of course.

Pause.

You're a Catholic then?

Phil   Was. I still do this though.

Tom   What is it, superstition or habit?

Phil   D'you not believe in souls?

Tom   I'm not sure.

Phil   I do. I believe in reincarnation.

Tom   Is there anything you don't believe in, Phil?

Phil   Acupuncture. And the Tory Party. But I still go into churches sometimes, light a candle for my mam. And I just think about her for a few minutes. I give her all my attention. I think attention's a form of prayer.

Tom   Oh. Right.

Phil *laughs.*

Phil   You think I'm mental, don't you?

He blows the candle out.

Tom   No, no, don't do that, no please, light it again –

Phil *tosses him the matches.*

Phil   You do it.

Tom *lights the candle and sets it on a packing case. They both sit on the floor and look at the flame. Silence for a while.*

Phil   How's the wife's ethical crisis?

Tom   Still bubbling along nicely.

Phil   I had a thought.

Tom   Did you?

Phil   Aye.

Pause.

Tom   What was it then?

Phil   Bar codes.

Tom   Sorry?

Phil   Well, along those lines. Like, you know, if they can map your genes before you're born, they'll soon be wanting a little plastic card with your DNA details on. And if it says anything dodgy, it'll be like you're credit blacked. And then imagine this, people'll say I can't have this kid because it'll never get a mortgage. I mean, that's bloody mad, that. I bet your wife hasn't thought about that, has she?

Tom   I think she's starting to –

Ellen *and* **Kate** *come in, wearing outdoor clothes.*

Ellen   What on earth are you doing?

Phil *gets up.*

Phil   Just messing around. I'd better take this downstairs.

He goes over to his ladder, picks it up and goes out.

Ellen   Did I say something?

Tom   He was going anyway.

He goes back to packing.

Kate   That looked very cosy. Doing a bit of male bonding, were you?

Tom   We were talking about the body in the basement.

Ellen   I wish you wouldn't call it that.

Kate   She probably wasn't murdered. She was dissected. That's why some of her's missing.

Tom   How did you come to that conclusion?

Kate   I remember years ago, they had to dig up an old

cemetery near us, to widen the road. And when they came to move the coffins, lots of the really old ones were empty. The bodies had been snatched. Probably by medical students, before the Anatomy Act, which was about eighteen thirtysomething.

Ellen So why then bury her in our garden?

Kate I don't know. Nearest place maybe. It'd be a bit risky trying to put her back in her grave. Risky enough getting her out in the first place.

Ellen There you are, Tom. Not a murder victim at all. Just the equivalent of leaving your body for medical research. Feel better now?

He stares into the candle flame, and blows it out. Blackout. They leave.

Roget *and* **Armstrong** *enter, in outdoor clothes, carrying racquets. The two men blow on their hands, stamp to keep warm.* **Roget** *takes a shuttlecock from his pocket and they begin to play.*

Armstrong You should have been there. A growth the size of a potato.

Roget Jersey or King Edward?

Armstrong Bigger in fact. As big as my fist. In the upper abdominal cavity. Smaller ones in the lungs. The smell was abominable, of course.

Roget Where did you get him from?

Armstrong Who?

Roget The unfortunate stinking corpse.

Armstrong I've no idea. Farleigh saw to it.

Roget Ah.

Armstrong Ah what?

Roget Was it still in its grave clothes by any chance?

Armstrong It was stark naked on a slab. I don't know why you're playing holier than thou.

He stretches for a shot and misses, crashing his racquet down on the table.

Damn.

Roget   Mind the table!

He goes over and rubs at it with his coat sleeve. **Armstrong** *picks up the shuttlecock and bats it back to* **Roget**.

Roget   The whole thing sticks in my craw ever since two students in Edinburgh acquired for us a lovely fresh corpse which turned out to be our tutor's grandfather. The poor man clean fainted away when he pulled back the sheet.

Armstrong   What difference does it make if they're dead? The dead are just meat. But meat that tells a story. Every time I slice open a body, I feel as if I'm discovering America.

Roget   I do see the relatives' point. If you believe in bodily resurrection, the minimum requirement is a body.

Armstrong   I'd happily allow you to slice mine into porterhouse steaks, as long as I was definitively dead.

Roget   When's Farleigh's next demonstration?

Armstrong   Depends on the supply. D'you want to come?

Roget   I'm torn. I'm fascinated by the thing itself but slightly uneasy at the methods used to procure the bodies.

Armstrong   We've got our eye on an undersized fellow, about three foot tall. He's not at all well. He'll not see out the winter.

Roget   You seek out potential cadavers before they're even dead?

He catches the shuttlecock and stops playing.

Good God, man, that's appalling.

Armstrong   Needs must. We can have any number of average, everyday corpses. They're two a penny. Literally, at this time of year, when people are dropping like flies. But an unusual specimen must be ordered in advance. I thought you knew that?

Roget   I suppose I didn't think about it. I didn't ask where they came from, I assumed . . .

Armstrong   What? That they climbed on to the dissecting table of their own accord?

Roget   No no no, of course not, I just . . . well, I suppose I chose not to wonder.

He bats the shuttlecock to **Armstrong**.

Armstrong   You didn't want to sully yourself with thoughts of such vile trade. You're a romantic, Roget –

Roget   I think more precisely, I am a man of delicate sensibilities –

Armstrong   Useless, not to say dangerous, qualities in a man of science.

Roget   D'you never have qualms? D'you exist solely in the burning fires of certainty?

Armstrong   Digging up corpses is necessary if we're to totter out of the Dark Ages. You can dissect a stolen body with moral qualms or with none at all and it won't make a blind bit of difference to what you discover. Discovery is neutral. Ethics should be left to philosophers and priests. I've never had a moral qualm in my life, and it would be death to science if I did. That's why I'll be remembered as a great physician, Roget, and you'll be forgotten as a man who made lists.

Roget *passes him a drop shot which he fails to anticipate and misses.*

Armstrong   Bastard.

Fenwick *appears. They stop playing, guiltily.*

Roget   Sir – we were just, er –

Armstrong   It was very cold outside, sir.

Fenwick   Useless girls, both of you. Anyway. Supper's about to be served.

They go with him.

Lights down. **Maria** *reads a letter over the scene change.*

Maria   'Dear Edward, You are right, England is cold and
bleak, and so, I might add, is my heart. Either distance has
dimmed your perception of me, or you never looked properly
at me from the start. Imagine my eyes again, Edward. Now
write and tell me what colour they appear in your
imagination. Your early letters were so full of longing for me
and for home, but now I sense a reluctance to return which
cannot entirely be explained by the prevailing weather
conditions. I hear, via a Mr Roger Thornton, who has
recently returned from Lucknow, that a certain Miss
Cholmondely has stayed in India rather longer than expected.
Could this be the same musical creature you mention in your
letters? She who sinks into a dead faint when confronted by
native antiquities? Her eyes, I gather, are a quite startling
blue. I note that when you think of England now, you
remember dead boys frozen in the top meadow. Hitherto you
imagined soft sunlight and balmy breezes and gentle
Englishmen full of decorum and equanimity. I now realise that
your vision of England was as flawed as your recollection of
my eyes. Yes, it is true that here we may freeze to death in
winter. Indeed our summers are mild. But temperate we are
not. Need I remind you that we have had bloody riots here for
at least six months, and that my father, the finest Englishman I
know, has never been anything less than passionate. As you
know, Edward, I have long been regarded as the mild,
perhaps even silly, half of the heavenly twins, very much in
Harriet's poetic shadow. That, presumably, is what attracted
you to me in the first place. (But Miss Cholmondely is clearly
the better swooner.) I find now, however, that anger has
provoked my intellect like a spark igniting a long-dormant
volcano. I await your reply with interest. Sincerely, Maria
Fenwick.'

Scene Three

Lights up on a long table, lit with candelabra.

Fenwick, **Susannah**, **Maria**, **Roget** *and* **Armstrong** *seated.*
Supper is over, and they are eating fruit, drinking. **Isobel** *is clearing*
away plates and glasses. Everyone is a little the worse for wear,
particularly **Susannah**.

Fenwick   When you've finished, Isobel, you may come and
join us if you wish.

Susannah   You prefer to talk to the servants than to me,
Joseph.

Fenwick   Don't be ridiculous, Susannah.

Susannah   I am not being ridiculous. It's patronising to ask
the girl to fetch and carry on the one hand and join us for
elevating conversation on the other.

She pours herself more wine. Hands **Isobel** *the empty bottle.*

Bring up another bottle please, Isobel.

Isobel   Yes, madam.

She goes out with tray of crockery, etc., as **Harriet** *comes in wearing her*
bonnet with the chimney. The chimney is now belching puffs of steam.

Harriet   Papa, Mama! Here you are. Look! I told you I
would get it to work.

They all look. Murmurs of delight.

Fenwick Oh, well done, Harriet –

Roget   I say! Look at that!

Susannah   Look at what? What am I supposed to be
looking at?

Maria   Her bonnet, Mama!

Susannah   What about it?

Armstrong   The steam, madam, the steam –

Susannah   Good God –

The steam stops puffing.

Harriet   Oh. It's stopped –

Roget   Nevertheless, Harriet, a remarkable achievement –

Harriet   Papa? Are you proud of me?

Fenwick   Impressed beyond words. It was almost worth sitting through that dreadful play, if this is one of the serendipitous results –

Susannah   But when would you wear such a thing, dear?

Harriet   That's not the point, Mama, the point is that through experiment I have made a discovery –

Susannah   But a singularly useless one –

Fenwick   Susannah, shut up. Harriet, my dear, sit down and have some wine. I'm delighted and impressed.

Harriet *sits down, glowing.*

Susannah   Mark the contemptuous way my husband speaks to me, gentlemen –

Fenwick   Susannah, that's enough –

Susannah   Tell me, Mr Roget, do you think my husband a saint?

Roget   I'm sorry?

Susannah   St Joseph of Newcastle upon Tyne. How would that suit him?

Roget   I think him an exemplary man, a great scientist and fine physician. However, sainthood would seem to be stretching a point.

Susannah   But you think him a man of great principle, with a finely tuned conscience, considerate to servants, indulgent to his family, yes?

Roget   Well . . . on balance, I would say so, yes.

Susannah   Then allow me to tell you how profoundly wrong you are.

Fenwick   Susannah –

Susannah   Don't worry, I'm not about to reveal any scandal. Oh, gentlemen, if only he were scandalous, but I'm afraid he's much too dull for that. What he is, is indifferent. To me. And what wife can stand that?

Armstrong   I wonder if we should perhaps retire to the drawing-room, Roget –

He begins to get up.

Susannah   Sit down!

Armstrong   Of course.

He sits down again abruptly.

Harriet   May Maria and I be excused, Papa?

Susannah   No!

Silence.

Fenwick   Susannah –

Susannah   And because you all admire him, that makes you indifferent too! It is intolerable. In my own house to be constantly ignored, to be held in no account –

Roget   Madam, I assure you that this is not the case, please. I beg of you –

Susannah   And if I am a little drunk, what of it, you too would be drunk ifyou had to bear what I must bear –

Fenwick   Susannah, no one is indifferent to you –

Susannah   Liar!

Isobel *returns with more wine* **Susannah** *takes it from her, pours herself more.*

Susannah   You don't love me.

Awkward silence. **Isobel** *hovers.*

Fenwick   What's this nonsense now?

Maria   Mama, we all love you. Indeed we do.

Susannah   The most respected man in the region, the most philanthropic, whose learning is universally admired, has no time for his own wife.

Armstrong   I'm sure you are grossly mistaken –

Susannah   He has turned me into a joke. I could play patience stark naked and he'd not notice.

Roget   Madam –

Susannah   And neither would you.

Harriet   Mama, please!

Susannah   I even embarrass my own children. I sit in a corner and chirrup away like a canary. Why don't you get a cage for me and a nice bit of cuttlefish. In fact, when we had a canary, he paid more attention to it than to me, he thought it intriguing and fascinating, all the things he once felt about me –

Fenwick   You have had a little too much wine, Susannah –

Susannah   I am shut out from everything you do. You think me a fool!

Fenwick   Of course I don't think you a fool –

Susannah   Because I care more for Shakespeare than for Newton.

Fenwick   They are not in competition, Susannah. One does not cancel out the other. They form a complementarity, not a state of siege.

Susannah   I admit I had little education when I married him, but that was no fault of mine. I painted, read poetry and plays, a little Greek of course, but obviously that counts for nothing.

Roget   On the contrary, it sounds quite admirable.

Susannah *gets up and thumps her breast theatrically.*

Susannah   I am an artist, gentlemen! I have a soul!

Silence.

Maria   Mama, do stop it.

Susannah   I am full of feeling and passion and I am wedded to a dried cod.

She sits down again in tears.

Isobel   Um. Will that be all, sir?

Fenwick   Of course, Isobel, off you go.

He gets up.

Please don't feel you must stay, gentlemen. My wife is a little overwrought –

Susannah   Overwrought!

Fenwick   Harriet, Maria, go with the gentlemen into the drawing-room, will you?

Harriet/Maria (*together*)   Yes, Papa.

They get up.

Roget   Madam.

Armstrong   Madam.

They get up to leave.

Susannah   That's right, go. Leave me to fend for myself –

Roget *and* **Armstrong** *hesitate.*

Fenwick   We'll join you presently, gentlemen.

They all go out. Silence. **Susannah** *continues to cry.*

Fenwick   Susannah –

Susannah   I'm sorry. I'm sorry, Joseph.

Fenwick   So you should be.

Susannah   Don't speak to me like a child! I am not a wayward infant to be scolded indulgently, I am your wife! Listen to me when I talk to you, take notice of what I say. Do not dismiss it as precocious whimsy! I want you to take me seriously, do you understand, Joseph?

Fenwick *is flustered.*

Fenwick   I'm very . . . I'm sorry, Susannah –

Susannah   So you should be.

Fenwick   Very well, now we're all square.

Susannah   Stop it! Stop patronising me. It's like a twitch, Joseph, you do it without thinking.

Pause.

Fenwick   I don't know what you want me to say, Susannah.

Susannah   When you married me, Joseph, you thought me beautiful.

Fenwick   I still think that.

Susannah   But you never mentioned any other requirements. The fact that I knew nothing of politics or science seemed a matter of supreme indifference to you, in fact you found my ignorance delightful, charming even.

Fenwick   I didn't know it was ignorance. I thought it an affectation of your sex and class.

Susannah   You loved me, Joseph, you pursued me with such tenderness, such dogged devotion, how could I not love you in return? Because the choice was not mine, d'you understand? I never had the freedom to choose as you did –

Fenwick   I didn't force you to marry me, Susannah –

Susannah   I was a passive thing, waiting to be filled up with love and ooze it out in return. That is what young women do, Joseph, they wait to be loved, they wait for a man to bestow his mysterious gift upon them. I loved you because you loved me. That was my criterion. What else did I have to go on? What else did I know? You caused this love in me! You planted it in me and then you abandoned it!

Fenwick   I haven't abandoned you, Susannah.

Susannah   But that is what it feels like, Joseph. I am lonely. It is a lonely thing to be married to you.

Pause.

Fenwick   It seems I've been remiss in my affection, and I am most profoundly sorry. Perhaps I've been too bound up with my work –

Susannah   Bound up? You have given your entire life over to it! Oh, certainly you have feelings, indeed you do, you are stuffed to bursting point with feelings about this injustice here, that cruelty there. You have feelings for every passing stray but none whatsoever for me. I've watched you weep bitter tears, I've watched you tear your hair at the misfortunes of utter strangers, whilst my most palpable misery goes sublimely unacknowledged –

Fenwick   It was never my intention to make you unhappy, Susannah –

Susannah   How could you love me so much then and so little now? Am I not the same person? Perhaps the woman you professed such tenderness towards then was an invention, a construct of your imagination –

Fenwick   I did love you, Susannah –

Susannah   Did? What good is did to me?

Fenwick   Do, I do love you, but perhaps we interpret the word in different ways. You talk of tenderness when you talk of love, you talk of dogged devotion, you make it all sweet nothings and new hair ribbons –

Susannah   I dispute the last, but for the rest, what else is love but tender devotion –

Fenwick   I was in thrall to you, Susannah. Sick, weak with
longing at the merest hint of your presence. I couldn't sleep
for thinking of the web of veins that traced the inside of your
arms. I dreamt of the scent of your neck, the soft, suckable
lobe of your ear. I wanted to crush your mouth against mine, I
wanted to run my tongue down the cleft your breasts –

Susannah   Joseph, please, this is bedroom talk –

Fenwick   – I wanted to lose myself inside you. Your beauty
possessed me, it made my blood dance. I could watch the
pulse flickering in your wrist and feel sick with desire. But
because you were beautiful I imagined you to be wise, and yes
I know now, as I knew then, that one has nothing to do with
the other. I asked myself even then, do I love her because she
is beautiful or is she beautiful because I love her. I couldn't
answer and I didn't care. Passion distorts, it makes things seem
what they are not. Because you had the face of the Madonna,
I imbued you with her qualities. You had no conversation
then, and I told myself that still waters run deep. Your looks of
blank incomprehension I read as philosophical musing. When
I talked of politics or science, and your face betrayed no
expression whatsoever, I saw it as profound spiritual calm, a
stillness which put my passion to shame, I saw in you a
wisdom which I could never hope to attain. The less you said
the easier it was to invent you. You could have sat at my side
and warbled in Japanese and I would have hung on to your
every word. I dreamt of your flesh, I wanted to lick your eyes,
I wanted to leave children inside you . . .

Pause.

Susannah   Joseph, if you bear any vestige of that love for
me, you must make it manifest. You must talk to me in a
language which does not exclude me. Do not shut me out.
Do not humiliate me in front of your friends, but include
me, ask my advice, my opinion. I know I behave
ridiculously, don't imagine I am unaware of it. I loathe the
role I have taken on, but you forced me to it, d'you
understand? It's the only part you have left open to me and
I have played it to the hilt. You talk always of equality. Why

don't you practise it? I want to be your equal, not a
fawning, yapping lap dog –

Isobel *appears. Screaming and shouting offstage.*

Isobel I'm sorry, sir, madam . . .

Harriet *and* **Maria** *come hurtling in, screaming at each other and
wrestling each other to the ground.*

Maria Take that back! Take it back!

Harriet Never! Argh . . . get off me, get off – Papa, Papa –

Susannah Girls, girls, what on earth –

Harriet *manages to disentangle herself slightly.*

Harriet Edward is a fickle fool, Maria, anyone could have
told you that, the whole world knew of his passion for Miss
Cholmondely apart from you –

Maria *goes for her again.*

Maria How dare you, how dare you –

Fenwick Harriet, Maria!

They ignore him and continue fighting.

Maria I hate you, I hate you –

Fenwick *grabs* **Maria** *and* **Susannah** *drags off the struggling*
Harriet.

Susannah Stop fighting immediately!

Harriet Stop it, stop it, get off me –

She tries to kick **Susannah**.

Fenwick Harriet, for once in your life, listen to your
mother and do as she says –

Harriet *is so stunned she shuts up. Both girls are carted offstage.*
Maria *bawling 'I hate her! I hate her!'*

Isobel *begins to clear away the rest of the debris from the table.*
Armstrong *comes in, unnoticed. He tiptoes up behind her, puts his*

arms around her waist. She gasps, and he puts his hand over her mouth, turns her round towards himself and kisses her passionately. He pushes her over the table.

Armstrong   Isobel . . . I adore you, Isobel . . . I adore you . . .

He kisses her again.

I want you to take this. It belonged to my mother.

He hands her something wrapped in a piece of silk.

Just tell me, I just want to know, that's . . . Just tell me that you might be able to love me.

Pause. **Isobel** *clutches the gift and speaks in a shy whisper.*

Isobel   I believe I might, sir . . .

She kisses him. He pushes her on to the table, kisses her again. Suddenly **Roget** *appears.*

Roget   Armstrong? What in God's name d'you think you're doing?

The two spring apart. **Isobel** *pulls herself together and slithers off the table.*

Isobel   Excuse me, sir, excuse me –

She dashes out. **Armstrong** *straightens his clothes and pours himself a drink.*

Armstrong   You shouldn't burst in on people like that.

Roget   What were you doing?

Armstrong   I was kissing her passionately. What did it look like?

Roget   How could you?

Armstrong   It was quite easy actually, she didn't object in the least. Why should she?

Roget   You can't play with her like this.

Armstrong   Oh, I think perhaps jealousy rears its ugly head.

Roget   It's nothing of the sort, I just can't bear to see the girl led by the nose.

Armstrong   She knows the state of play, she's not stupid.

Roget   Far from it, but she's ignorant when it comes to these particular matters, and you know it.

Armstrong   I enjoy her company.

Roget   So do I.

Armstrong   I think you might find she enjoys my company rather more extravagantly than she does yours. I'm sorry, but there it is. What can I do about it?

Roget   What do you want from her?

Armstrong *laughs.*

Armstrong   I love her, it's as simple as that.

Roget   So you love her. But not enough, I presume, to marry her.

Armstrong   Marriage is a different thing entirely. I'll probably marry a woman with a face like a horse but a great deal of money in the bank. I don't expect it will have anything much to do with love.

Roget   What is it that you particularly love about Isobel?

Isobel *appears in the doorway. Neither notice her. She stays in the shadows and listens.*

Armstrong   Oh, this and that. Who can say really? Love's such an indefinable thing, isn't it, I mean . . .

He begins to giggle.

Oh, for God's sake, Roget, I can't keep this up another minute, of course I don't bloody love her.

Roget   I knew you didn't.

Armstrong   I almost had you convinced though, didn't I?

Roget   Not for a moment actually.

Armstrong   'Oh Isobel, Isobel I adore you!'

He giggles.

God, I don't know how I managed it. She really is very hard work.

Roget   So why in hell's name are you doing it to her?

Armstrong   It's all in a good cause, I assure you.

Roget   What cause?

Armstrong   There's nothing sinister in it, honestly, it's all rather innocent actually. I don't know why you never thought of it yourself. So. I tell her I love her and so forth, right?

Roget   Yes . . .

Armstrong   I flatter her, look suitably love struck when she comes into a room, I call her beautiful –

Roget   But why? –

Armstrong   And eventually I get her into the sack.

Roget   That would seem to be a logical, if cynical progression. It's not in itself an explanation.

Armstrong   Oh, for God's sake, man, I get her in the sack which means she takes off her clothes –

Roget   Not necessarily –

Armstrong   I make sure she takes them off, that's the whole point because then I get to examine her beautiful back in all its delicious, twisted glory, and frankly that's all I'm interested in. D'you know the first time I saw it I got an erection?

Roget   You find it arousing?

Armstrong   In the same way that I find electricity exciting, or the isolation of oxygen, or the dissection of a human heart.

Roget *stares at him.*

Armstrong   I told you it was all in a good cause, didn't I?
I mean, obviously she's not the sort to just take her clothes off
and let me have a look for a few bob, I spotted the
Presbyterian bent right away. In fact I almost scuppered my
chances at one point, before I'd got the full measure of her.
I had to make up some awful rubbish about my mother being
dead, which of course she isn't. So unfortunately we have to
go the long route. Farleigh showed us a similar torso once but
it was much milder. Extraordinary malformation of the upper
vertebrae, with resultant distortion of the rib cage. And hers,
you see, is much more severe, much more interesting, I mean
it's exquisite, it's almost a poem –

Isobel *runs off, stifling a cry.* **Roget** *turns round.*

Roget   What was that?

Armstrong   What? Nothing.

Roget *looks at him.*

Roget   Can I say something?

Armstrong *grins.*

Armstrong   Go ahead.

Roget   You are amoral, corrupt and depraved. You are
cruel, heartless, mean-spirited, barbarous. You are
treacherous, despicable, and vilely contemptible. You are a
low-down seducer. You're a cunt, Armstrong. A complete and
utter cunt.

He goes out. **Armstrong** *shrugs, genuinely baffled at this response.*

Armstrong   Why? What have I done?

Lights fade. He goes out. Enter **Maria** *who reads a letter over scene
change.*

Maria   'Dear Edward, Thank you for your sloppily written
missive. I note that you and Miss Cholmondely have indeed
become "firm friends" and I am not at all sorry that you will

no longer be returning to England. You have recently been the source of great animosity between my dear sister and myself; for which rupture I blame you entirely. Our quarrel resulted, I am sorry to say, in no small degree of violence. I long for something similar, but more extreme, to light upon yourself; and only wish I were able to deliver the blows myself. Please do not write to me again. Maria Fenwick.'

Scene Four

1999. Lights up on same room as before, one tea chest left. The table bears the remnants of a meal, as in the previous scene. **Tom** *is sitting at the head of the table, in what was previously* **Susannah**'s *place.* **Ellen** *is next to him.*

Tom   I suppose I should say congratulations.

He raises his glass.

What was it tipped the scales? Goodbye schizophrenia or hello big bank balance?

Ellen   You don't think I'm a murderess then?

Tom   Would it make any difference if I did?

Ellen   No. It's just a word. I can live with it.

Pause.

I know you think I'm hyper-rational, but d'you want to know the real reason I'm going to take the job? Because I can't resist it. It's too exciting. It wasn't an intellectual decision at all. It was my heart. I felt it beat faster when I thought of all the possibilities.

Tom   D'you think the heart *is* involved in the choices we make?

Ellen   What d'you mean?

Tom   Literally. I read it somewhere. That your heart's not just a pump. It's what defines us. Apparently, if you give someone a new heart, they quite often take on some of the characteristics of the donor. That's a scientific fact –

Ellen   Have you been talking to Phil?

Tom   Well, why shouldn't it be true? When you talk about grief, you talk about heartache. Same when you talk about love. You just said it yourself. You said you took the job because your heart told you to.

Ellen   You make it sound poetic.

Tom   Isn't it?

Ellen   Science is supposed to be cold and considered and rational.

Tom   But it's not, is it?

Ellen   Up to a point. But maybe you're right. I suppose my urge to pursue it is a passion, it's intense, the same as yours for George Eliot or John Webster. Actually, it's more than that. It's sexy. It makes me fizz inside. To me it's a form of rapture. Yeah, you are right . . . To me, an exquisitely balanced formula is a poem.

Tom   So we're not that much different after all. Art and science, waves and particles, it's all the same thing.

Ellen   But the bottom line is: I don't actually think science is value-free, I don't think it's morally neutral. Kate does, but I don't –

Kate *comes in with two more bottles of wine.*

Kate   What do I do?

Tom   You're unscrupulous, ambitious, and you'd dissect your own mother if you thought it might give you the answer to something.

Kate   Yeah, I probably would. But only if she was dead already.

Tom   So where would you draw the line?

Kate   Well, I wouldn't kill. I wouldn't murder. But apart from that . . . white or red?

Tom   Red, please. But would you have worked on developing the atomic bomb, say –

Ellen   She's a geneticist, Tom.

Tom   You know what I'm getting at –

Ellen   You can't not pursue something. You can't say the road might have complications so I won't go down it. Once you know something, you can't unknow it –

Kate   The thing is, Tom, I can't make you see the world the way that I do. For me it's all potential, it's all possibility, everything's there to be unravelled and decoded. We're discovering things so fast now, we're falling over our feet. It's like for me everything is total possibility and for you everything is total remembrance.

Tom   Well, I don't know, shall I just cut my throat now? Why wait?

Kate   I want to eat up the world, I want to tear it apart and see what it's made of. And you're just conscious of this weight all the time, of the past bearing down on you –

Tom   The past's always with us –

Kate   There's nothing wrong with Milton, there's nothing wrong with Shakespeare –

Tom   I'm glad we've sorted that out then –

Kate   But it's history, and I'm hooked on the future.

Tom   Don't you think there is something to be said for acknowledging the weight of history?

Kate   Yes, but –

Tom   No you don't, you don't even know what history is –

Kate   Oh please –

Tom   You don't respect ambiguities –

Kate   What on earth does that mean?

Tom   You bandy these words about, like manic depression and schizophrenia, and you don't even know what they mean. Schizophrenia is just a label, it's not a finite quantifiable thing –

Kate   Schizophrenics stab people in tube stations –

Tom   Most of them don't, and not that you care anyway, I mean, that's not why you do it, is it –

Kate   No, why should it be –

Ellen   Tom, we've been through this –

Tom   James Joyce probably had a schizophrenia gene, his daughter certainly did. It's a continuum, at one end you get poetry and at the other confusion, you can't just swat it like a fly.

Kate   Tom, that's a very nice romantic idea, but it's not necessarily true, you're hopeless, you're a dinosaur –

Tom   Yeah, well, we look around, us dinosaurs, and we know we're old and tired, a bit cynical, a bit ironic, but we know the score, we can see the arc of things. We've seen things come and go. And one of the things we know is that the Messiah's not coming. We know that much.

She laughs and hands him his wine.

Kate   How d'you know? How come you're so certain?

Tom   Oh, for goodness sake –

Kate   I'm telling you, Tom, we don't know anything, but it's out there now, within our grasp. Does that not blow your mind?

Tom   Not in the way you'd like it to –

Phil *appears.*

Phil   Right, I'm off then, have a good New Year.

Ellen   Phil, stay, have a drink before you go –

Tom   Have one to see in the new century, stop us arguing, for God's sake –

Phil   Oh, go on then, a quick one –

Kate *hands him a glass of wine. They all drink.*

All   Cheers –

Phil   In twenty-four hours it'll be the twenty-first century then. It doesn't feel like it, does it?

Tom   How's it supposed to feel?

Phil   I don't know. Futuristic. Not like this. It feels a bit old-fashioned, like. You know, you think it's going to be robots and everything shiny-white and new and clean. That's what it's like in the films. The future. But it's just the same old shite really, isn't it?

He looks at his watch.

I'd better go. I've got to take my daughter to the hospital.

He downs his drink.

Thanks a lot then. Have a good New Year.

They get up and raise their glasses.

All   Happy New Year!

He goes out. The others are frozen, glasses aloft, as **Isobel** *comes in with paper and pencil and the silk-wrapped gift from* **Armstrong***. She opens it: a gold chain. She holds it up to the light and puts it around her neck. She reads through a letter she has just written.*

Isobel   'Loving words as I do, I now find my vocabulary insufficient to describe my anguish. How may I explain to you my fall from contentment to despair? I was never a loved thing; it was not a condition I had ever known. Recently, and most fleetingly, I discovered the rapture of that state. Now I know it to have been a fiction. My life stretches before me, and it is now a bitter road. All pleasure's pale now that I have felt love and may never feel it again. You will say that it was not a real love, and I would agree. It was a lie and it was moonshine, but how happy I was to bathe in its watery glow. Now my mouth is full of ashes. He caused dreams in me where none had thrived before, and I am without hope or consolation. Isobel Bridie.'

Isobel *folds the letter. Blackout.*

Scene Five

Lights up. **Isobel** *is hanging from a rope in the middle of the stage, the chair overturned beneath her dangling feet.*

Maria *comes on. She screams.* **Armstrong** *comes running on.*

Armstrong   Oh my God, oh my God –

He runs to the body, climbs on the chair, tries to get her down. **Maria** *is frozen with horror.*

Help me, help me, Maria, for God's sake –

She helps him and together they get **Isobel** *down.*

Maria   Oh, Isobel, Isobel, I don't understand –

She feels for a pulse. **Armstrong** *puts his ear to* **Isobel**'*s chest.*

I can feel a pulse, it's weak but it's there –

Armstrong *takes off his coat and places it under* **Isobel**'*s head.*

Armstrong   Fetch help, Maria, find your father, anyone –

Maria   They're out walking –

Armstrong   Well, find them!

She goes. **Armstrong** *feels the side of* **Isobel**'*s neck for a pulse.*

Isobel? Can you hear me?

There's no response. He hesitates. Then puts his hands over her nose and mouth, presses down. Her heels flutter almost imperceptibly. In a second it is over. He feels for her pulse again. He gets up, shakily, and notices the letter lying underneath the chair. He picks it up, unfolds it. Reads.

'Loving words as I do . . . '

He reads to the end, then crumples the paper and puts it in his pocket. **Fenwick**, **Roget**, **Harriet**, **Maria** *and* **Susannah** *come in.*

Armstrong　She's gone. I couldn't save her.

Fenwick *and* **Roget** *go to her. The three women hold on to each other in horror.*

Fenwick　Why? Why did she do this?

Susannah　She left no note, no explanation?

Armstrong　It seems not.

Fenwick　Isobel, did we not care for you enough? Were we harsh? What did we do?

Susannah *goes to her.*

Susannah　Oh, her poor neck.

She takes her hand.

Are you sure she's dead, Joseph?

Fenwick　Gone. Snuffed out.

He picks her up in his arms. Tears run down his face.

I'll take her to her room. She should lie on a soft bed, not a cold floor. Come with me.

He goes out. The women follow. **Roget** *and* **Armstrong** *are left. Silence.*

Armstrong　Why did you tell her, you stupid fool?

Roget　I didn't. She was at the door. She heard what you said about her.

Pause.

Armstrong　Well, how was I to know? It's not my fault, I didn't know she was . . .

Roget　What?

Armstrong   Unstable. I didn't know. Don't say anything, eh?

Silence.

I mean, we don't know for a fact that it was me who drove her to it, do we? It could have been anything.

Roget   Of course it was you.

Armstrong   Where's the evidence?

Roget   You disgust me.

Armstrong   I never wished her dead.

Roget   Much more convenient that she is. I expect she won't be in her grave five minutes before Farleigh has her dug up.

Armstrong *giggles nervously.*

Armstrong   Oh, well. Waste not want not . . .

Roget *walks over to him and punches him hard in the stomach. He doubles over in agony as* **Roget** *walks out. He staggers out after him as* **Tom** *and* **Ellen** *come in. They look round the empty room.*

Ellen   We could still pull out. Contracts aren't signed yet.

Tom   No. Let's sell up and get out. Let's start again.

Ellen   Are you sure?

Tom   Yes. It's just a house. I think they should knock it down actually.

Ellen   What?

Tom   It's had its day. It's worn out. You can't keep adapting this bit and converting that bit. Knock it down and build something new. Something wonderful. There was a medieval almshouse on the site before they built this place and they knocked that down with confidence. Kate thinks I worship the past but I don't. I just liked this house, but fuck it, I want to be free of it now. I'm sick of being shackled to dry rot and deathwatch beetles. We'll start again. It could be exciting even.

Ellen   You'll get another job.

Tom   I doubt it. I'm going to sail into the twenty-first century as a middle-aged redundant man supported by a younger sexier wife who works at the cutting edge of technology. Maybe there's a sort of poetic justice to it.

Ellen   You're only redundant as an English lecturer. You're not redundant as a human being.

Tom   I keep thinking about the dead girl, do you? No upper vertebrae. Missing ribs. That's the bit I don't understand.

Ellen   I don't suppose we ever will.

Tom   No.

Pause.

This time next year, this room will be full of Scandinavian businessmen leaping out of saunas and drinking schnapps and shouting skol.

Ellen   I bet it's not. They'll probably run out of money by June. This time next year there'll be pigeons in here and security fences outside. And in five years' time they'll pull it down. And build a car park.

Tom   I keep thinking about the dead girl. No upper vertebrae. Missing ribs. I don't understand.

Ellen   I don't suppose we ever will.

Tom   Let's go and put the champagne in the fridge.

They go out as the lights dim. Music, distant sounds of what could be celebrations, or could be riots. Chandelier descends, **Roget** *and* **Armstrong** *carry on* **Isobel**'s *open coffin.* **Harriet** *and* **Maria** *follow them with tall flickering candles. The coffin is placed gently on the table. They gather round to look at her.*

Harriet   Poor Isobel.

Roget   She looks almost beautiful. Pale as wax. One might hardly notice her poor back. It seems, now, the least significant thing about her.

Armstrong (*gazing at her, fascinated*)   She is exquisite. She
makes a beautiful corpse.

They took at him.

As Roget said . . . So pale and waxen.

Maria   What time is it?

Harriet   It must be almost midnight.

Fenwick *and* **Susannah** *come in. They go to the coffin.* **Fenwick**
kisses **Isobel**'*s forehead,* **Susannah** *strokes her hair.*

Fenwick   So this is how we're seeing out the century. Not
the way we'd imagined it, not with a flurry of trumpets and
beacons blazing. I thought it would be a golden night, full of
hope and anticipation, and instead, this. Groping blindly over
the border in a fog of bewilderment. The future looks less
benign now, Isobel. We're a little more frightened than we
were.

He kisses her again. **Susannah** *strokes her hair.*

Susannah   I don't understand . . . I don't understand . . .

Fenwick   Goodbye, Isobel . . .

*The lighting changes as then gather round the coffin, to the chiaroscuro
effects of the very first montage. Their positions and attitudes once again
suggest the painting, but this time* **Isobel**, *in her coffin, has taken the
place of the bird in the air pump. The rioting continues from outside.*
Fenwick *looks at his pocket watch.*

Susannah   Are they rioting or celebrating out there?

Fenwick   It's hard to tell . . .

*He lifts his right arm for silence as the bells ring out the chimes of
midnight.*

Fenwick   Here's to whatever lies ahead . . . here's to
uncharted lands . . . here's to a future we dream about but
cannot know . . . here's to the new century.

Music. Hold on montage. Lights fade.

Ancient Lights

Ancient Lights was first performed at the Hampstead Theatre, London, on 29 November 2000. The cast was as follows:

Tom	Don McManus
Bea	Joanne Pearce
Kitty	Gwyneth Strong
Tad	Dermot Crowley
Iona	Ruth Gemmell
Joni	Sheridan Smith

Directed by Ian Brown
Designed by Tanya McCallin
Lighting by David Hersey
Sound by Nicholas Gilpin

Act One

*A black void bursts into life with the sound of wild talk-show applause, cheering. Back projections of flickering black-and-white stills and grainy video images of **Tom Cavallero** in various film roles, publicity shots. The images are jumbled and constantly changing. They wash over the set, distorting it, disguising it and blurring its boundaries. Spotlight up on **Tom**, slumped in a swivel leather armchair, floating in a sea of himself. He's wearing dark glasses, expensive casual suit, open-necked shirt, light tan, stubble. He looks like what he is: an American movie star. He's slumped in laid-back, chat-show pose, raises a hand in recognition of the applause, smiles at the audience with a kind of lazy bewilderment and delight. The applause dies down.*

Tom Thank you very much . . . Thank you . . . Hey, who says the British are tight-assed? Am I allowed to say that on TV? Excuse me? . . . My pleasure, totally, it's great to be here, Michael. I love England. I did a couple of years here as a student and I totally fell in love with just about everything. That whole experience has kind of resonated down my life, you know? I always knew I'd come back, it was just a matter of when . . . I mean, like, to stay a long while . . . maybe take a house . . . Excuse me? . . . I'm over to see some old college friends actually . . . we were like the three musketeers, shared a house for two years, me and two women, knew each other inside out. Still do. It's good to get together occasionally . . . I remember this thing from like twenty years back for some reason, I've never forgotten it. I was walking along a river bank in England this time, on a beautiful breezy summer's day, and there was an old house right there on the towpath, with chestnut trees and honeysuckle, and roses falling over the gate, and on the side of the house, high up, near the roof, was a wooden sign that said 'Ancient Lights'. And it struck me like a poem, like an echo of something long gone, kind of pagan and all tied in with this old, old river and this tumbling greenery, and it's just, I guess, kind of stayed with me, it's kind of reverberated inside of me all these years, you . . . Excuse me? Sorry, sorry, I just got in from LA, so I'm a little tired, a little slow on the uptake. Have you tried melatonin? Some kind of mineral or vitamin or maybe it's an herb. I don't think it's chemical. Something to do with your pineal gland. It kind of takes the edge off jet lag. I'm double-dosing. Maybe I should triple-dose. There's some other thing where you shine a light at the back of your knee, d'you know if that works? But right, yeah, the weather . . . well . . . it's pretty scary after California, but I kind of like it. Real snow. I haven't seen snow for, like, ten years. I mean, I can't believe it. Real fucking snow . . . Well, what can I say?

Big sky . . . it did pretty good business in the States, so we're hoping, you know. . . Right, I play Joe Washington, he's a paraplegic forensic guy whose marriage is in a mess and he's drinking too much and there are some really weird killings going on and you know he gets to thinking . . . I don't know, basically I play a cripple in an Armani suit who gets to have sex with a lot of women.

Snap blackout, snap lights up on:

Evening. Softly lit, uncluttered space, suggesting a large room. (Maybe one large Georgian window?) In the corner, a huge, half-decorated Christmas tree. One kitchen chair, and lots of large floor cushions, rugs. **Bea**, *fortyish, is sitting amid a pile of recipe books, fruit and vegetables, and a large uncooked goose.* **Tad**, *fiftyish, is sitting in the chair, reading. A bottle next to him.*

Tad   Did you know that at the moment of death, there might be an involuntary emission of semen?

Bea   I didn't, no. D'you think these chestnuts are organic?

Tad   And partially digested food might be regurgitated –

Bea   Jesus, what are you reading?

Tad   It's a sort of Pathology for Beginners. What happens when you cop it. Also you get an involuntary release of waste products. Involuntary. I love that. Death means never having to say you're sorry. And then, quite shortly after you're dead, depending on the weather, you take on a sort of greenish tinge –

Bea   Depending on the weather?

Tad   If it's hot it happens quicker, anyway, that's your gases and your fluids breaking down, and dispersing through the body. And then shortly after that you begin to smell –

Bea   Chestnut-and-prune stuffing, what d'you think? Although I'm worried about the prunes –

She looks at the packet.

Sulphur dioxide, what's that? No wonder fish are growing penises and everyone's got cancer –

Tad   Not that you get much experience of stinking corpses these days, it's all sleight of hand, they whisk you away and shove you in a fridge before you know you're even dead –

Bea *looks at the goose.*

Bea   I suppose I'll have to cook this on a rack, there's so much fat, although it says here you can freeze it –

Tad   You should live with a body, sit with it, have a wake, you know –

Bea   – frozen goose fat, what would you do with it, I mean, how much cassoulet can you eat –

Two telephones ring at once. **Tad** *picks up the one nearest to him, while* **Bea** *searches frantically for her mobile.*

Tad   Hello, Charnel House here . . . no, sorry . . . Charnel . . . you know, the place they . . . right, right . . . sorry . . . this is Thaddeus . . . hi, no, we've not met . . . no . . .

Bea *has found her phone. She has a phone voice which is slightly grander than her normal one.*

Bea   Hello?

Tad (*to* **Bea**)   It's Kitty –

Bea (*hand over receiver*)   Ask her what train she's getting. (*Back to mobile.*) Sorry . . .

Tad   Did you hear that?

Bea (*into mobile phone*)   Max, there's going to be a problem
with those questions for Tom, I just know there is. He won't
talk about his private life . . . I know, I know it's hard to avoid
it but basically can you just go easy on the stuff about the
underage sex?

Tad (*still talking to* **Kitty**)   Would you like me to come and
get you? . . . You what? . . . I should warn you though, I'll
have probably had a few jars by then . . . You what?

Bea   OK, OK, OK, but he really is worried about the
picture shoot . . . I mean, I might be able to persuade him but
what we have to avoid is anything remotely *Hello!* magazine.
No toxic technicolour, OK? No showing you round his lovely
toilet with en suite jacuzzi.

Tad (*picking up the bottle and looking at the label*)   Have you ever
tasted this stuff. . . 'Sercial Madeira' . . . it's called . . . I could
live on it . . . Oh right, I'm with you now . . . Second left after
Burnside Farm, no, you have to go through Rothbury . . .

Bea   OK, Max . . . pleasure . . . and to you too . . .

She puts the phone down.

Tad   Right, see you tomorrow –

He puts the phone down.

She'll be here just after lunch.

Bea (*looking at her watch*)   Right. Everything's more or less on
schedule . . . all that's worrying me now is did I pack the
oyster knife –

She rifles through her bags.

Tad   In cold weather like this, a body can stay recognisable
for several months if the coffin's sturdy, did you know that? If
you're not in a coffin of course, if you're out in the open, foxes
and that sort of thing will be after snacking off you. They
always say in the papers, don't they, 'the body had been
disturbed by animals'. Have you noticed how delicate the
language of death is? It's like ballet. You have to do the whole

thing on tiptoe. If they just said 'eaten', we'd know where we were.

Bea When Tom and Iona get here, d'you think you could lay off the pathology for a while?

Tad Iona. Jesus. She's not a crystal clutcher, is she?

Bea Off-limit topics include death, dying, mortuaries, post mortems and bizarre funeral rituals. Also decay, putrefaction and bodily fluids.

Tad They might be interested.

Bea They won't.

Tad It's research.

Bea It's unhealthy.

Tad If he's such a regular guy, as you keep saying, why are you so worried about me upsetting him?

Bea Because it's important that this visit goes well. Trust me, it's extremely important. And because he's coming here for a rest, and he might have been into a lot of different things in his time, but as far as I know necrophilia's not one of them.

Snap blackout. Snap lights up on **Tom***, same position as before, same projections, still doing his talk-show routine. He leans forward confidentially to the audience.*

Tom Listen, can I just be straight with you guys? Can I do that, Michael? I just want to like really lay it on the line here . . . about the . . . with regard to . . . the situation I find myself in, which you might be wondering about in some way. Because of the newspapers and so forth. So. Right, OK. Let me just be completely straight and honest here. No bullshit, no pre- whatever, prevaricating. Just the fucking – excuse me, just the truth.

He swigs a glass of water.

First. It's taken this woman ten years to lodge this complaint. I mean, come on. Yeah, I slept with her. I had a brief relationship with her. Like three weeks. So what? Because, second, she told me she was twenty. She looked twenty-five. No way did she look sixteen. She had breast implants, for Christ's sake –

The images vanish, as **Iona** *comes in with a camcorder to her eye:* **Tom** *is sitting in his chair with some hand luggage at his feet, blinking at her.*

Iona   Time to go, Tom, come on. We have one hour to get to the airport.

Tom *looks at the camera.*

Tom   Is that turned on?

Iona   What do you think?

Tom (*trying to laugh*)   Iona, come on . . . are you shooting this?

Iona *laughs.*

Iona   Were you talking to yourself just now?

Tom   No, I was running through some lines –

Iona   What lines?

Tom   Is there tape in that?

Iona   We've got an hour. The car's waiting.

Tom   Iona –

Iona   I'm not shooting you, I'm just fooling around –

Tom *looks at his feet and then round the room.*

Tom   What happened to my shoes?

He begins searching for his shoes. She follows him with the camera.

Iona   A day in the life of a movie star, what did I tell you, it's just work work work, he's running through lines and he hasn't made a movie in six months –

Tom   Yeah, very amusing, I thought you said it wasn't going to be ironic –

He locates his shoes.

Iona   So, he's found his shoes, he's putting them on those beautiful, tan, pedicured feet – show us your feet, Tom –

Tom   Take a hike –

He goes to the door.

Iona   OK, some other time with the feet. And now, he's got his shoes on, he's going to the door – but no – he's remembered the hand luggage – he's turning back, he's picking it up – hold on, he's hesitating – should he leave it for the bellhop? OK, what the tuck, he'll take it himself, he's a regular guy honey, talk to me, will you?

Tom   Iona, I thought there was a car waiting –

Iona   Just tell us why we're going to England, will you –

Tom   Who is 'us'?

Iona   The people who'll be watching the movie –

Tom   You said it wasn't turned on –

Iona *flicks a switch.*

Iona   It is now.

Tom *forces a smile, and goes into professional mode.*

Tom   We're heading for England, for a little Christmas break. We're going to promote my movie, to get a little spiritual peace, to get away from . . . all sorts of stuff basically, to see my oldest friends . . .

He looks at his watch.

Honey, I think we have to get out of here –

Iona   OK, OK.

She turns off the camera.

You're going to England to find your true self. That's what you said last night.

Tom   Last night I was drunk.

Iona   Hey, and today you're not?

Tom   How else do I ever get on a plane? We're not just talking scared here, scared doesn't even begin to approach what I'm going through, we're talking cold sweat, heart-stopping primal oh my God we're all going to die terror –

Iona   This is just ridiculous –

Tom   I know it's ridiculous, I know it is –

Iona   You have to get over the idea that planes only stay in the air because passengers will them to. It's technology, Tom. Some really smart people figured it out.

Tom   Look, can we just get out of here? Can we just get on the plane so I can take a sleeping tablet and wake up in London? So if we do fall out of the sky and into the ocean, I'll be unconscious before I hit the water.

He goes out. **Iona** *puts the camera to her eye.*

Iona   And he's leaving the room, heading for the lobby, the limo, then the airport, leaving behind the Pacific Ocean, the Californian sun, the beautiful women with virtual breasts and bonded teeth and native spirit guides. Heading for England where no one's heard of orthodontists and they're having the worst winter in living memory. And where he's aiming to find his true self. My God. What is this man on?

Snap blackout. Simultaneously snap lights up on **Tad** *and* **Bea** *almost as before, but next day, around lunchtime.* **Tad** *is lying on a cushion, reading and drinking whisky. The goose is now on the chair.* **Bea** *is using a hairdryer on it.* **Tad** *is reading his book.*

Bea   It helps to make the fat crisp.

Tad   There's a type of white fatty substance –

Bea   Well, it works with duck anyway –

Tad   – you find it in bodies that have been buried in damp spots, it's called adipocere, listen to this –

Bea   God, if Tom's gone vegetarian I'll cut my throat –

Tad   – 'the corpse had been submerged in shallow, cold water for at least three months' –

Bea   Last time I saw him he could only eat bananas, peanut butter and turkey, plus eight litres of water a day, I hope he's given that up –

Tad   – 'wrapped in polythene, and weighted down with rocks' –

Bea   – maybe I should make a nut loaf, just to cover all eventualities –

She turns off the hairdryer.

Tad   – 'it had also been partially eaten, in the exposed parts, by aquatic life' –

Bea   Tad, why are you so obsessed with what happens to you after you're dead? Why d'you want to know these things?

Tad   Why d'you want to not know? Anyway, it's research.

Bea   For what?

Tad   I think the new book's going to have a pathologist in it.

Bea   So suddenly you're moving into genre fiction? When did this happen?

Tad   It's more in the line of a philosophical investigation. Did Tom really sleep with a twelve-year-old?

Bea   Sixteen-year-old. She said she was twenty. And I could wring her neck for starting all this, the little shit. I've put an embargo on all newspapers for the duration. So don't you dare bring it up, OK?

Tad   All right, all right –

Bea   All that I require for inner happiness is that things run according to plan –

Tad   And you live next door to an incredible delicatessen that sells arcane bits of dried this and that from a single backyard in an obscure region of Italy. I mean, bottarga, what the hell is it?

Bea   – I don't need shrinks, I don't need yoga or shiatsu or Rolfing. I need a coherent schedule that runs seamlessly and without hitches. That is the true meaning of the word contentment. Bottarga is dried fish roe. And you've made a complete mess of that tree.

Tad   It's not finished yet, I got sidetracked.

He gets up and begins to rearrange the tree haphazardly. **Bea** *opens another recipe book.*

Bea   I don't know what he's going to make of it when he gets here. I tried to tell him Northumberland wasn't like Surrey, which is essentially a golf course, and that's the only bit of English countryside he knows. This weather'll kill him. They're snowed in up on the moors, they're dropping hay bales by helicopter.

Somewhere, a phone rings out the '1812 Overture'. **Bea** *picks up the mobile. It's not that.* **Tad** *looks round puzzled. She looks under cushions, empties her bag.*

Tad   Have you bought another bleeding phone?

Bea   Fuck –

She rushes out. **Tad** *pours himself some more whisky. He takes a chocolate star off the Christmas tree, eats it and goes back to his book.* **Joni** *comes in looking like Bambi. She's wearing a skimpy cardigan with a tiny skirt and a lot of eye make-up.*

Joni   Got a cigarette?

Tad   Your mother doesn't like you smoking.

Joni   It's Christmas.

Tad   I don't have any.

Joni   Liar.

She goes to his jacket and takes out a packet and lighter. Lights up.

Tad   Well, that's it. You'll get cancer and die.

Joni   You'd like that. You could use me as research for your next book.

Tad   Fame at last. You'd love it.

The phone stops ringing.

Joni   Yeah, I would actually. But only if I recovered. It played 'Annie's Song' when she first got it, you know.

Tad   What?

Joni   The phone. She's reprogrammed it. D'you realise she's got six different numbers now? When she dies, I'm going to get her a headstone in the shape of a telephone. And on it, I'm going to write: 'Sorry I can't take your call right now.'

She shivers.

I'm freezing, aren't you?

Tad   You don't think that might have something to do with what you've got on?

Joni   It's this stupid house. I hate it up here. It's full of sheep. It's freezing. It's crap. Why couldn't we just have stayed in London?

Tad   Your mother and her roots. You know what she's like.

Joni   She comes from a council house in Whitley Bay. What's a Georgian mansion got to do with her roots?

Tad   You don't really get the notion of landscape and memory if you come from Hammersmith.

Joni   Whitley Bay doesn't have landscape. It has amusement arcades. Anyway, I can't stand landscapes. I like streets and cinemas and department stores and lights. Thank God I'm going to Dad's on Boxing Day. I'm going to refuse to come next year. Did you see me on the telly?

Tad   When?

Joni   At the weekend. Did Mum not tell you? They were doing this news thing because you know that boy in year ten brought three hand grenades to school, and so they sent cameras and everything, and I was just hanging around with loads of other girls, and they interviewed me. And the cameraman said afterwards that there are two types of people: those whose skin absorbs light and those whose skin reflects it, and I reflect and that's the best. That's what all the movie stars have. He said I looked luminous. He had really horrible teeth though.

Tad   How old was this cameraman?

Joni   About as old as Mum. But not as ancient as you. Are we going to be in this film, d'you think?

Tad   What film?

Joni   That Tom's girlfriend's making.

Tad   What's it about?

Joni   Him.

Tad   Why, what's he done?

Joni   God, you're so irritating.

Tad   Are you thinking of auditioning then? D'you think you might wow them with your new-found luminosity?

Joni   I've met him before, you know.

Tad   I know.

Joni   Aren't you going to ask me what he's like?

Tad   No.

Joni   He's really handsome but dead normal. His eyes are exactly like mine. Except he's got a kind of aura thing, you know?

Tad   Ah, right. A class of archangel.

Joni   He makes your throat go dry. You can't think of anything to say. You feel like you might faint or something.

Tad   I can't wait.

Joni   But I was really really immature then, I hadn't even started my GCSEs or anything.

Bea *comes back.*

Bea   Right, the cab got lost but Kitty's on her way. Tad, keep off the subject of death, and, Joni –

She takes her cigarette and stubs it out.

Joni   Mum, it's my right to get cancer if I want to, OK? God . . .

She stomps out.

Tad   Did you know the suicide rate soars at Christmas? All those poor fuckers quietly sawing through their wrists in front of *The Sound of Music.* I bet you the murder rate goes up too.

Bea   Tad.

Tad   Sorry.

She goes to the tree, pushes him out of the way and starts to sort it out herself.

So. Kitty. What's she like then?

Bea   I met her in the registration queue my first day at university. She was wearing an army greatcoat, and I had an Afghan. Neither of which had been seen in London since before the Boer War. I saw her in the queue looking self – conscious, and my heart leapt: oh thank God, I thought, someone else who's got it wrong and knows it. We can form a gang. We both read English, and both went into journalism.

Tad   So why didn't you stick it?

Bea   She went the serious route. I got sidetracked. One minute you're trying to be Martha Gellhorn and the next you're at a party with a glass of champagne, interviewing someone about kitten heels and having her pubic hair waxed by some woman who comes over from New York every other Thursday but she's booked up for a year. And they're paying you loads of money for it and you've never had any before. You kind of get caught up.

Tad   God, you're exotic. That was probably around the time I had a temp job, administering ECT treatment at St Columba's Psychiatric Unit.

Bea   Jesus, you've had some weird jobs.

Tad   The pork-pie factory was worse.

Bea   Anyway it dawned on me that what I was doing was essentially PR, and that I was better at it than most of the people I was dealing with. Of course, Kitty thinks what I do is trivial and stupid because it involves socialising and parties.

Tad   A reasonable proposition.

Bea   Actually it's bloody hard work, it requires enormous diplomacy, and phenomenal organisational skills. Neither of which are Kitty's strong points, I think even she would admit that.

Tad   'Good evening. I'm fierce, I'm tough, I'm uncompromising. I go where grown men fear to tread. I don't take no for an answer and I'm standing here, surrounded by machine-gun fire and mortar bombs, wearing a bulletproof vest and no mascara. Mess with me if you dare. This is Kitty Percival, BBC News, Kosovo.'

Bea   She doesn't do that any more. She's presenting a series about road accidents.

Tad   I bet she's seen loads of bodies, has she?

Bea   It's all reconstructions. She's not filming real accidents, for Christ's sake.

Tad   I mean, when she did wars.

Bea   This death jag you're on, are you doing it expressly to irritate me?

Tad   No. People think that sex is the thing that really gets us going. The old Freud bollocks. But it's not, it's death. That's the lad that drives us on –

Bea   Have you been eating these chocolate stars?

Tad   No –

Bea   There's supposed to be fifty, and there's only thirty-seven. Tad, these stars are covered in real gold leaf –

Tad   Well you're an arse for buying them then, aren't you, but listen –

Bea   – I wanted fifty, not thirty-seven –

Tad   – if death wasn't looming out there, you'd never get out of bed in the morning. If you're a painter or a writer or a pathologist, you do what you do because of your attitude towards death. Art's bound up with it, success is bound up with it. D'you not think that?

Bea   No. It's not the sort of thing I think about.

Tad   I'm forcing myself to face the absolute, objective reality of dying. What's wrong with that?

Bea   If you're thinking of it as an inoculation, I have to tell you you're doomed to failure –

Tad   De Gaulle took a quarter of a grain of arsenic every day, did you know that? To prepare himself for the poisoned croque-monsieur he was expecting any moment.

Bea   All it is in your case, is obsessional morbidity.

Tad   Look, I'm not into digging up body parts and making them into pendants. I don't want to be sleeping in cemeteries so I can be closer to the dead –

Bea   Thank Christ for that –

Tad   There are people who do that, you know, ask any policeman about the number of people who sleep in graveyards because they like it –

Bea   Why do you know such weird, sick things?

Tad   I read a lot.

Bea   Why can't you read *Hello!* magazine?

Tad   I don't need to. I live with you. Look, I'm writing about a pathologist. A pathologist opens up a body and tries to find the story of a life that leads to a death. He's looking for patterns and signs and hidden disturbances, he's looking for a story, right –

Bea   Are you frightened of dying, is that it?

Tad   Of course I'm fucking frightened.

Bea   You've got years yet.

Tad   I'm at the age when I hear a wonderful piece of music and I don't think, great, I'll have that on my *Desert Island Discs*, I think, great, I'll have that at my funeral.

Bea   I've always done that. I'm having 'Into the Mystic' by Van Morrison.

Tad   There you are, you're making preparations. Everybody does. We can all see the end of the road out there.

Bea   But what difference does it make to me if I go green after I'm dead?

Tad   Are you going to be cremated or buried, d'you think?

Bea   I've no idea. I'm not interested.

Tad   Ah come on, you must be.

Bea   I'm not. I'll be dead. I Won't care.

Tad   If you care about your funeral music, you must care about where you're going to be while they're downing bottles of stout at the wake. Up the chimney or six feet under?

Bea   Tad, none of it matters because when you're dead things don't. In general, one of the things the dead don't do, is care. Now. Remember that new book programme?

Tad   Yes . . .

Bea   I spoke to them earlier.

Pause.

Tad   And?

Bea I think they want you too. I wasn't going to tell you until it was a hundred per cent, but what the hell.

Tad Oh. Right.

Bea Is that all?

Tad What d'you mean?

Bea D'you know how many strings I had to pull to set this up? D'you realise how many people I had to take to lunch?

Tad Ah Jesus, it sounds like hell –

Bea People with Palm Pilots who've been on BBC management courses, people you'd rather die than spend an hour with under normal circumstances –

Tad Sorry, no, I didn't mean it, it's fantastic, sure, it's great, it's just . . . ah fuck it, it doesn't matter.

Bea What?

Pause.

Tad I don't really like doing these TV shows, you know –

Bea Oh, for God's sake, d'you want to sell any books or not?

Tad Of course I do, it's just I keep thinking of that Faulkner thing, you know, 'It's my ambition to be, as a private individual, abolished and voided from history, leaving it markless, no refuse save the printed books.'

Bea Well, it didn't work then, did it, because everyone's heard of Faulkner, but if you go on like this no one will ever have heard of you. I worked my arse off to get you this deal.

Tad But I talk bollocks on those programmes.

Bea A) That's not true, and B) even it was, who cares? You're out there, in the public eye, you're visible and that's all that matters.

Tad I'm not sure I'm so keen on this visibility thing.

Bea   If you're invisible, you might as well be dead, I'm sorry, but that's the way it is.

Tad   Tolstoy never had to do this.

Bea   Tolstoy doesn't need to. He's the literary equivalent of Guinness. Not everyone's tried it, but everyone's heard of it. With you, we have to get your face on the screen, we have to get people talking about you otherwise, by this time next year, you'll be remaindered.

Tad   But the conversations you have to have. They're ridiculous. 'What were you trying to say in this book?' 'I thought you'd just read it?' 'I have.' 'So that's what I was trying to say.' Jesus. What do they want? Simultaneous translation? A parallel text? Anyway, the writer's the last person you should ask. What happens, right, is you get to the end of your book or whatever and you look at it and think, well, it seems to be a class of aardvark, and I'd a notion it might be more in the line of a mongoose. But there it is, what can I do?

Bea   That's why they want you on their programmes, because that's very entertaining.

Tad   But it's not true. I just made it up.

Bea   It doesn't matter if it's not true.

Tad   Why doesn't it?

Bea   Because it's a TV programme, it's entertainment, not moral philosophy.

Tad   Radio Four. I like that. Couldn't you get me on there? I bet you I'd be really radiophonic. People like Irish voices, there's loads of them on Radio Four.

Bea   Exactly –

Tad   Sure they'd love me.

Bea   Look, they love you because you're televisual.

Tad   And I'm a great writer.

Bea   That's secondary.

Tad   Are you saying I'm a crap writer?

Bea   No, of course I'm not.

Tad   Because I'm not interested in being some literary fucking pin-up –

Bea   You're not that good-looking.

Tad   I'm serious –

Bea   All I'm saying is charm sells. Count your blessings.

Joni *brings* **Kitty** *in, wrapped in huge coat, scarves, gloves, etc.*

Joni   Mum –

Kitty *looks wan.*

Kitty   Hello . . .

Bea   Kitty! Thank God you got here. Tad, this is Kitty –

Kitty *bursts into tears.*

Bea   Jesus, what's happened? Are you OK?

Kitty *continues to sob.* **Tad** *pours her a drink.*

Tad   Have some whisky. Sit down. What happened?

He sits **Kitty** *in the chair.*

Bea   Kitty? What's wrong? What's going on?

She puts her arm around her. **Kitty** *heaves and sobs.*

Joni   Something to do with the taxi driver.

Kitty   The taxi driver . . . he . . .

She sobs.

Bea   He what . . . what did he do?

Joni   Shall I call the police?

Kitty (*sobbing*)   . . . he . . . he . . .

Bea   What? . . . Oh my God, what?

Kitty (*through sobs*) . . . it's stupid . . . it's stupid .

Bea   No it's not, try to tell us, come on . . .

Kitty (*through sobs*)   . . . he shouted at me . . .

Tad   The taxi driver shouted at you?

Bea   He shouted at you?

Kitty (*through sobs*)   Yes . . .

They all look at each other.

. . . he called me a rich bitch because I only had a fifty-pound note and he didn't have any change . . .

She continues to sob. **Tad** *and* **Bea** *exchange a delicate look.*

Bea   Tad, she needs a large whisky –

Tad   I've just fucking given her one –

Bea   – She needs hot water in it, with honey and lemon –

She takes the whisky from **Kitty** *and goes out.*

Kitty   You must think I'm really stupid –

Tad   Not at all, here – (*Taking her coat.*)

Kitty (*sniffing*)   I've been having a really horrible time, I'm sorry –

Joni   There's a girl in my class who's really depressed and her doctor put her on Prozac –

Kitty (*looking round*)   Where's the furniture?

Tad   She got rid of it. All the cushions are full of organic hops.

Kitty   Jesus wept . . .

Tad   It was after she went to Morocco . . .

Bea *comes back.*

Bea I've put the kettle on. Now. What's going on? What's with all the weeping? So a taxi driver shouted at you. Why didn't you shout back?

Kitty I can't help it, I cry all the time, anything sets me off. He just refused point blank to give me any change and eventually I got so frustrated, I threw the money at him and said, 'Oh, keep the fucking change, for Christ's sake, and a merry Christmas to you too, pal.'

Bea How much was the fare?

Kitty Fifteen quid.

Bea You gave him a thirty-five-pound tip?

Kitty He wasn't even nice to me then, the shit, he still didn't help me with my bags.

Bea This is outrageous. I'm going to report him.

She picks up a phone.

Kitty Don't, he'll lose his job.

Bea I bloody hope so.

Kitty Bea, don't, he's probably got fourteen children, and they'll end up as child prostitutes and it'll all be my fault. Because I've got a wallet stuffed with fifty-pound notes that I don't deserve.

Tad Ah now, steady on there, Kitty. I think that's going a bit far.

Bea You can't just go throwing money at people –

Kitty It doesn't matter, let's just forget it.

Bea It's insane, if everyone did that, the whole . . . I mean, the entire –

Kitty – economy would collapse. No it wouldn't. There'd just be less poor people.

Bea And less rich ones –

Kitty   D'you never look at people and think there's something unbalanced here that I should be so comfortable and they should be so desperate?

Bea   Kitty, he was a Geordie taxi driver, not a legless child beggar in Calcutta –

Kitty   But there's something not right. There's something out of kilter, I feel it all the time –

Bea *gives her a beady look.*

Bea   You're depressed, aren't you?

Kitty   No.

Bea   Any word from Duncan? Where exactly is he?

Kitty   Covering a civil war, and a famine, in that order. So at the very moment you're carving the goose, he'll be watching someone starve to death in front of his eyes.

Bea   She's depressed.

Tad   There you go, Kitty, concern about the world at large is no longer considered a valid response to the inherent contradictions of capitalism, it's just a sign your mental feng shui's up the pole.

Bea   You ask these impossible questions, Kitty, you've always been like this.

Kitty   Always been like what?

Bea   Why do some people have to sell their kidneys to pay the rent while someone else picks at an arugula salad before knocking off a little magazine article about pedicures, thus earning more in a minute than the other one earns in a year? This is what you do when you're depressed. Round and round, on and on. But life's unfair and horrible, and unspeakable things happen, but there's only so much you can do about it. If you think like you do, you go mad and have to check into very expensive clinics, which of course is one way of offloading a substantial proportion of the cash you're feeling so guilty about –

Tad   Some people become nuns. Or social workers –

Kitty   What's wrong with having a conscience –

Bea   It's this ridiculous fucking Catholic thing –

Kitty   It is not fucking ridiculous.

Tad   I'm with you there, Kitty, the Christian Brothers never did me any harm –

Bea   Joni, go and see if the kettle's boiled –

Kitty   What's fucking ridiculous about it?

Joni *goes out reluctantly.*

Tad (*desperately*)   Why don't we all have a drink and calm down –

Bea   What's the point of a conscience if that's all it is? Ooh, I feel so guilty, I've got far too much money –

Kitty   Well, we have –

Bea   So give it away, endow a charitable foundation, burn it, but stop blahing on about it –

Kitty   Oh, fuck off.

Tad   Come on now, Kitty, d'you take a drink?

Kitty   Anything except blue Bols, Malibu or crème de menthe – although I have been known –

Bea (*looking at her watch*)   How long have you been here? Ten minutes, and we've already reached the fuck-off stage –

Tad   Have you two always been like this?

Kitty   She threw a jug at me once. A big jug. With water in it.

Bea   It didn't actually hit you –

Kitty   It might have done –

Bea   You gave my cashmere jumper to a man who said he needed contributions to a strike fund –

Kitty   That was twenty years ago, why d'you always have to bring this up –

Bea   Look, can we stop this –

Kitty   You started it –

Tad   I thought you said you were best friends?

Bea   We are –

Tad   So shut up then –

They both turn on him.

Bea/Kitty   Who asked you?

Tad   Jesus, I was only saying calm down.

Joni *comes back with the hot toddy, hands it to* **Kitty**. **Tad** *pours himself a drink.*

Bea   You behave as if I just loll around eating grapes all day while the world starves. But I don't do nothing. I organised a breast cancer charity ball last week.

Kitty   Were you for or against?

Bea   We all do what we can –

Kitty   Organising a ball, for Christ's sake –

Bea   Subject closed, OK?

Silence. **Tad** *picks up a bowl.*

Tad   Anyone fancy a Twiglet?

Bea   They're not Twiglets, they're pretzels.

Tad   Pretzel then.

Bea   No.

Silence.

Kitty (*conciliatory*)   The tree looks nice.

Bea   No it doesn't. He ate half the decorations.

Tad   Covered in gold fucking leaf. My insides are like
Tutankhamun's tomb.

*Kitty sips her drink, sniffs. A phone rings. They all reach into bags and
grope under cushions. Bea finds one, as does Kitty.*

Bea   Hello?

It continues to ring.

Kitty   Hello?

The ringing continues. Tad picks up a phone. The ringing stops.

Tad   Hello? . . . Oh right . . . right . . .

He looks troubled, awkward. He looks at Bea.

Excuse me a minute, will you?

He goes out with his phone. Kitty blows her nose.

Kitty   D'you cry a lot now? Seriously. I mean, more than
you used to? Is it our age or something?

Bea   I don't cry at all.

Kitty   What, never?

Bea   I can make a little dry grunty noise, but that's it. The
last time I really gave it a go, it was like weeping sand. I can't
do it.

Kitty   I can't stop.

Bea   Maybe you're having an early menopause –

Kitty   Beggars, shabby people with inadequate footwear,
people adding up all their items at supermarket checkouts, in
case they don't have enough money, all that desperate
arithmetic, I can't bear it. People casually glancing into trash
cans, rubbing at scratch cards in newsagent's shops, it kills
me. I've become emotionally incontinent. And it's getting
worse.

Bea   Depressed, what did I tell you? Go straight to your
doctor and ask for a year's supply of Prozac.

Tad *comes back.*

Tad You're supposed to be depressed at Christmas. It's all part of the festive spirit.

Bea Who was that on the phone?

Tad My aged dad.

Bea In Dublin?

Tad Where the fuck else would he be?

Bea OK, OK, don't be so snippy. Kitty, don't be depressed, it's silly, your show's doing really well, it's on prime-time TV, for God's sake.

Kitty It's a pile of shite.

Bea Eight point four million people watch it.

Kitty Lots of people voted for Hitler, it doesn't make it a good idea.

Bea Oh, stop being such a whingeing drip –

Tad Have you ever thought of taking up counselling?

Kitty Christmas carols. They slay me as well.

Tad So the holiday's looking like a bit of a minefield then.

Kitty And if I'm not weeping surreptitiously, I'm shouting at the television, or screaming at the radio.

Bea So, no change there then.

Kitty Every morning I wake up and yell at the *Today* programme. Shut up, you smug, stupid, ill-informed, self-referential bastards, you tiny-minded bunch of dicks, God, I fucking hate you and your nasty, cynical, self-congratulatory world, your wall-to-wall opinionation about everyone and anything whether you know the first thing about it or not, jostling for your two minutes of airtime so you can tell us how you feel about the health service or teenage mothers or why the prime minister should be castrated because he smiles too much, and it doesn't matter what you say anyway

because the interviewer is honour bound to disagree no
matter what –

Joni (*off*)   Mum –

Tom *and* **Iona** *come in, followed by* **Joni**. **Iona** *is filming.* **Bea**
leaps up.

Bea   Tom!

She goes over, beaming, and hugs him.

Tom   Hi, guys. We made it! We didn't die!

Kitty *is still streaked in teary mascara as she gets up and gives him a
kiss.*

Kitty   Hi. How are you?

Tom   Great, we're great, good to see you, you all look
terrific. You know, the Brits are a very ugly race –

Bea   Thanks –

Tom   No, not you, I mean en masse, at Heathrow. I know
in the States we do fat, but over here, I always forget. All these
stumpy little pig folk –

Bea *pushes an awkward* **Tad** *forward.*

Bea   Tom, this is Tad, luckily, he's Irish –

Tad *is smiling for his life.*

Tom   Hi!

Iona   Hi, Tod!

Tad (*still smiling*)   Tad –

Tom *hands his coat and scarf to* **Tad**.

Tom   And this is Iona –

Iona *keeps filming.*

Bea/Kitty/Tad/Joni   Hi, Iona . . .

Iona   Hi, everyone . . .

Awkward pause. They all look at the camera.

Tom   She's making a documentary. Didn't I tell you?

Bea   Of course you did –

Iona   You're doing great so far.

Kitty   A documentary about what?

Tom   Me.

Bea   It's going to be shown on television.

Kitty   Are we in it?

Bea   Look, why don't you give me your coats, and sit down, it looks like a book launch –

She takes their coats and goes out.

Tad   Would you like a go of the chair?

Tom   What? Oh . . . no . . . I'll just . . . what happened to the furniture?

Kitty   Filled with organic hops. The cushions.

Tom   Really? Why is that?

Kitty   One of the great mysteries. Try sitting on one. It's like being trapped in a brewery. A brewery in a souk.

Tom *sits down on a cushion.*

Tom   Can someone get me some chocolate? I have low blood sugar.

Tad *looks around helplessly.*

Tad   Chocolate . . . chocolate.

Iona   Organic hops. what do they do?

Tad   Search me. I'm sticking with the chair.

Joni (*shouting*)   Mum? Have we got any chocolate?

Tad *grabs a handful of chocolate stars from the tree and gives them to* **Tom***.*

Tom   What is this?

Tad   Chocolate. Covered in real gold leaf.

Tom   Isn't that dangerous?

Tad   Well, it hasn't harmed me.

Iona *trains the camera on the cushions.* **Kitty** *looks at* **Tom**.

Kitty   So you're making a film. And we're in it? Hey, thanks
for asking us, Tom, thanks for the consultation –

Tom   Iona, maybe you can pick this up later –

Kitty   What if we don't want to be in it? What if we object?

Iona   Well, I film you objecting.

Tom   OK, Iona, just take a break for a while, come on –

Joni   Why don't you film me instead, I don't mind –

Iona *turns off the camera and puts it down.*

Iona   OK, look, I'm sorry, I should have warned you. Not
too sensitive, I admit it. I just wanted to get the reunion bit,
that's all, but now I have, and that's fine. I'll edit that little
spat out.

Tom   And maybe edit the pig folk out, I don't want to erode
my British fan base entirely.

Iona *holds out her hand to* **Kitty**.

Iona   Kitty, I'm really pleased to meet you, I've heard so
much about you.

Tom   Yeah, it's great to see you, Kitty. I didn't know for
sure you were going to be here.

Kitty   I wasn't. I had a – my plans fell through.

Tom   Great. Do we get to meet your husband at last?
Douglas, is it?

Kitty   Duncan. He's covering a civil war. He might be being
shot at this very moment. Which is one of the reasons I'm a
touch tense.

Tom   Oh. Right. Hey. That's awful. But you don't look tense. You look great.

Kitty   Bollocks. I look a hundred years old.

Tom   I don't think I like this chocolate. Can someone get me something different? Like a muffin or something?

Joni   Mum, have we got any muffins?

She hurries out.

Tom   You look great, Kitty, because you're still in a furious rage about something, it's a relief, I'm sick of people mellowing, it's kind of depressing –

Kitty   I'm not in a furious rage –

Iona   I wish I was getting this on tape, it's so authentic.

Kitty   I'm sorry?

Tom   Iona's a postmodernist.

Iona   I mean authentic in the authentic sense, dick brain –

Tad   D'you take a drink, anyone?

Tom   I guess you'd know all about that, wouldn't you?

Tad   What? Drink?

Tom   Postmodernism. You're a writer, OK?

Tad *laughs inordinately.*

Tad   Oh, right, right, I'm with you, great, that's really funny . . .

Tom   It is? Why?

Tad   Oh, right, no. I don't even know what postmodernism is. I mean, I do but, you know, not consciously.

Tom   Right . . .

Tad   Yeah . . .

He laughs even more. No one else is a laughing. He stops.

Anyway.

Bea *comes back with a tray of champagne and Guinness, and some cakes for* **Tom**. **Iona** *turns on the camera again.*

Tom (*to* **Tad**)   She ever tell you we were all in a production of *The Seagull*?

Bea   I wasn't in it, I was the stage manager.

Tom   Kitty was Nina, and I was Konstantin. She mumbled and I shouted.

Kitty   I wasn't Nina, I was Masha. In mourning for my life.

Tom   Remember when Trigorin came on and the tree fell on him?

Kitty   And Bea shouting over the tannoy: 'Actor down, we have an actor down.'

Tom   You were lying in the wings saying 'I'm going to die, I'm going to die –'

Bea   And I got very cross with you, and told you it was unprofessional –

Tom   That was the summer, remember, sitting up there on the roof, in pigeon shit, listening to Bruce Springsteen for the first time? D'you remember that blast? Tramps like us –

Bea/Kitty (*singing*)   – 'Baby we were born to run, duh dang dang dang –'

Joni   No, Mum, don't start, I'll be sick, honestly.

Iona   Oh, sing it, go on –

Kitty   Tom, what is this, why do we have to have this camera going?

Tom   It's just a little film, you know.

Kitty   Why?

Tom   Why what? This muffin is weird.

Kitty   Why are you making this little film?

Tom   Well, because . . . you know . . . is this banana?

Kitty   Because what?

Bea   Kitty – I think it's bran or something, Tom –

Kitty   No, I don't know what he means –

Iona   This is great, you're so aggressive, no one's ever aggressive to Tom. No one ever says no to him –

Tom   Iona, will you stop trashing me –

Iona   He could go into a restaurant and ask for a little dry toast and a boiled baby, and they'd say, our pleasure, you got it, take a seat Mr Cavallero.

Tom   This is Iona's film. Kind of *cinéma-vérité*. About me. My life. The real me or something. You know the kind of stuff.

Iona   A documentary, not a biopic. I mean, I hate biopics, we're not talking hagiography here. We're talking what it's actually like to be someone like Tom.

Kitty   Yes, but why?

Tom   Excuse me?

Kitty   Why d'you want to do that with your life? Why not, just, you know, have a life? Why d'you have to make a movie out of it?

Bea   Kitty, stop being a pain in the arse –

Tom   Because Iona makes documentaries, that's what she does. She did one about a vulcanologist who got engulfed, it was awful –

Iona   But it was incredible, I actually got it on film, the moment when the lava rolled right over him like something from the black lagoon.

Tom   We met when I went to judge her film school project –

Iona   And d'you know what he said about my piece? He said he it was a total mess –

Tom   I didn't mean it like that –

Iona   It was a mess, I was into alternative scenarios, randomness, weird timescales, you know when you're twenty-three and you just want to trash the world and put it back together in a different order –

Kitty   And what about now?

Tom   Now we're just making a movie. A little bit *cinéma-vérité*, but basically a movie.

Iona   Documentaries always pretend to be actuality, as if this was the way it happened. But they ask people to do things again, to say things they maybe don't mean, they edit stuff out, they splice it together to fit a preconceived notion –

Kitty   Whereas you're going to what?

Iona   I'm hoping it's going to be more truthful, that's all.

Kitty   I spend my life in front of cameras, Tom, I'm supposed to be on holiday –

Bea   Kitty, there's definitely something wrong with your hormones at the moment, you're being ridiculously bad-tempered –

Iona *turns the camera on* **Tad**.

Tad   No, no, don't train that thing on me –

Iona   Don't be so shy . . . come on . . .

Tad *tries to dodge away from the camera.*

Tad   If you point it at me long enough I'll confess to something –

Iona   Like what?

Tad   I don't know, anything. I'm a defrocked priest who used to be a woman. I cheated on my wife with a lesbian go-go dancer. I was born with three penises but now I've found love with a Dobermann pinscher. Cameras scare the fucking pants off me. God knows what I'll admit to.

Tom   You're a funny guy. You're great. I like you.

He looks at **Bea**.

Should I tell him?

Tad   What?

Bea   Go on.

Tad *looks suspicious*.

Tad   Tell me what?

Tom   I want to buy the film rights to *Plunket's Causeway*.

Tad (*floored*)   What?

Bea   He wants to play Padraig.

Kitty   I thought Padraig was a man in a tweed suit from Tipperary?

Tad *looks at her*.

Kitty   She sent it to me.

Tom   So, what d'you think?

Tad   Well, I . . . I mean . . .

Tom   OK, I know, you don't think I can do the accent, right?

Tad   No, no, I mean –

Tom   Guess where I was born?

Tad   Idaho? Palm Springs? Albuquerque? I give up.

Tom   County Down.

Tad   The Cavalleros of County Down?

Tom   I was going through my Robert De Niro phase. So listen, I'd be honoured, truly. I love your book, I mean that bit where the priest throws up on the deathbed, that is just so, anyway, I'm rushing ahead here, what d'you say, Tod?

Tad   Tad.

Tom   Didn't I say that?

Bea   Tad, could you try and sound a bit more thrilled?

Tad   I am, I am, I'm just, you know, a bit taken aback, but sure, it's great –

Tom   I thought we could do some research together in Ireland.

Tad   Right, that'd be great, yeah –

Tom   Can we shake on it? I mean, I know we have to talk to your agent and stuff, but I'd be so thrilled –

Tad   Sure, right, OK –

He shakes **Tom***'s hand, awkwardly.*

Tom   Slainte.

Tad   Great. Slainte.

Kitty   Congratulations, Tad –

Tad (*still awkward*)   Thanks.

Iona   Hey, Mr Hollywood –

Tad   Ah come on now. Take the camera away, can't you? Can a man not be thrilled in private?

A phone rings.

That's mine, excuse me, can you?

He hurries out with his phone.

Joni   Why don't you film me now? I don't mind.

Iona *moves the camera round to her. She gives it a sultry took.*

Joni   Hi, I'm Joni –

Iona *moves the camera round to* **Bea**.

Bea   Are you looking at me now? Oh, don't please, I hate it, I can't bear seeing myself, it's my teeth or something, and my little scrabbling hands, don't you hate that –

Kitty   I don't have little scrabbling hands –

Iona *keeps the camera on her, and* **Joni** *struggles to find a way to keep in the frame.*

Bea   You imagine you're rather composed and elegant and you see yourself on screen and you realise you're a twitchy little graceless person with a mouth like your mother's and huge fat arms –

Iona   You look great –

Bea   No, please, I hate it, I feel sick when I look at myself, I'm such a disappointment and completely the wrong age – no, no, especially sideways, I look like a malevolent tortoise with a grudge –

Iona   OK, OK, so listen, here we are, it's December twenty-third, we're in this beautiful house in Northamptonshire –

Joni (*desperate to get the camera back on her*)   Northumberland –

Iona   Which is near Scotland, right?

Joni   Yeah.

Iona   And they have the weirdest accent I ever heard. That guy at the airport, I thought he was Russian. Do it for us, will you, Bea?

Bea   What?

Iona   That accent. Northumberland.

Bea   I can't, honestly.

Joni   She can when she's drunk.

Bea   Look, could you point that at someone else, d'you think?

Iona   OK, OK, you don't feel easy with impersonations. So, tell us about yourself, Bea.

Bea   No, honestly, ask someone else. I don't like this, I really don't.

Iona   This is weird. What's with you guys? Ask your average American to talk on camera and he'll tell you his life story.

You won't even tell me your name.

Tom Come on, Bea, lighten up.

Bea (*briskly*) All right. I help Tom out bit when he's in Europe, I'm in PR . . . So, anyway, we've known each other since college, and. . . that's about it. Ask someone else, I can't think of anything else to say.

Joni God, Mum, you're so pathetic –

Iona *trains the camera on* **Joni**, *who beams gorgeously.*

Joni Have you heard of Joni Mitchell? Some hippie chick my mum's obsessed with, anyway, I'm named after her, and when Mum gets drunk she always sings 'I could drink a case of you and still I'd be on my feet' –

Bea Joni –

Joni Which is really ironic because she's always lying on the sofa by this point, totally unable to move –

Bea I hope you're going to edit this out –

Iona You're very photogenic, Joni.

Joni I've got a light-reflecting complexion. Also, I'm a Libra, which is supposed to be the most beautiful sign in the zodiac, well, that's what it says in this book I've got. I'm not really sure if it's true though –

Tad (*returning*) It's not. The Elephant Man was a Libran.

Joni This is Tad, my mum's boyfriend, he's a Celtic person who writes books. I haven't read any of them.

Kitty Is this going to go on all night? I mean, do we at least get to sit on the lavatory in private?

Tom I don't. Tell us what you've been up to, Joni.

Joni I'm learning to play the guitar.

Tom Really? That's great. I used to play the guitar.

Joni Yeah, I know. I've written some songs. I'm going to form a girl band with my mate Nubs. I could play some of them for you if you want –

Bea　I think that's enough now, Joni, you've been absolutely fascinating but you can have too much of a good thing –

Tom　Maybe just wrap it up now now, Iona. It's kind of irritating after a while.

Joni　Shall I play my songs, Mum?

Bea　Not tonight, Joni.

Joni *exits.*

Iona　OK, guys, just carry on. You won't notice me if you just pretend I'm not here.

Kitty　How can you pretend there's not a camera in the room?

Iona　Just talk amongst yourselves. Stop being so self-conscious. Go on. Talk. Do what you'd be doing if I wasn't here.

Silence.

OK. Tod –

Tad　Tad –

Iona　What part of Scotland are you from?

Tad　I'm not Scottish, I'm Irish. We've just had a long conversation about it.

Iona　Oh, I'm sorry, I get confused. I'm not so hot on British accents.

Tad　That's OK, I'm Irish.

Joni *comes back with her guitar.*

Bea　Joni, please don't play that now.

Joni　God, any normal mother would be proud –

Bea　It's very distracting, that's all, when there's a room full of people –

Joni *throws her guitar down with a crash, muttering.*

Joni   All right, all right, I'm not going to, OK? God, you're such a pain –

Bea   I think we need more alcohol –

She picks up a bottle desperately and refills glasses.

Tad   So how was the trip then, Tom?

Tom   Excuse me?

Tad   The flight, you know.

Tom   It was . . . a regular flight.

Tad   I bet you got on the plane and turned left, did you?

Tom   Excuse me?

Tad   You'd be in first class.

Tom   Well . . . yeah . . .

Tad   So what's it like?

Tom   I'm sorry?

Tad   First class. I always go steerage. I always want to ask them if I can have a quick glance upstairs, you know, when I get on the plane. I mean, d'you get double beds and Filipino handmaidens and that sort of thing? Or just a polyester sleep suit and a copy of *Hello!* magazine?

Tom   Well, it's . . . OK . . . I mean, you don't get there any quicker. If the plane crashes you still die.

Tad   Have you ever travelled steerage?

Tom   Economy? Not for around twenty years.

Tad   It's the most disgusting and demeaning form of travel known to man.

Tom   Yeah, I guess . . . but it's kind of difficult for me, you know, because of my . . . because people kind of bug me . . . I mean, when I travel, I like to be left alone –

Kitty Really? I like spending eight hours next to a man weighing seventeen stones, in a seat designed for a midget. Preferably next to the lavatories. I really really love that –

Tom I mean, people can be weird, you know –

Tad Yeah, yeah. Right. I know what you mean, fans and that kind of thing. They can drive you mad, can't they?

Joni What would you know about it?

Tad I've had experience of this sort of thing, not as much as Tom, obviously –

Joni *shrieks with laughter.*

Joni Who'd be a fan of yours?

Bea Joni –

Tad I've done a book signing –

Joni – in Croydon –

Tad There were some very weird people there, I'm telling you –

Tom Like they're over-friendly, you know, or they're really aggressive.

Tad Yeah, exactly, I know exactly what you mean –

Tom *looks at him.*

Tom I don't think you do.

Tad Well, I –

Tom You cannot begin to imagine what I mean.

Tad No, obviously, I just –

Tom One guy comes up to me in the airport, d'you remember this, Iona? He comes right up to me and says: 'Hey, pal, all your movies stink. So don't get superior with me. Plus, my dick is one hell of a size. So up yours, buddy.' I never met the guy before in my life.

Iona   Tell them about the sandwiches, Tom.

Tom   Oh Jesus, the sandwich, yeah. That was just weird.

They look at him expectantly.

Does anyone have a cigarette? And maybe another muffin, I still need sugar.

Bea (*going out*)   A muffin, a muffin –

Tom   Make it low fat –

Joni   Mum, you said he didn't smoke.

Tom   Tom Cavallero doesn't, but I do. You know what I mean?

Joni   Tad's got some –

She rushes to **Tad***'s jacket and brings out the packet. Offers them to* **Tom***.*

Tom   D'you mind?

Tad   No, go on.

Tom *lights up.*

Tom   We're in New York this time. In a deli, right. So I'm sitting eating my pastrami with French mustard, a side order of latke and sour cream, because I'm depressed and I've just trashed my diet sheet. I bite into my sandwich, OK, and I think what the hell is this? And I take out of my mouth this kind of paper streamer or something, about so long. I unravel it and it says: 'Tom, I really want to fuck you. I want to have your children.' I open up my sandwich and it's full of messages, on little pieces of paper. And I look up and the waitress opens her shirt and shows me her breasts. Just for like a split second. I smile, I figure it's always best to smile, in case they have a gun, and we get out of there quick. And when I tell my therapist he doesn't believe me. He says, are you seeing these sort of messages anywhere else right now? Like on billboards, for instance? Maybe in the *Wall Street Journal*? So I fire him. Who needs a therapist who thinks you're crazy?

Tad   That's a great story.

Tom   It's not a story, it's true.

Tad   No, I know that.

Tom   It really happened to me.

Bea *comes back with a plate of muffins.*

Tad   Yes, I know, I only meant, Jesus, there's a lot of fucking mad people out there.

Tom   And all of them are attracted to me. Thanks.

He takes the muffins.

Bea   I think this happens to almost everyone in your position, Tom. It's not specific to you. By the way, supper's almost ready.

Tom   Listen, other people get schoolteachers from Wyoming, they get beautiful young women, they get movie buffs, what I get is psychotics. People who collect cake stands and thimbles, and musical dogs, they hold the world record for lying in bathtubs of maggots, they're nudists, they believe the government's bugging their bathroom. They're basically not the sort of people you'd have over for supper. And they love me.

Iona   They don't love you, they don't know you.

Tom   You mean if they did know me they wouldn't? Is that what you're trying to say?

Iona   They're in love with a construct, Tom. Does someone else want to take this, so I can be in it for a moment?

Bea *looks at her watch.*

Bea   Is anybody hungry?

Kitty   She's been cooking for three weeks –

Bea (*briskly*)   Because I think I should serve supper soon, I don't mean to be rude, Iona, but we need to eat. Joni, can you show Tom and Iona and Kitty their bathrooms?

Kitty   Wow, are we dressing for dinner?

Bea   I thought you might want to get washed, that's all.

Kitty   OK, OK . . .

She gets up, as do **Tom** *and* **Iona**.

Joni   Follow me. Yours has got a really stupid bath, Kitty.
It's pale green plastic . . .

She goes out, they follow.

Tom   How long? Fifteen, twenty minutes?

Bea   That's fine.

He goes. **Tad** *lights up a cigarette, edgily, as* **Bea** *tidies up glasses, etc.*

Tad   Did I make a complete eejit of myself? I did, didn't I?

Bea   You did do some over-enthusiastic laughing at one
point –

Tad   I can't help it. Famous people turn me into a complete
dick. Something happens when they come into a room. The
molecules regroup, there's some sort of atmospheric shift. I
talk shite.

He puts his head in his hands.

Over-enthusiastic laughing. Jesus. I'm a fifty-year-old
published author, I've had an article about me in the
Independent. Tom Cavallero walks into the room and I'm
infantilised.

Bea   You could have sounded a bit more delighted about the
film. A few monosyllabic grunts. What happened to your
famous Celtic charm?

Tad   Bea, listen –

Bea   I mean, he wants to come over and meet your family
and everything –

Tad   *Plunket's Causeway*'s not about my family –

Bea   No, he knows that, but he also knows it comes from
somewhere in you –

Tad   Bea, would you ever just stop?

Bea   What is the matter with you? What's wrong?

Pause. **Tad** *looks at her for a long time.*

Tad   I don't know how to say this.

Bea   What is it? Tad, I've got to get the supper sorted out –

Tad   Fuck the supper.

Bea   What!?

Tad   I have to tell you something, Bea –

Bea   What?

Tad   I mean, if I told you something . . .

Bea   Like what, for Christ's sake?

Tad   I mean, you know, if . . . I told you . . . something about . . . if I told you quite a big thing . . .

Silence.

Bea   What . . . ?

Tad   Or maybe it's not so big . . . I suppose it depends how you look at it –

Bea   Tad, cut to the chase, will you?

Pause. **Tad** *is in an agony of indecision.*

Tad   I need to tell you . . . I can't not . . . I'm just, I mean, oh Jesus, oh Jesus, I can't do it.

Bea   What? Can't do what?

Silence.

What are you trying to say?

Tad   Nothing.

Bea   For Christ's sake! What are you trying to tell me?

A beat.

You've met someone.

Tad No –

Bea She's younger, she's thirty-two, she wants children. All that stuff you said about never wanting a family, you've changed your mind. She has no cellulite and pert breasts and you're leaving me. She has nine-inch hips and a flat stomach and a PhD. I knew this would happen, I was waiting for it, oh Jesus –

Tad No, for fuck's sake! It's not that.

Pause. **Bea** *looks at him.*

Bea Well, what is it then?

Long pause.

Tad I'm not . . . what . . . I'm not . . . oh fuck . . . I don't know how to say this . . . I mean . . .

Pause.

Bea What?

Pause.

Tad I'm not actually Irish.

Pause.

Bea What?

Tad I'm not Irish.

Bea I don't know what you mean.

Tad I'll spell it out for you. I-am-not-Irish.

Pause.

Bea I'm still not sure what you mean.

Tad Jesus fucking wept. I'm not bleeding Irish.

Pause. **Bea** *is very confused.*

Bea You mean you were born somewhere else?

Tad   I'm from Hull.

Silence.

Bea   I don't understand what you're saying. You were born in Hull, so what?

Tad   No, I am from Hull. D'you see what I'm getting at?

Bea   Not really, no . . .

Tad   But the thing is, I couldn't get anyone to publish my stuff when I set it in Hull. It's not sexy or something. I was on my uppers. I went to Ireland and dossed about. This was twenty years ago. And you know. Sort of slipped into it.

Bea   What?

Tad   Being Irish.

Bea   You 'sort of slipped into' being Irish?

Tad   That's just about the size of it.

Bea   But you're not Irish?

Tad *looks agonised.*

Tad   No.

Bea   So –

Suddenly the lights go out. It's pitch black.

Fuck! Tad, are you having me on?

Tad   I'm not codding you.

Tom (*off*)   What's going on?

Bea   Hang on. There are candles somewhere.

She stumbles around looking for candles. **Kitty** *appears in the doorway.*

Kitty   Does this happen often?

Bea   Is that you, Kitty? It's the weather. Go back upstairs. Where're those fucking candles . . .

Tom (*off*)   Is somebody going to fix this?

Joni *comes in.*

Joni   This house is pathetic, Mum.

Iona *and* **Tom** *appear, in bathrobes.*

Tom   Isn't there a maintenance guy?

Kitty   Oh, for God's sake, Tom –

Bea   Look, go and get dressed, they'll come on again in a minute –

Tom   It's black as fuck up there –

Bea   Tad, can I speak to you in private, d'you think?

Tom   Where're the fucking candles?

Iona   This is wonderful. I love it. Is this place haunted?

Tad *strikes a match.*

Tom   Iona, shut the fuck up.

Tad   It is actually.

Bea   Tad, I need to speak to you

Joni   You mean there's something in the house?

Bea   Tad –

Tad   Not so much the house as the grounds. Out there, not in here.

Bea *finds a candle and lights it.*

Tad   That's what they say.

Bea   Stop it, will you?

She lights another candle.

Tom   What? What's out there?

Iona   When do we get some light back?

Bea   Oh for God's sake, it happens all the time, it's nothing. Tad –

Tom   This is medieval, you can't live like this, someone get it back on, will you?

Bea   Tom, stop panicking, it's OK. We're just going to sit in the dark for a while, that's all –

Tom   OK, OK –

Kitty   What's this story, Tad?

Bea   Kitty, please, I like ghost stories but not when they're about my own house, OK?

Tad   This one's really fucking weird. I was completely spooked when I heard it.

Tom   Will I be able to sleep? I mean, will I have to keep the light on all night?

Kitty   You'll be lucky.

Tad   Don't worry. Whatever it is, it's not in the house, it's outside. Can I get anyone a drink?

He goes round with the bottle. The candles flicker and gutter. They all look at him expectantly. He sits down on the chair and lights a cigarette. Silence.

Bea   So? I thought you were going to tell us one of your stories, Tad?

Tad   I thought you didn't want to hear it.

Bea   Oh, for fuck's sake, what's outside the bloody house?

Iona   Hold on, hold on –

She picks up her camera. Turns it on.

OK. Go.

Tad   Well, if you're sure you want to hear it . . . do we need another candle, d'you think?

Bea   Tad –

Kitty   Oh, for God's sake –

She finds another candle and lights it.

Tad   Maybe it's a bit too bright now.

He snuffs it out again. Then another. Leaves just one candle, which he holds, flickering in front of him.

That's better. So. Where was I?

Kitty   'It was a wild and stormy night – '

Tom   I'm feeling kind of spooked here.

Tad   I haven't started yet.

Bea   Well, bloody start then.

Tad   OK, OK. The story comes from before this house was built, when this was common land on the edge of the moors. So it's very ancient, it's as old as the land itself. It's not complicated. The place is visited by a fetch.

Tom   Excuse me?

Tad   A fetch. The wraith of a living person. A doppelgänger. You know, your uncle Arthur appears to you at the very moment of his death on the other side of the world. But this, right, is not quite the same thing. This is a much more unusual manifestation. Here, you meet your own self out there on the moors. Your own doppelgänger. According to this story, it's happened twice this century and a score of times in the past.

Kitty   I don't get it.

Pause.

Tad   In 1923, a man called Thomas Earlby was out walking his dog at about five o'clock on a December evening. So it was dark, the way it is in the country, no light except the moon which kept dipping behind clouds. And the moors, you know, are pitch black. There's a frost prickling the ground and the two feet and four paws crunch and crackle over the coarse tussocks. Crunch, crunch. Pad, pad. Suddenly the dog stops, and refuses to go any further. Earlby coaxes him: 'Come on lad, come on.' But the dog starts whining, and giving little uncertain barks, and Earlby looks up and sees a vague, bluish light coming towards them across the moors. The dog cowers now. He won't move an inch. The light gets closer and Thomas Earlby makes out the figure of a man, carrying a lantern, with a strange glow the colour of moonlight. But the curious thing is that the man makes no sound as he comes towards them over the frozen ground. Earlby calls out, 'Who's there?' But the figure keeps coming until it's only a few feet away. And Thomas Earlby is transfixed, rooted to the spot: for the man before him is his own self. But himself white-faced and gaunt, sick-looking, his lips drawn back from his teeth. And this other self beckons to Thomas Earlby. Beckons to him, like this . . . (*He beckons.*) The hairs stand up on the back of Earlby's neck and he turns on his heel and flees, the dog scurrying alongside him giving a low whimper. And when he gets home he tells his wife and his old dad, who lives with them, about what he'd encountered out there on the moors. And the father goes pale, and walks out of the room, goes upstairs to his bed, without a word. And the next morning Thomas Earlby is dead.

Silence.

Tom   But like . . . I mean, that's not really a haunting, right? I mean, it's not like there's a ghost out there, right?

Tad   I wouldn't call it that, no. It's more that this is a place where such things occur. You meet your own doppelgänger who beckons you to your doom. Apparently. Maybe that's why it's called a fetch. Because it comes to fetch you. Your own self comes to fetch you . . .

He snuffs out the candle. Blackout.

Tom   Holy shit.

Act Two

Scene One

Later. **Bea** *and* **Tad** *are alone at last.* **Bea** *is in shock.*

Bea   Tad, please tell me this Irish thing is an elaborate joke.

Tad   It's not.

Bea   But for Christ's sake . . . I mean . . . you sound . . . everything about you . . .

Tad   I know. I'm spongy. I absorb stuff. And the whole thing of it is, I feel Irish. It's not as if it's hard for me. I mean, really, I might just as well be. Except I'm not. And you know, being on the television and all that. You putting me on all those programmes. It's only a matter of time before someone from Hull . . . you know . . .

Bea   What . . . ?

Tad   Recognises me.

Pause.

Bea   I can't take this in . . . I mean . . . So who . . . ? Who the hell are you?

Tad   Me. I'm still me, it's just, you know . . .

Bea   But Thaddeus Kennedy's an Irish name.

Pause.

Tad   It's not the one I started out with.

Pause.

Michael Armstrong. That's my, you know . . .

Bea   You're really called Michael Armstrong?

Tad   Yeah.

Bea   Jesus Christ . . . I've been . . . Who the fuck have I been sleeping with for the last six months?

Tad   Me.

Bea   But you're not who I thought you were.

Tad   I am. Essentially I am. It's just the details that are a bit different.

Bea   Details? Is that what you call them?

Tad   Well, you pretend to be middle class and you're not, you pretend your hair's naturally that colour, you talk in an accent that's completely made up –

Bea   That's not the same thing at all –

Tad   Why isn't it?

Bea   You lied to me, that's the difference –

Tad   I omitted a few facts, I never lied about anything –

Bea   But everything about you's a lie –

Tad   Couldn't you look at it like this, I mean, I feel comfortable being Tad, it feels right, it doesn't feel like a lie. Maybe I'm the cultural equivalent of a transsexual. An Irishman trapped in an Englishman's body.

Bea   Oh, don't be so fucking ridiculous.

Tad   Micheál MacLiammóir was a great Irishman and he came from Kensal Rise. He never set foot in Ireland till he was twenty-three.

Bea   I don't understand . . . I mean . . . why?

Tad   I told you, it felt right. And as soon as I started writing in my Irish voice, it felt true, it felt like mine. When I was writing about England, it didn't seem authentic, it's like my identity was liquid, it just ran through my fingers. I couldn't seem to define myself. Plus I couldn't get a fucking thing published. And I was just the same writer. Except I'm better now. I've got a voice now.

Bea   You're mad.

Tad   I'm not. I'm not mad at all. But I had to tell you, d'you know?

Bea *stares at him.*

Bea   If you're from Hull, talk to me in your real voice.

Tad   This is my real voice.

Bea   You know what I bloody mean.

Tad (*Hull accent*)   The rain in Spain falls mainly on the plain. (*Irish accent.*) Now you do your real accent. Go on, give us a blast of the old Geordie.

Bea   Losing an accent's nothing like what you've done. You can't equate social mobility with out-and-out deception –

Tad   Social mobility my arse –

Bea   But what about your parents, your family?

Tad   My mother's dead. My dad . . . we never got on . . . he was a complete bastard . . . knocked my mother and me about, you know . . .

Bea   So where is he?

Tad   In Hull . . . I see him maybe once a year. He's eighty-five, for fuck's sake.

Bea   And he's in on this, is he?

Tad   No. He doesn't watch the sort of programmes you get me on. He doesn't read broadsheets. He doesn't have a clue. He thinks writers are a bunch of jessies. But now . . .

Bea   What?

A beat.

Tad   It doesn't matter. I just know I should have told you, that's all.

Bea   Everything I thought about you, everything that makes you what you are has just disintegrated –

Tad   I'm still everything I was before except I'm not Irish, not in the strictest sense of the word –

Bea   But that was what I loved about you –

Tad   Thanks a fucking bunch –

Bea   I mean, I loved all the stuff that comes with that – I mean, you're not real –

Tad   I thought I could get away with it, being a writer and all that. You know, I thought, it's a quiet, invisible sort of profession, it's not like being a film star. And that's what it was for years. A few short stories. Novels that never made much of a splash. Eking out a living, with a bit of this and a bit of that. But suddenly I'm all over the papers. The more visible you want me to be the more scary it gets. I kept thinking I'll stop, I'll tell her, I'll get out of this. But it's like a drug, you know? Cars picking you up, make-up people taking all that trouble over you, cameras, applause, it's like slipping into a big warm bath of affirmation and aren't you fucking marvellous. But all the time I'm thinking any minute now the whole lot's going to come down. I'm being launched into the stratosphere and someone is going to fucking recognise me, Bea. And I just want to get on with my work in peace.

Bea *has poured herself a large whisky. She knocks it back.*

Tad   I mean, it doesn't change the way I feel about you –

Bea   But those feelings are suspect, for Christ's sake! They come from some fabricated person, I've been in love with a glove puppet –

Tad   It's me. I'm still me.

He goes towards her. She holds out her hand to ward him off.

Bea   No, don't try and be smoochy with me –

Tad   Bea.

Bea   No . . . fuck off . . . d'you know I was going to bake soda farls tomorrow, especially for you, but fuck them, fuck you and your champ and potato cakes, and your Irish stew –

Tad Bea –

Bea – and your fucking peat briquettes, fuck you –

Tad Bea, peat briquettes are a type of fuel –

Bea – and your pints of plain and bowls of malt, fuck you
and your crubeens, whatever they are, your bacon and
cabbage, your Celtic twilight bollocks and your poetic soul
that's forty shades of green, you treacherous fucking
Yorkshireman –

She bursts into tears.

And now look, now look what you've done, look at me, I don't
do crying, I haven't cried since 1982, you impostor, you shit –

She sobs. **Tad** *watches awkwardly.*

Tad Bea. My dad's ill. They've given him two months.

Pause. **Bea** *is still crying*

Bea What?

Tad My dad's dying.

Bea (*sobbing*) Which one? The one in Hull or some surrogate
leprechaun?

Tad My real one. The only one I've got.

Bea So . . . ? And . . . ?

Tad I don't like him. I used to hate him. I used to want to
kill him. But he's part of me, you know? . . .

Pause.

Bea, I don't know what the fuck to do.

Blackout.

Scene Two

Lights up, later. Two a.m. Spotlight on **Joni** *posing by the chair in her nightdress. Wild applause, wolf-whistles, camera bulbs flashing. Screen images washing over the set. She strikes a series of provocative poses as the applause dies down.*

Joni   Yeah, I'm really really happy that the truth's out at last. Yeah, he gave me this ring. (*She holds out her hand.*) It belonged to his mother, so you know, it seemed right. Right, it's incredible, I know, my first film and I'm nominated for an Oscar, I can't believe it, it's been an amazing year. Well, I've known Tom since I was tiny, so I've never been in awe of him or anything, and getting the film was nothing to do with our relationship because I'd already got the part before all this happened. Yeah, I met Iona a couple of times, and it was really terrible about the car crash and everything, but I think the relationship was more or less over by then. Decapitated. She never knew what hit her. I think I probably helped him to get over it. Well, it takes a bit of getting used to being over here in Beverly Hills with all the palm trees and everything, it's not much like Hammersmith, I can tell you. And getting mobbed by fans and not being able to leave the house. I've had a couple of stalkers, you know, the usual, God, it's so boring. I can't go places like the supermarket any more, but we have staff and everything. Would I take my clothes off on film? I think that's a very difficult question, but yes, if the part demanded it –

Lights change abruptly as **Tom** *comes in, still in his bathrobe, clutching his mobile phone and a glass of whisky. He's sniffing, as if he's taken coke, and is obviously mid-conversation.*

Tom –

Tom   Joni, sorry, I didn't realise you were still up –

Joni   I was just going to bed, goodnight –

She dashes out, mortified.

Tom   Hey, you don't have to go because of me –

He goes back to his conversation.

Sorry, Charlie –

He picks up a book, and throws himself down on the cushions. During the conversation, he's trying to snort coke from a line he manages to lay out on the book.

Yeah, he's thrilled. Thinks I'd make a great Padraig. All we need now is a screenplay. But Charlie, listen, I'm calling you because I can't sleep. Have you ever heard of a fetch? (*He looks at his watch.*) It's three a.m. What d'you mean you're going out? You're my agent, you're supposed to make soothing noises when I make irrational calls in the middle of the night. Hold on –

He moves away from the phone, and snorts the line of coke.

No, truly, I'm serious, I'm having a crisis here, I'm in the middle of fucking nowhere, it's colder than North Dakota, and we've had a power failure. I come all this way, to some county I've never heard of, full of people who sound like Vikings, I've no idea where I am, left of Norway or somewhere, and there's a fetch outside. A fetch . . . It's a spook. It's a doppelgänger and it's in the garden.

Iona *appears in her dressing gown with the camera to her eye.*

Iona   Tom –

Tom   I am not fucking drunk! Listen to me. Can you imagine anything more horrible than to see someone coming towards you and it's you? . . . No, not you, me . . . No, *I* meet me. *I* run into myself . . . no, you don't come into it at all . . . you're not in this scene OK . . . I'm talking about the fetch . . . I just told you for fuck's sake . . . I'm not in bed, I'm in the living room . . . because it's three a.m. and I don't want to wake Iona . . .

Iona   So stop shouting then –

Tom You see, you woke her up –

She takes the phone from him. Continuing to film.

Iona   Hi, Charlie, it's me . . . no, he's OK, he's jet-lagged and tired, that's all . . . yes he's warm enough . . . The house has heating, Charlie, we don't have to sleep in our clothes . . . I'm sorry . . . really . . . ? That sounds pretty unusual . . . yeah, why don't you go on out to dinner . . . boy, you don't know how good that sounds, the sun dipping down over the Pacific, I'm so jealous . . .

Tom   Tell him to call me tomorrow –

Iona   He says to call him tomorrow – OK, goodnight, Charlie . . .

She turns off the phone.

Tom   What did he say? Did he say I was drunk?

Iona   No.

Tom   Did he say I sounded emotional?

Iona   No. He said did you bring cashmere socks because a friend of his went to Scotland and got frostbite and had to have his toe amputated. And cashmere socks would have saved that toe.

She goes.

Tom   Iona?

She doesn't respond. He yells at the top of his voice.

Iona!

Iona *comes back.*

Iona   What?

Tom   D'you think that thing, the fetch? D'you think it ever gets inside the house?

Joni *appears in the doorway wearing her dressing gown and with a joint in her hand.*

Joni   Tom. Can I speak to you a minute?

Iona   It's three a.m., Joni, you should be asleep.

She looks at **Joni**.

Are you smoking dope?

Joni   I'm allowed.

Iona   Are you sure?

Joni *looks at* **Iona***'s camera and puts the joint behind her back.*

Joni   Don't film me though.

She hovers awkwardly.

I can't get to sleep.

Tom   Me neither.

Joni   Why?

Tom   Just a little jittery, that's all.

She offers him the joint.

Joni, I don't think you should smoke that, you're way too
young –

Joni   When you get cross you look exactly like I do when I
get cross.

Tom   I do?

Joni   Can I put some music on?

Tom   Sure, but don't you think you should be asleep? –

She goes to the CD and puts on some hip-hop music.

Iona   Joni, I think you should go back to bed, come on, I'm
going up –

She takes **Joni***'s arm but* **Joni** *shrugs her off.*

Joni   I want to talk to Tom about something.

Iona   OK, I give up on both of you. I'm exhausted.

She goes out. **Joni** *begins to sway to the music.*

Joni   D'you think my skin really is luminous?

Tom   Sure.

Joni   Is it true, all that stuff about reflecting light?

Tom   Probably.

Joni   I really love dancing, don't you?

Tom   Yeah.

Joni   But I'm also quite a spiritual person.

Tom   Right.

Pause. She stops dancing.

Joni   Tom. I know.

Tom   Excuse me?

Joni   I know.

Tom   What?

Joni   It's all right. Mum didn't tell me, I just worked it out.

Tom   Worked what out?

She comes over and tentatively sits at his feet.

Joni   I know you're my dad.

Tom *is taken aback. He sits up.*

Tom   What?

Joni   I know you're my –

Tom   Joni, no, hey, hold on –

Joni   But I know – .

Tom   Joni, Philip is your dad –

Joni   It's OK, I know he's not. I don't look like him, I look like you –

Tom   I don't think you do, honey, I think you're just – listen, I'm not your dad, I swear to God I'm not –

Joni   Why are you denying it?

Tom   Because it's not true. I am not your father.

Joni *is confused and embarrassed.*

Joni   But I worked it out! You were in London when I was conceived and I know you were staying with Mum because I found photographs of you with the date on and you have your arms round her, and you look, you look –

Tom   Joni. Listen to me. I am not your father.

Kitty *and* **Bea** *come in.*

Bea   Joni, what are you doing? And what's this bloody awful music that's waking everyone up?

She turns off the music. **Joni** *and* **Tom** *both get up, covered in embarrassment, as if they've been caught out.*

Joni (*tearfully*)   You'll never speak to me again now, will you –

Tom   I will. I promise. It was a mistake, that's all, honey. Now get some sleep.

Bea   What's going on?

Joni *looks at her.*

Joni   Nothing. It's private, OK? It's just a thing between me and Tom, all right?

She goes out.

Kitty   What's she talking about?

Tom   Nothing. Forget it.

Kitty   Were you chatting her up?

Tom   Oh, for Christ's sake, of course I wasn't –

Bea   Of course he wasn't –

Kitty   D'you know somehow that's less convincing coming from a man with an underage sex charge round his neck –

Tom   I was not trying to seduce Joni, or any other young woman –

Kitty   So how come you've got one suing you, and another one practically sitting on your face?

Tom   She was not sitting on my face –

Kitty   Only because we walked in before you got her pants off –

Tom   She thinks I'm her dad, for Christ's sake.

Bea   What?

Kitty   Where did she get that idea from?

Tom   Search me.

They both look at **Bea**.

Bea   It's nothing to do with me.

Kitty   You're not, are you?

Bea   Of course he's not.

Tom   Of course I'm not.

Kitty   Jesus, so you're trying to seduce her and she's thinking she's your daughter. No wonder she's upset –

Bea   Kitty –

Tom   I wasn't trying to seduce her, how many times d'you want me to say it. Jesus wept, underage girls are not my problem –

Kitty   Hah!

Bea   Oh, for Christ's sake, Kitty, he wasn't trying to seduce Joni, now will you just forget the whole thing –

Kitty   Why are you on his side? Why aren't you defending your daughter's honour?

Bea   Because, oh, for God's sake –

Kitty   What?

Tom   listen, I don't have any kind of problem with young girls. That is not my problem, OK?

Kitty   So why are they suing you?

Bea *and* **Tom** *look at each other. A considered pause.*

Bea   Men . . . are his problem.

Kitty   What d'you mean, men?

Tom   I fuck them.

Pause.

Kitty (*uncertainly*)   Yeah. And my mother's the Empress of Russia.

Tom   I'm serious.

She looks at **Bea**.

Kitty   Is he serious?

Bea   Yes.

Pause.

Kitty   And you knew this?

Bea   He wouldn't let me tell you, he wouldn't let me tell anyone –

Kitty   So he sleeps with men. Since when?

Tom   Since for ever.

Pause.

Kitty   But you've slept with me.

Bea   He's slept with *you*?

Tom   And I also sleep with men –

Bea   *When* did he sleep with you?

Tom   – which is not an admissible orientation for someone in my position –

Bea   Obviously, he's not, in the past, been the most committed homosexual seeing as he's also slept with me.

Kitty   Jesus Christ, Tom, is there anybody you haven't slept with? Are our pets safe? *When* did he sleep with you?

Bea   Years ago. When we were at college –

Tom   Listen, can we forget about the when and the where –

Kitty   Because that would be so much more convenient for you, wouldn't it. Bea, I can't believe you never told me this –

Tom   Christ, this is a big deal, d'you understand? I come out to my oldest friend and what does she do? She argues about who fucked who when –

Kitty   And what about all this underage girl stuff?

Tom   It's a scam. Iona and Bea cooked it up with my agent.

Kitty   So it's not true? It's just horseshit?

Bea   Well, no, there is a woman –

Tom   I mean, she's real –

Bea   It's just –

Tom   She's an old friend, my yoga teacher. She said she would spin this story about how I broke her heart, it was a fun thing, we laughed about it, she was my beard. And then fuck, what happened, she got carried away, suddenly she's claiming she was sixteen years old, she's making up all sorts of things –

Bea   I think she liked the attention.

Tom   Invented a whole load of shit, a whole scenario that never happened, things we did in bed, hotels we went to, how I picked her up from high school, I mean, you know, she's a fucking yoga teacher, she told me she was on the path to enlightenment –

Bea   When actually she's mad as a bag of snakes, Jesus, I wish you'd let me meet her before you got into this, Tom, I'm a professional, I know a fantasist when I see one –

Tom   Anyway, it's over, we paid her off: She wanted a nose job, and to go to some ashram in the Hindu Kush because she mistakenly thinks Mel Gibson once hung out there. Let's hope she fucking stays.

Kitty   And what does Iona get out of this set-up?

Tom   Iona doesn't really go for men –

Kitty   Of course not. How stupid of me to think she did.

Tom   She gets to make a movie –

Kitty   Which will be bullshit from start to finish –

Tom   I play straight leading men, Kitty.

Bea   He can't afford to come out.

Kitty   Let's just get this right. You're bisexual. You've always been bisexual?

Tom   Yeah. Except I'm increasingly inclined towards, you know . . .

Kitty   Gaydom.

Tom   Yeah.

Kitty   But you're going to suppress this, for the sake of your career?

Tom   That's what I've always done.

Kitty   For Christ's sake, Tom –

Tom   We're talking about Hollywood here. We have gay rights, we have gay pride, we have gay marriages, but we don't have gay movie stars.

Kitty   James Dean.

Tom   You're allowed to come out if you're dead. Or British.

Kitty   Tom, this is a hall of mirrors –

Tom   Listen, I like women, you know that. I don't even mind having sex with them. It's just I also like having sex with men, and stories get around. Hence the young girl.

Kitty   I can't believe you went along with this, Bea. And you never told me –

Bea   He wouldn't let me, it's not my fault –

Kitty   Why didn't you trust me?

Tom   It's a fire that needs to be contained. There was no need for you to know –

Kitty   Excuse me –

Bea   D'you know something? I need to lie down. Believe me, this is the least of my worries right now. Christmas isn't really panning out that well for me at the moment. I'll be in the spare room at the back if there's anything else you need to get off your chest.

Kitty   Why aren't you sleeping with Tad?

Bea   Because we're not actually on speaking terms.

She goes out.

Kitty   Can I just sort something out here? Sorry to bother you with the vulgarity of the when and where, but when you slept with me –

Tom   Listen, things got pretty wild afterwards, you know . . . I mean, I was kind of out of control and making a picture and I guess . . . I'm sorry, OK. I should have called you.

Kitty   I'm surprised you even remember it.

Tom   Oh, come on. It was a whole week.

Kitty   Ten days.

Tom   Yeah, well, you didn't call me either.

Kitty   You didn't give me your number.

Tom   You're kidding me? Why didn't you get it from Bea or someone?

Kitty *looks at him.*

Kitty   Hi, I bumped into Tom in New York, we got ripped and spent a week in bed together. Now I need his phone number to find out why he never calls me.

Tom   Were you really waiting for me to call?

Kitty   Well, it would have been polite, you know? And because even if I did have your number, I couldn't have called you anyway.

Tom   Why not?

Kitty   Because you're Tom Cavallero. –

Tom   We've known each other for twenty years, for Christ's sake. Twenty-three, to be accurate.

Kitty   And in all that time you never told me you were gay –

Tom   Half gay –

Kitty   What I'm saying is you're a movie star. I don't know how to be with you. I don't know how I'm supposed to behave. I do angry, because it's better than doing embarrassment.

Tom   You should have called me.

Kitty   I should have called you?

Tom   Kitty, this is getting circular –

Kitty   Fifteen years ago I tried calling you in LA. I got your secretary who said, 'How did you get this number?' When I said I was your friend she said, 'I'm sorry but you don't appear on Tom's list of bona fide people, I'm afraid I can't pass on your message.' Are you surprised I didn't try and track you down this time?

Tom   Was her name Maribel, this secretary?

Kitty   I've no idea.

Tom   Maribel I had to fire. She refused to put my mother through. Plus she had this weird personal hygiene thing, she was always cleaning her hands on these anti-bacterial wipes, and disinfecting the telephone. Also she stole my clothing, like socks and stuff. After I fired her I ran into her in a bookstore and she was wearing my jacket. Can you believe that?

Kitty   Your nose is bleeding.

Tom   Shit.

He wipes it.

Has it gone?

Kitty   Yeah.

Tom   Listen, I just want to say –

Kitty   Forget it, OK, it was three years ago, it's stupid.

Pause.

It's just . . . the reason I'm here is I've had a fight with Duncan.

Tom *looks at her.*

Tom   Who's Duncan?

Kitty   He's my fucking husband, how many times do I have to tell you this?

Tom   OK, OK, I'm sorry –

Kitty   We went out to a party one night and got, you know, that sort of drunk when you can sort out the Balkans and dance like Ginger Rogers. I thought, hey, I'm invincible and in love, this man understands me like no one on earth, let's have no secrets. So in a moment of champagne-fuelled love and honesty, I told him I'd had this thing with you. I thought I could tell him anything and he'd understand. I thought he loved me enough. And instead he just went very quiet, like I'd thrown a bucket of water over him. He worked out that it happened just after I'd met him. And instead of us spending a quiet Christmas together in London, he's gone off to some bloody civil war to punish me. He hasn't even phoned.

Tom *gropes around for his phone.*

Tom You want me to call him? What's his number? I'll call him and tell him it's OK, I'm a faggot, how would that be?

Kitty I don't know why I told him. I didn't think he went in for jealousy. Jesus. I spend one week with you three years ago and my whole life goes down the toilet –

Tom Kitty, I'm not taking the rap for this. You told your husband you slept with a movie star –

Kitty I did nothing of the sort –

Tom He'll get over it. He'll come back. If he doesn't he's an asshole. Fuck him.

Kitty You probably would actually. He's quite handsome.

Tom Listen, I'm sorry I didn't get in touch. I've been, you know, under a lot of pressure lately. I've been worried about a lot of things, my career for one . . . you know, there's all these young guys coming through, all these focused Scientology types, I mean, I don't know where to . . . I don't know how to . . .

Kitty What?

Tom I don't know.

Pause.

I don't know how to live. That's it. I don't know how to live. D'you think I'm insane?

Kitty You're a homosexual pretending to be straight. To me, that's insane. No wonder you're miserable. I mean, look at the state of you –

Tom Kitty, are you happy?

Kitty Of course I'm not.

Tom Why?

Kitty I just told you why. Duncan's sulking in the middle of a civil war. If he gets killed it'll be my fault, for sleeping with you and telling him about it. Also my job's so stupid I could die.

Tom   Have you seen my last movie? Stupid is flattering.

Kitty   I'm ashamed. I'm embarrassed. I host a programme that does dramatic reconstructions of terrible accidents, and how people escaped by the skin of their teeth. It is entirely without merit.

Tom   Right. It's not good then?

Kitty   It's banal, anecdotal and mindless. At best it panders to curiosity, and at worst voyeurism. Its original tide was 'Close Shaves'. Then they discovered a porn mag with the same name. I'm earning a fortune.

Tom   So, that's why you're doing it.

Kitty   No. I lost my nerve for the other stuff. I was doing a report from one of the new republics from the ex-Soviet Union. Civil disturbances, looting, snipers, mortars, reports of torture. All par for the course. Then this day I was filming with a camera crew and I realised the soldiers behind us were beating up a bunch of young boys for us. Because we had a camera. Not just a punch and a slap. They were beating them unconscious with rifle butts, with their boots. Blood was spurting from noses, teeth flying. And the soldiers were shouting: 'Look, this is what we do to looters, this is how we treat them, put this in your report.' And the guys just kept on filming. I said, no, stop, stop filming, they're going to kill them. But they didn't stop. They said it was reporting but it wasn't, it was something else. It went out on televisions all over the world as actuality, and what it was, was a performance. Afterwards they told me I'd copped out, that I'd lost my nerve. I don't know. Maybe I have. Anyway, they all got awards for that report. And I just felt confused. But if I didn't have the stomach for that stuff, I sure as hell don't have the stomach for what I'm doing at the moment. And I'm supposed to be filming the day after tomorrow.

Tom   D'you know something? You're the realest person I know. Apart from Iona. No. You're even more real than she is.

Kitty   Tom, when was the last time you touched base with 'real'? Iona's a lesbian pretending to be your girlfriend.

Tom   Actually I think she's asexual. But one thing, right, about being, you know, in the weird position I'm in, is you get to fuck a lot of people –

Kitty   Thank you, that makes me feel very valued –

Tom   No, listen to me, you get to fuck, like, anyone.

Kitty   And this is supposed to make me feel better, is it?

Tom   No, I don't count you in this. What I mean is that I find it depressing. You know most of them will do almost anything, they'd do back flips with an iguana if I asked them, because I'm Tom Cavallero. Whoever the fuck he is.

Kitty   Tom, you wanted this more than anything. At college, all you were ever going to be was famous.

Tom   I know. I thought the alternative was a kind of living death. To live your whole life and not be known. Like obscurity, what's the point?

Kitty   Well, there's no obscurity for you now even if you want it. No matter what you do or where you go, someone, one day, will say, Hey, didn't you used to be Tom Cavallero? And then you'll be a has-been which really is a living death. There's no escape.

Tom   This guy I slept with, sorry to get back to this but it bugs me, right, this one guy, he said, 'Your dick's much smaller thin I thought it was going to be,' and I said, 'What d'you mean, it's a completely normal size, what's wrong with it?' And he said, 'I know but I'm used to seeing you on screen where your head's like fifteen feet across, so you know . . . '

Kitty   Why d'you sleep with these people?

Tom   Because I can.

Pause.

Because I'm bored. I don't know.

Pause.

You get jaded, you know? You get bored with people who'll just do anything for you. You want a challenge or something. I went out with this woman once who wanted me to do really bizarre things with an electric toothbrush, right –

Kitty   Like what?

Tom   The batteries were flat, so we never did it. But she bossed me around, you know? She ordered me, do this, do that, and I kind of liked it, it was different. But outside of that she wasn't very interesting, plus she was a really bad actress, which kind of turned me off. We split and she sold the story to the *National Enquirer*, which made it sound like it was me who had the thing about domestic appliances. She got killed skateboarding down a freeway with half a ton of prescription drugs inside her, so I guess there's some justice.

Kitty   The thing is, Tom, you have everything you ever wanted.

Tom   There's this guy ghost-writing my autobiography, right –

Kitty   What?

Tom   Yeah, I know, listen, it's just one of those things, and I didn't have time to do it myself –

Kitty   Is he going to mention the men at all, or is he just writing a complete fiction?

Tom   What do you think? So anyway, he gets to the final chapter, right, and I've read the other ones by this time, and I think, hey, I think I could get the hang of this guy's style, so I write the final chapter myself.

Kitty   So?

Tom   So I've mastered the style of a ghost-writer, who's pretending to be me. Basically, I'm a man pretending to be a man who's pretending to be me. It completely scrambled my brain.

Kitty   So you thought you'd better take half a ton of cocaine to unscramble it –

Tom   Could you be sympathetic for like a nanosecond?

Kitty   I'm sorry for you. Your life is unbearable, it's hell.
How you struggle through I don't know, maybe you'd like an
honorary knighthood for your services to recreational drug
use –

Tom   Listen, I came here for some . . . I don't know . . .
some . . .

Kitty   What?

Tom   Have you ever seen a sign on an old building that says
'Ancient Lights'?

Kitty   Yes.

Tom   I saw it twenty years ago on a house on the banks of
the Thames. It's kind of haunted me. It's so poetic. It's so
mythic.

Kitty   It just means you can't build another house within
fifty yards because you'll block the light to the windows. It's a
form of building regulation.

Silence.

Tom   You're kidding me?

Kitty   No.

Tom   Oh my God. That is just so . . . Jesus . . . you're telling
me that for twenty years I've been haunted by a building
regulation?

Kitty   What did you think it meant?

Tom   I don't know. I just thought it was so . . . English and
historical and mysterious. Those words have such resonance.
Ancient Lights. I though they were about place, and
rootedness, and belonging. Like the way Tad carries his
Irishness so lightly because it's who he is, it's his history. I
thought those words had some atavistic meaning that only the
English could truly understand. They're part of what brings
me back here.

Pause.

This is terrible.

Kitty Sorry.

Tom That's OK.

He starts to cry. **Kitty** *is appalled.*

Kitty Tom, look, I'm sorry. I mean, I could be wrong. In fact I am, I'm wrong, I'm completely wrong about this.

Tom You're not. I know you're not.

Kitty I didn't realise it would be so upsetting.

Tom Forget it. It doesn't matter . . .

He wipes his eyes. Silence.

You're a Catholic, right?

Kitty Lapsed.

Tom Same here. When you were a kid, did they ever tell you what heaven was going to be like?

Kitty We'd sit at God's right hand for ever and ever, and there'd be no more tears and no more want, and everyone would be happy more or less permanently. And bliss. We'd all be lolling around in great vats of it, ad infinitum.

Tom No more want. Everything you ever desired or dreamed of. Permanent fucking bliss. Just one thing wrong here.

Kitty Several actually.

Tom I mean, the nature of bliss is that it's, you know, fleeting. Otherwise it's just . . .

Kitty What?

Tom Completely and utterly intolerable . . . D'you know what I mean?

Blackout.

Scene Three

Seven a.m. Christmas morning. Same room. **Bea** *is straightening up the room in her dressing gown, beating something in a bowl. Christmas-morning carols are playing on the radio.* **Tad** *comes in.*

Tad   Happy Christmas.

Bea   Morning.

Tad   You're speaking to me then?

Silence.

Can I do anything?

Bea   You could spontaneously combust. That would solve all my problems at one fell swoop.

Tad   Right.

She beats whatever's in the bowl furiously. Silence. **Tad** *is stranded, awkward.*

Bea   So. You asked me what you should do.

Tad   I did, yeah.

Bea   Go to Hull. Spend Christmas with your dad.

Pause.

Tad   What?

Bea   Have lunch and go.

Tad   But –

Bea   There won't be another Christmas. You won't have another chance.

Tad   I don't want to make my peace with him, if that's what you mean. That's just bollocky sentimental crap.

Bea   He's dying. Swallow your pride.

Tad   I can't.

Bea   You can.

Tad   I don't want to.

Bea   Take the leap. Think of it as making peace with yourself.

Tad   Say goodbye to him, and say goodbye to Michael Armstrong you mean?

Bea   I didn't say that. You did.

Pause.

Also, Tad, I'd quite like you out of my hair for a while.

Tad   Ah. Right.

Bea   I need a bit of time to get used to this . . . new development, you know?

Tad   I can't really blame you, I suppose.

Pause.

Bea   What was he like, this Michael Armstrong?

Tad   Jesus, we were two peas in a pod. Anyone would have taken us for brothers. Same sense of humour. Same mole, here. Same knocked-about mother who wanted the best for us.

Bea   So what's the difference between you and him?

Tad   I'm the successful one.

Pause.

Bea   When you see your dad, who are you going to be?

Tad   What? Who am I going to be? . . . Me . . . I'm going to be me.

Bea   And who the fuck is that?

Tad   I usually kind of morph into Michael by degrees, you know what I mean? I can manage such a smooth transition now, I can hardly see the join myself.

Pause.

If I go, will you still want me when I get back?

Pause.

Bea   I might.

Tad   You'll be living with a liar and a conman.

Silence.

On the other hand, no one else needs to know that.

Bea   And what the world doesn't know doesn't count?

Tad   Something like that. The work's what counts.

Bea   What gets me, is that you're a brilliant writer and it's based on what? Thin air.

Tad   All writing's based on thin air.

Bea   There's no need to take it to extremes.

Tad   D'you think you could live with the fact that I've invented myself?

Bea   Fuck, I don't know. On the other hand, why not? I'd be out of a job if people didn't reinvent themselves.

Pause.

But I also don't want to lose you. I know that's pathetic, I know it is, but I don't. There, I've admitted it. If I was the person people think I am, I'd throw you out on the street. But I can't imagine my life without you, it's too bleak to contemplate. My heart drops like a stone when I think about it. I've done years of being alone. All those empty Sundays that last three weeks. I'm in too deep now.

Tad   Maybe in the night, you know, with your legs wrapped around me in the dark . . . only you and I will know what we know . . .

Bea   You're never going to tell anyone else . . . are you?

Tad   No . . . it's our secret . . .

Bea   But when we make love, I'm going to call you Michael . . .

Tad   Wouldn't that be very confusing?

Bea   Just for those moments I want to be sure of who you are. And for you to be sure too. When I call you Michael, and you respond, I'll know you're mine.

She kisses him, long and deep.

Michael . . .

Tad   I think I'd prefer Mike;

Bea   And I want you to take me seriously.

Tad   OK. Sorry. Michael. OK. You can call me that under the duvet.

Bea   It's our secret.

Tad   Of course if I ever, you know . . . let you down in any way, you could . . .

Bea *looks him in the eye.*

Bea   Yes. I could.

Tad   Not that you're blackmailing me or anything.

Bea   As if.

A beat.

Tad   So. I'm going to Hull then?

Bea   How will you feel about him dying?

Tad   I've been thinking a lot about that.

Bea   Yes, I know.

Tad   I think what I think is this: that death's not just something that happens at the end of your life, it's something that happens from moment to moment. Every moment's a birth and a death. I'm not the man I was twenty years ago. My dad's not the man he was. From moment to moment, we start again. Maybe if I bear that in mind, I'll resist the temptation to punch him.

Blackout.

Scene Four

Christmas Day. Four p.m. A post-prandial tableau: **Tom** *and* **Kitty** *have crashed out on the cushions. Everyone is wearing paper hats out of crackers.* **Bea** *is clearing away wrapping paper, glasses and general detritus.* **Joni** *is sitting in the kitchen chair wearing a new leather coat and looking at herself critically in a hand mirror.* **Iona***'s camera is on the floor with a pile of videotapes.*

Joni   I've decided what I want to do when I leave school, Mum. If the band doesn't work out, I mean, it probably won't, but anyway, I'd rather be an actress, or if not an actress, I'll do the breakfast programme on the television or something like that, you know, be a personality, but I just know in my heart, Mum, that what I want more than anything else, right, is to be so famous I can't leave the house.

Bea   Could you pass me those glasses please?

Joni   More famous than Tom. Much more. Tom is going to be asking me for my autograph. I might give him a wave from my stretch limo as I glide past. Just think. You'll be the mother of a famous child, won't it be great? You might even get quite famous yourself because of me, and people will want to see the bedroom I slept in and things like that, I might even let you be my manager, except I'll probably have to live in America, God, I can't wait –

She smiles at herself in the mirror.

D'you think Dad would give me the money to have my teeth straightened?

Bea   No.

Joni *gets up sulkily and begins to sort through the videos on the floor.*

Bea   Kitty . . .

Kitty *shifts slightly.*

Kitty   What . . . ?

Bea   You won't sleep tonight if you don't wake up now. And you've got a car coming for you in the morning.

Kitty   I'm not going.

She turns over.

Bea   Not going where?

Kitty   Filming. I'm not going.

Bea   What d'you mean? Have they cancelled or something?

Kitty   No. I have.

Bea   What are you talking about?

Kitty   I'm breaking my contract. They'll have to sue me. Fuck them.

Bea   Are you out of your mind?

Kitty *sits up blearily.*

Kitty   Actually I might have to say that. I might have to claim insanity. D'you know any good doctors who might vouch for the parlous state of my mental health?

Bea   Kitty, you can't break your contract. It's completely unprofessional.

Kitty   Watch me.

She picks up a bottle of water and takes a long swig.

One more series of whoops I nearly got killed, and d'you know what I'll be doing next? Pet programmes. Cute pets get cured of impetigo. No thanks. I'm too old.

Tad *comes in with a suitcase.*

Tad   I suppose I'd better get going then.

Joni (*still sorting through the videos*)   Bye. I hope your dad gets better.

Kitty   Are you sure you can get a flight on Christmas Day?

Tad   I'm driving –

Bea   There's a ferry first thing –

Tad Six o'clock.

Kitty So where will you stay tonight?

Bea His brother.

Tad Yeah, my brother.

Tom *stirs. He's still wearing his paper hat.*

Tom My neck . . . what time is it?

Bea It's still Christmas Day. Tad's going to see his father.

Tom Oh. Right. Right.

He gets up unsteadily and picks up a bottle of whisky. Pours himself a large one.

Good to meet you, Tad. Give my love to the old country, will you.

Tad Right. I will.

Tom I can't wait to make this movie.

Joni *has slipped a cassette into the video recorder.*

Tad Sure it'll be great. We'll have great craic.

Tom Excuse me?

Tad Craic. You know. Craic.

Tom Yeah, right. Great. I –

He breaks off as the video suddenly whirrs into action, the sound up way too high.

Bea Joni, what are you doing –

Joni It's just one of Iona's tapes –

Tom Where the fuck did you get that from?

Joni It was lying on the floor.

They all stare in horror at the screen: **Tom** *slumped in the living room, coked out of his head, talking to his agent on the phone the night before. He looks appalling.*

Tom (*on tape*)   . . . I am not fucking drunk! Listen to me. Can you imagine anything more horrible than to see someone coming towards you and it's you? . . . No, not you, me . . . (*etc.*)

Kitty   Oh dear, I hope she's going to edit that out.

Bea   Joni, that's enough, turn it off please –

Joni   Ah, Mum –

Tom *is transfixed.*

Tom   Jesus Christ. Is that what I look like?

Tad   Listen, I think I'd better get going –

Kitty   It was the middle of the night, Tom, no one looks good at three in the morning.

Tom   I don't think I need this . . .

Bea   Joni, turn it off, for Christ's sake –

Tom   No, no, no, no –

He goes to the video and wrenches it out. He kneels on the floor and tears the tape from the casing in shining black coils.

Bea   Tom –

Bea *and* **Kitty** *try to gather up the tape as* **Iona** *comes in. She looks at* **Tom** *in horror.*

Iona   What are you doing?

Bea   I don't think he liked that particular bit of film.

Tom   I'm sorry, Iona, I don't think this movie's such a good idea any more –

Tom *has now started on the other tapes. There are coils of black tape everywhere.* **Iona** *tries to wrench them from him.*

Iona   Tom, stop it, please, don't fucking do this –

Bea   Joni, go upstairs to your room –

Joni   Ah, Mum –

Bea Now!

She goes.

Tom It was a stupid idea, Iona, I look a complete asshole –

Iona I was going to edit that stuff out. We had a deal, you promised –

Iona *tries to wrest the tapes from him. He pushes her over.*

Bea Tom, you made your point, stop it –

Iona This is three months' work, Tom –

Tom (*still shredding and tearing*) Let's just forget the whole thing. Make another film, make ten other films, but leave me out. I want this stuff burned, I want it obliterated –

Kitty Tom –

Iona They don't want some other film, they want this one, they want a film about you, you asshole, Jesus, Tom, the whole point of everything is that the film's about you. It was your idea, for Christ's sake –

Tom And it's my idea to stop right now. OK? It's over. The project is abandoned.

Iona Tom –

Tom I said it's over!

Iona *begins to cry. She picks up an armful of tape.*

Iona I can't believe you've done this . . . all my work, wasted –

Tad Look, I'm really sorry to butt in like this but I have to go –

Iona *gets up, weeping.*

Iona Tom, you're an asshole.

She goes out. Silence.

Tom I guess she's a little put out.

Bea   Will she be OK?

He sits down on the cushions.

Tom   Fuck knows. She'll probably write a story for the *National Enquirer* about how I ruined her career.

He picks up a handful of tape and tries to shred it.

So, here I am. This is me. *Cinéma-vérité.*

Bea   Tom –

Tom   D'you ever look in the mirror and you don't recognise the person looking back at you?

Tad   Look, I'm off, right? I really am this time. Great to meet you all, but, you know, my dad and everything –

Kitty   Sorry, Tad. I'm sorry about your dad. Give my love to Dublin.

Tad   Sure.

She kisses him. He shakes **Tom***'s hand.*

Bye, Tom. Sorry about the er . . .

He looks at the mess.

Anyway. Bye. See you.

Tom   See you in the Emerald Isle.

Tad   Great.

Bea   I'll see you out.

She goes out. **Tom** *starts to roll a joint. The telephone rings.* **Tom** *looks round to see where the noise is coming from.*

Kitty   It's OK, it's mine.

It continues to ring.

Tom   Aren't you going to answer it?

Kitty   No. You are.

It continues to ring. She finds it and hands it to **Tom**.

Tell them I've left for London, and I didn't seem too well –

She picks up the phone and thrusts it at **Tom**.

Tom   Hi? . . . No . . . this is a friend of hers . . . she must have left it behind . . . no, she left . . . maybe two, three hours ago? . . . think she said London . . . she said she wasn't feeling too good . . . OK . . . I will . . . OK . . . bye . . .

He turns off the phone.

Kitty   Tom, you saved my life.

Tom   This morning I ruined it. My, how times change.

Bea *comes back, throws herself down on the cushions and the reels of tape.*

Bea   Jesus, what a fucking Christmas, the whole thing's been a bloody disaster –

Tom   Bea, it's been great, what are you talking about. Apart from Tad's old man. And Iona. And the film.

Bea   Why did you do that, Tom? Iona's in bits.

Tom   I didn't like what I saw.

Kitty   You wanted reality and that's what you got.

Tom   Fuck it. Fuck reality. You know what I saw there that I've never seen before?

Kitty   Tom Cavallero on screen without make-up.

Tom   No.

Pause.

I looked camp. I looked fucking camp.

Bea   You don't look camp, Tom –

Tom   Say what you like, I know what I saw.

He lights up the joint and hands it to her. Throughout the following scene the joint is passed round.

And I never want to see it again. But I have this horrible

feeling I will. Tell me, do I sound camp to you? Give me the truth. Do I sound like a screamer?

Kitty   No. You do not sound like a screamer.

Tom   I don't know whether I believe you.

Bea   You do not sound camp.

Tom   You don't detect a kind of inflection? A little louche thing? Just a hint of something around the shoulders, that tiny facial quirk which says –

Kitty   No. Have some of this.

She hands him the joint. He takes a drag.

Tom   OK.

Pause.

Even my teeth looked gay –

Bea   Well, you are gay, for Christ's sake –

Tom   I looked irrational, raving, drunk. And camp.

Kitty   Can we change the subject?

Tom   OK, hey, what a truly great Christmas –

Bea   Oh, shut up –

Tom   Seriously. Apart from fetches and power failures, and the realisation that I'm turning into Liberace –

Kitty   Stop –

Tom   – it's great being here with the snow and all. Christmas never feels real in LA. It's great being in the place where Christmas actually began.

Kitty   That was Bethlehem.

Tom   Yeah, but if we were in Israel it wouldn't feel right, would it? It'd be pretty much like LA, which like I said just doesn't get when it comes to Christmas. You have to be here with the log fire and the real tree and the thatched cottages with all the snow on them.

Kitty   There aren't any thatched cottages up here.

Tom   I've seen them.

Kitty   Where?

Tom   Everywhere.

Bea   You imagined it. There are no thatched cottages up here, period.

Tom   This is England, for Christ's sake.

Bea   You only get thatch further south, Tom.

Tom   Jesus . . . Maybe my therapist is right. He says I create realities.

Bea *hands on the joint.*

Bea   Neurolinguistic programming.

Kitty   What?

Bea   It's a type of therapy.

Kitty   Yeah, but what does it do?

Bea   No idea.

Tom   Freudian. Kleinian. Episcopalian. Tried them all.

Kitty   Go back to Catholicism. The priests have the best outfits. Greek Orthodox, even better. Great outfits and great beards.

Tom   But how d'you get . . . you know . . . the thing . . . faith . . .

Kitty   Actually, Bea, you could found your own church. The First Church of Christ the Chef.

Bea   I wish I did have a religion.

Kitty   A different job would do me.

Bea   I'm serious.

Kitty   So am I. Look at what we all do. What is the point of any of it?

Tom   Iridology. Healers. Bio-feedback. I had someone read my feet once. Can you believe that? Read my feet, I want to know the answers to the big questions, go on, read my feet and tell me, I know it's all there somewhere.

Bea   What did they have to say for themselves?

Tom   Oh, you know. You're basically a good person, but sometimes people take advantage of you. Oh, and your kidneys are fucked. Thank you, that'll be three hundred dollars.

Bea   Channelling. Tibetan chanting. Fire-walking.

Tom   Done them all. Psychosynthesis.

Bea   What's that?

Tom   I can't remember. The therapist was called Skippy.

Kitty   You went to a therapist called Skippy?

Tom   My judgement wasn't good at the time. That's why I was in therapy.

Bea   Was she any use?

Tom   What do you think? I've tried my body's a temple low sodium drug-free spring water organic fruit and jogging routine but it got so I could imagine how clean my intestines were and I was frightened to eat anything in case I messed them up. Plus I even bored myself. I only really start functioning after I'm three beers in.

Bea   So where to now?

Kitty   In the old days, we'd have joined the International Marxists or something.

Bea   Well, you would.

Tom   I don't know. Buddhism. What d'you think?

Kitty   You'd be crap at Buddhism. You have to live in the moment which is not possible if you're turning your whole life into a major motion picture. Plus for you, almost every moment is a lie.

Tom   Get over it, Kitty. I have a friend who says that golf's very Zen if you do it right. What d'you think?

Kitty   Everything's very Zen if you do it right.

Bea *begins to giggle.*

Bea   I set up this interview for you, Tom, and I had to pretend you wouldn't answer any questions about the underage girl thing, and they got so fed up, so when you apparently relent mid-interview, they're going to think it's such a scoop.

Tom   Hey, I have the whole spiel worked out – 'D'you know this woman's been hounding me? She sent me a paperweight with her pubic hair set inside it. She sat in some uncooked dough, baked it and sent me the results: a loaf of bread in the shape of her vagina. And now she's suing me?' Actually, I didn't make that up, someone did that to me once.

Kitty   That is disgusting.

Bea   Are you really breaking your contract, Kitty?

Kitty   Yep. I'm going to sort things out with Duncan. Even if I have to go to Africa to do it. Then, I don't know. Take it from there. Find some work that makes some sense. If you don't have religion, work's all you've got.

Bea   That's depressing.

Kitty   It is if you do what we do.

Bea   Children. Children are what's important. And lovers and friends and families.

Tom   But just sometimes, you want a little bit of transcendence, you know. I thought being a movie star would do it.

Bea   Doesn't it?

Tom   Do I look like I'm transcending anything?

Bea   No. Do I?

Tom   You're a great cook. You're a great organiser.

Bea   That'll look really great on my headstone. What a

summing-up: Beatrice Davies, a good organiser. She went to a lot of parties. Fuck.

Kitty   Kitty Percival, she made some terrible television shows.

Tom   Tom Cavallero. Briefly famous.

Kitty   Ah well. Forty-three next birthday. Soon be dead.

Bea   Tad says death's a process, not an event.

Pause.

Tom   Shit. I guess it is.

Kitty*'s phone rings again. They ignore it.*

Tom   Shall I roll another joint?

Bea   Yeah, why not.

He starts to do so. The phone continues to ring.

Tom   It was a dark and windy night. Thomas Earlby was walking his dog across the moors at around five o'clock in the evening, when the dog suddenly stopped, cowering and whimpering and giving little uncertain barks. And Earlby looked up and saw a figure walking towards him with a strange lantern the colour of moonlight.

The phone stops ringing. As **Tom** *talks, a huge image of him (back projection) begins to develop on the walls behind him.*

And the strange thing was that this figure made no sound as it came towards him across the frozen ground. And as it got nearer, Earlby was rooted to the spot, for the man standing before him was his own self, white-faced and gaunt, and beckoning to him, like this . . . Earlby turned on his heels and fled. When he reached home, shocked and shaken, he told his wife and his father what he'd seen out there on the moors, and his father turned white, and got up from the table. He went upstairs without a word. And the next morning, Thomas Earlby was dead . . .

By now the image of **Tom** *fills the back of the stage. Fade down lights, leaving only the image. Bring up John Martyn music. Fade down image.*